THE USSR's MANAGEMENT OF FOREIGN TRADE

THE USSR's MANAGEMENT OF FOREIGN TRADE

V.P. Gruzinov

Edited with a foreword by
Edward A. Hewett

©M. E. Sharpe Inc. 1979
901 North Broadway
White Plains, New York 10603

Softcover reprint of the hardcover 1st edition 1979

This book is a translation of *Upravlenie vneshnei torgovlei: tseli, funktsii, metody* (Moscow: "Mezhdunarodnye otnosheniia" Publishers, 1975) and is published by arrangement with VAAP, the Soviet Copyright Agency.

Translated by Michel Vale

Published simultaneously as Vol. XIV, nos. 3 and 4 of *Soviet and Eastern European Foreign Trade*, edited by Mojmir Bednarik

All rights reserved. No part of this publication may be reproduced or transmitted, in any form or by any means, without permission

First published in the United States of America 1979
First published in the United Kingdom 1979

Published by
THE MACMILLAN PRESS LTD
London and Basingstoke
Associated companies in Delhi
Dublin Hong Kong Johannesburg Lagos
Melbourne New York Singapore Tokyo

British Library Cataloguing in Publication Data
Gruzinov, V P
  The USSR's management of foreign trade
  1. Russia—Commercial policy
  I. Title
  382'.0947   HF1557
ISBN 978-1-349-04834-2   ISBN 978-1-349-04832-8 (eBook)
          DOI 10.1007/978-1-349-04832-8

This book is sold subject to the
standard conditions of the Net Book Agreement

CONTENTS

Foreword
   by Edward A. Hewett   vii

In Lieu of a Preface: The Purpose of the Study   3

1. The Current Organization of Foreign Trade   9

2. Theoretical Foundations of the Management of Foreign Trade   36

3. The Current Organization of the Management of Foreign Trade and Ways to Improve It   65

4. Some Aspects of Introducing the Scientific Organization of Labor in the Ministry of Foreign Trade and Problems of Training and Advanced Training of Managerial Personnel   138

5. Controlling the Quality of Products Intended for Export   189

Conclusion   229

Notes   234

Glossary   238

About the Author   243

FOREWORD

Most Soviet writings on USSR foreign trade tend toward a dull, highly abstract, uninformative, and repetitive format. One searches in vain for serious, detailed discussions of how the Soviet planning apparatus generates decisions on foreign trade. To be sure, there are extensive discussions on how foreign trade decisions should be made (viz. the extensive literature on foreign trade efficiency indicators), but almost nothing on the actual decision processes. By far the blackest of the black boxes surrounding the institutions which make foreign trade decisions in the USSR is the one surrounding the Ministry of Foreign Trade (MFT). Organizational charts are available here and there, and the MFT's journal, Vneshniaia torgovlia, can be counted on for brief articles about various foreign trade organizations (FTOs) or about trade in certain product groups. But until now there has been virtually a complete blackout on discussion of how things are actually done.

V. P. Gruzinov's book is important because it pierces that blackout by providing a look into the black box called the Ministry of Foreign Trade; it breathes life into the organizational charts. The book summarizes the findings of an evidently extensive internal study of the bureaucracy of the MFT undertaken by a team of researchers under Gruzinov's supervision. Gruzinov (then a member of the ministry's All-Union Academy of Foreign Trade) and his team apparently enjoyed unlimited access to the entire central bureaucracy of the MFT, all of the

The USSR's Management of Foreign Trade

FTOs, and the records in both. Judging from the results reported in this book, this was intended to be a definitive "no-holds-barred" study of all aspects of the MFT's operations, the ultimate goal being to devise ways to streamline the bureaucracy. While there is no way of knowing for sure, one suspects that this is a very highly condensed, and somewhat sanitized, version of the full internal report.

Even in its possibly condensed and sanitized form, this book is full of rich, previously unavailable detail on the MFT. In the first place, the focus of the book is really on the administrations or directorates (upravleniia), which form the middle level of the MFT bureaucracy, below the minister and his deputies but above the FTOs. Of particular importance are the seven administrations which divide responsibility by product groups for all exports and imports. There is, for example, a main administration that supervises all exports of raw materials and therefore supervises the FTOs that export those products. Throughout the text one will find fairly general assertions, supported by anecdotal evidence, suggesting that these administrations are the formidable administrative bottlenecks that account for much of the inefficiency in the operation of the MFT. There is evidently a general tendency throughout the bureaucracy for higher-level officials to hoard their power instead of delegating it to subordinates. Not surprisingly this leads to frequent poor (and probably slow) decisions from overworked decision-makers. Also, many FTOs are supervised by more than one product administration, sometimes three or four, which must surely complicate the life of the FTO directors as well as the life of high-level administrators. The FTOs themselves also suffer from poor administrative organization, which Gruzinov discusses in some detail, with examples from actual FTOs to support some of his observations.

For those of us who have worked in a bureaucracy, many of the problems Gruzinov describes will sound all too familiar; they are hardly unique to Soviet foreign trade management, or to the Soviet Union for that matter. What is interesting about the book is that it gives the first account of which I am aware outlining

Foreword

the nature of the problems for the MFT. Furthermore, the book is important because it draws our attention to a previously neglected source of inefficiency in Soviet foreign trade: the bureaucracy itself. Western economists have emphasized the costs to the USSR of conducting foreign trade in ignorance of the actual opportunity costs entailed in various export and import decisions, an ignorance originating in the absence of meaningful domestic prices or meaningful exchange rates. But even if the prices and exchange rates were considerably improved, or even if a sophisticated set of foreign trade efficiency indicators were devised, the problem would still remain that the current bureaucracy of the MFT would tend to generate tardy and costly decisions on foreign trade flows. It is just as important for the USSR to reform the foreign trade decision-making process as it is to change the criteria on which foreign trade decisions are made (and in fact the two are inextricably intertwined).

When Gruzinov moves from describing what is to what ought to be, his message in its simplest form is that the MFT can streamline its work by adopting Western management techniques. Basically his argument is for more computerization, better division of supervisory authority within the bureaucracy, and substantial streamlining of the administrations and the FTOs. He discusses the possibility, for example, of establishing "large, financially accountable (khozraschetnye) export-import, foreign trade firms (predpriiatiia)," combining the functions of several FTOs. On the other hand, he suggests there is a fairly substantial body of opinion within the MFT which supports breaking up the Main Administration for Export of Raw Materials into three administrations, which would divide up responsibility for dealing with the more than twenty sectoral ministries and numerous FTOs now involved with that main administration. What emerges from Gruzinov's discussion of possible reforms is a conviction that the MFT and its FTOs should retain their monopoly over foreign transactions, but that they could considerably improve the way they administer that monopoly.

ix

The USSR's Management of Foreign Trade

Since the completion of the study, and quite possibly because of it, the Soviet government has announced a program to completely reorganize FTOs.[1] The three most important features of the resolution are:
1. The FTOs are to be converted to operations on a <u>khozraschet</u> basis, although what that means in this case is not clear;
2. Apparently FTOs will be merged into larger units;
3. The supervision of the operation of FTOs is to be in the hands of a board on which the MFT and sectoral ministries will enjoy equal representation. Evidently this supervision has no effect on the ultimate power of the MFT over the FTO, but rather relates only to decisions on how best to operate the FTO in light of plans sent down through the administrations.

It would appear then that, at least in part, Gruzinov's recommended reforms are beginning to be implemented. It is not clear if any changes have been made at the level of the administrations; the May 31 resolution only deals with the FTOs.

Anyone — businessman, government official, or academic — with an interest in Soviet foreign trade will find much to interest them in this text. In particular, now that the Soviets are undertaking a long overdue attempt to reform the foreign trade administrative apparatus, Gruzinov comes as a welcome and unique discussion of the considerations that lie behind the reform. One can only hope that this is the beginning of a trend toward more critical and interesting work on Soviet foreign trade by Soviet economists themselves.

Edward A. Hewett

Note

1. "O poriadke i srokakh reorganizatsii vsesoiuznykh vneshnetorgovykh ob"edinenii vo vsesoiuznye khozraschetnye vneshnetorgovye ob"edineniia, vkhodiashchie v sistemu Mini-

sterstva vneshnei torgovli" ("On the Manner and Timetables of the Reorganization of All-Union Foreign Trade Organizations into All-Union Financially Accountable Foreign Trade Organizations Belonging to the System of the Ministry of Foreign Trade"), Resolution No. 416, USSR Council of Ministers, May 31, 1978 (included as a supplement in the August 1978 issue of Vneshniaia torgovlia).

THE USSR's MANAGEMENT OF FOREIGN TRADE

In Lieu of a Preface:
The Purpose of the Study

This book was written on the basis of data gathered in research done by the author or under his supervision in a number of all-union associations and foreign trade departments. Its purpose is to collate the experience accumulated by foreign trade departments and organizations with regard to the rationalization of management and the organization of labor and to examine some methodological and practical problems entailed in improving the management system in foreign trade.

The present trends in foreign trade are shaped by broad and complex political and socioeconomic processes. The development of foreign trade now and in the future assumes the maintenance of a steadily increasing volume and scope while keeping the number of employed at a roughly constant level. This strategic problem can be resolved only if a systematic effort is made to intensify all aspects of foreign trade.

First of all we must determine the best way to organize labor as foreign trade grows, i.e., how we can ensure the fullest possible use of existing possibilities and resources. Efforts in this direction must take into account a multitude of political, economic, organizational, and legal factors. When to begin, how to get things going, and what problems must be dealt with — these are the questions that constantly confront those responsible for the effective management of foreign trade.

The matter is not simply one of improving some isolated or particular aspect but of improving the entire system of management, including the organizational structure and all the processes, modes, and methods of management (see Figure 1).

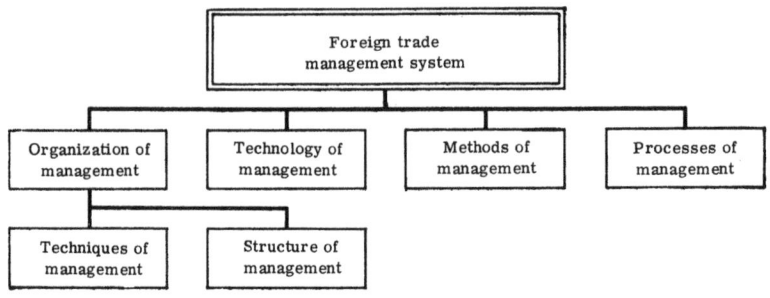

Figure 1.

Each of these aspects has its own distinctive features, the quality of which determines the level of organization of the managerial processes and the degree of refinement of the methods used. The efficiency of management will depend on how these various features are combined and on the specific form they take.

An intensive quest is currently under way in the USSR Ministry of Foreign Trade for better ways to manage foreign trade operations. In the process we have found that certain psychological barriers had to be overcome in the employees themselves, among whom there are proponents of everything new, skeptics, and direct antagonists.

One of the principal directions in these efforts to improve foreign trade management has been to find just the right balance between centralization and decentralization in management. Noting the importance of this problem, General Secretary L. I. Brezhnev observed: "The correct blend of centralization with the rights, initiative, and responsibilities of local agencies is a fundamental problem, a major policy issue."[1]
As it relates to foreign trade, the question involves determining how much greater range of independent action should be given to all-union associations in commercial operations and economic matters, and encouraging the staffs of these associa-

In Lieu of a Preface

tions to apply their ingenuity in finding ways to employ more efficiently the available internal resources for increasing the effectiveness of foreign trade operations.

This problem can only be resolved on the basis of a thorough qualitative and quantitative analysis and study of relations among the basic economic-commercial indices of the operations of all-union associations and the various departments of the Ministry of Foreign Trade. In particular, it is important to analyze the correlation between these commercial indices and the size of all-union associations, as well as the sheer number of channels existing between enterprises and the supplying ministries.

For example, the view is gaining ground that the general line to be followed in streamlining the organizational structure of management is to set up large, economically accountable export-import organizations by merging existing all-union associations that deal in the same general types of goods. The experience of the industrial ministries and other socialist countries in dealing with this question shows that only large, autonomous organizations can hope to effectively meet the requirements of the current scientific-technical revolution, taking into account the general interests of the state.

The effectiveness of setting up large export-import associations is basically contingent on the following factors:
— the ability to develop a sound policy for the sale and purchase of specific groups of goods and the improvement of ties with industry and other entities;
— staff maneuverability, centralization of functions, and installation of an automatic control system (ACS) for foreign trade;
— reduction in the number of centralized actions. This creates conditions for radical improvement in the work of the central administrative apparatus on meeting the nation's economic needs.

If large export-import associations are created, the existing apparatus for managing foreign trade (i.e., the ministry, with its various functional administrations, the commodity administrations [glavki], the all-union associations) must of course also be rationalized. In a certain sense the commodity administrations are a bottleneck. They are structural subdivisions under the central control of the ministry and tend to use administrative methods of management. However, since the commodity administrations and the all-union associations under their jurisdiction do not organizationally form a complete system, their power to exercise control over the operations of the associations is itself limited. Practically this means that the lines of authority are multiple. Therefore an effective revamping of the foreign trade administrative apparatus presupposes the development of scientifically sound criteria and indices that will facilitate the choice of more rational structures and will guarantee the flexibility and reliability of the foreign trade management system as a whole. Such criteria must be based on principles developed in the course of building socialism; the most important are: unified political and economic control, democratic centralism, and constant improvement in the management system.

But the concrete application of these principles in designing and improving a management system requires taking into account the distinctive features of foreign trade activity.

Unfortunately, until recently, no systematic research or elaboration had been done in this area. Our book, then, is the first attempt to inquire into how the general principles and guidelines of management of socialist production can be applied to foreign trade. We shall be concentrating mainly on an analysis of the experience accumulated in the practice of foreign trade, which contains much that is useful for generalizations. Our inquiry will concern three mutually interrelated areas.

The _first_ deals with the methodological and practical aspects of putting to work in foreign trade the general conclusions and propositions of the science of management; it dwells on the current system of management in foreign trade and its organization of labor.

The _second_ has to do with various methodological proposi-

In Lieu of a Preface

tions for the rationalization of labor and management in foreign trade. Lenin once said that "anyone who tries to deal with particular questions without first having solved the general ones will inevitably and unwittingly stumble across these general questions at every step. To do this, to stumble blindly over them in each particular case, means to abandon one's politics to the worst sort of vacillation and lack of principle."[2]

These general guidelines will provide the framework within which we shall attempt to stake out a rough path along which efforts to rationalize the management of foreign trade and its organization of labor should proceed. That in turn depends to a considerable extent on how intelligently a whole series of questions bearing on the organization of foreign trade are handled, which ultimately entail the efficiency of the management system and the abilities and skills of the managerial staff, specialists, and employees. It is now a truism that a thorough grounding in the science of management is essential if an institution or enterprise is to be managed efficiently. "At the present stage in our economic development," observed General Secretary Brezhnev, "we are no longer able to rely on past experience alone. Management is becoming a science, and we must master this science as quickly and thoroughly as possible through resolute study."[3]

Accordingly, the third area of our inquiry covers problems in improving the training and level of competence of those who work in the field of foreign trade. In this study we have drawn extensively on factual material accumulated in the all-union associations and main administrations, on official statistics, and on information found in the periodical literature. The book is intended for the broad ranks of those employed in foreign trade, particularly for all those employed in the departments of the scientific organization of labor and for specialists dealing with the problems of rationalization of foreign trade management. Scientific workers, teachers at institutions of higher education, and students and auditors in the advanced training colleges who may also be studying problems of management should also find it useful.

The USSR's Management of Foreign Trade

The first section of Chapter 3 and the second section of Chapter 4 were written in conjunction with V. M. Kostikov, A. A. Zolkin, and I. B. Erdynevskaia; the fifth section of Chapter 4 was written with V. A. Burenin, and Chapter 5 was written in collaboration with R. M. Tikhonov.

CHAPTER ONE

The Current Organization
of Foreign Trade

1. The Essential Features of Foreign Trade
   and Its Role in the Functioning of
   a Socialist Economy at Its Present Stage

Foreign trade is trade between countries. Its specific features, the way it develops, and its role in the economy are determined by the mode of production, as is the case with any other branch of the economy.

Foreign trade is a vital condition for existence under the capitalist mode of production. "Capitalism," said Lenin, "is merely the result of expanded commodity circulation, extending beyond the boundaries of the state."[1]

The uneven development in different branches of the economy and the fierce competition inherent in capitalism mean that as soon as a firm begins operations, it must be attuned to the foreign as well as the domestic market. Consequently, foreign trade does not accord with the interests and needs of the nation. Maximum profit, not the needs of the economy, is its driving force.

Under the conditions created by the scientific-technical revolution, foreign trade takes on new features. Its development today is steered not only by growth in production and in the comparatively inadequate capacity of the domestic market, but also by the expansion of international production relations, e.g., the steadily growing specialization and expansion of cooperation in production between monopolies in different countries that conclude agreements on production and scientific-technical collaboration, on licenses and patents, and so on.

One result of these trends is a more rapid growth in trade

among the industrially developed countries, wherein finished goods, the products of the manufacturing industries, and above all, machinery and equipment acquire an increasingly important place; on the other hand, this also means that the share of the developing countries in the total exports of capitalist countries declines. For example, about 70 percent of U.S. exports are to the developed capitalist countries.

The forms and methods of foreign trade have acquired many new aspects. The traditional procedures of foreign trade are becoming more and more diversified: for example, the financing of machinery and equipment export (France and Japan); new forms of trade that had not existed before are being rapidly brought into use (trade in patents and licenses, economic and engineering-technical consulting, mutual use of sales networks, international consortiums, leasing, etc.).

Scientific-technical progress has substantially altered the nature of foreign trade relations between countries. Whereas previously trade between nations was characterized by episodic transactions, i.e., single sales and purchases, now trade relations are increasingly becoming an ongoing affair. Thus when selling a piece of equipment, the seller must already be thinking about its next model so as not to lose the buyer. The introduction of aggregate unit installations of machinery and equipment, made possible by a high degree of unification and standardization of units, as a result of which there is specialization between countries, is also a factor that has contributed to the permanence of foreign trade relations.

Foreign trade also involves considerable export of capital, especially as direct investments; in this respect it is becoming increasingly lopsided. Under capitalism foreign trade not only contributes to but strengthens an international division of labor under which production and hence the export of finished goods, especially machinery and equipment, are concentrated principally in the industrially developed capitalist countries, while the backward countries are confined to the production and export of agricultural goods and raw materials. For example, more than 80 percent of the total volume of trade of finished products takes place among the economically developed countries (United States, Great Britain, Federal Republic of Germany, France, Italy, Japan, Canada, Netherlands, Sweden, Switzerland, Belgium, and Luxembourg).

Under socialism the role of foreign trade is quite different. It serves as a means for utilizing the advantages of the international division of labor, particularly the international socialist division of labor, in the interests of strengthening the socialist system. But this is not its only distinctive feature. It also stimulates the intensification of production and helps to improve its technical level.

Economic growth involves a number of factors[2] (see Figure 2).

The present stage of the process of creating the material-technical base of communism is marked by a steadily deepening intensification of production, the emergence and expansion of new sources of economic growth, involving in the first instance the exploitation of the achievements of the scientific-technical revolution. For example, whereas up until roughly the 1960s economic growth relied mainly on extensive factors (increase in the number of employed, a high rate of capital investment, the drawing of new lands and natural riches into the economic process, etc.), now it is intensive factors that constitute the main source of development of productive forces (increase in the productivity of labor, improved utilization of productive capacities, creation of a progressive structure for the nation's economy, multifaceted utilization of the achievements of science and technology, etc.).

During the Ninth Five-Year Plan, for example, 80-85 percent of the increment in national income, 87-90 percent of the increment in industrial output, 95 percent of building and installation expenditures, and the entire increment in agricultural output are to be achieved by intensification of production. Ultimately the net saving should amount to the equivalent of the labor of 32 million people.[3]

The course steered by the Communist Party of the Soviet Union, aimed at increasing the intensification of social production on all fronts, is already bearing fruit. It finds its

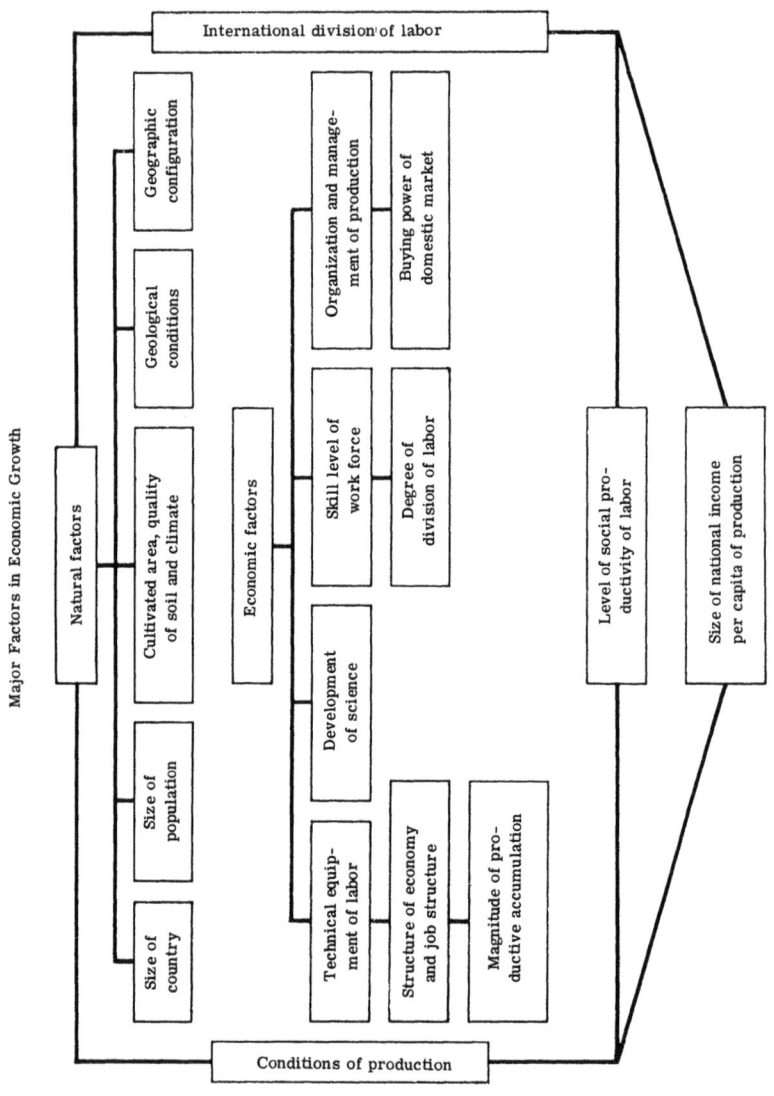

Figure 2.

The Current Organization of Foreign Trade

expression in the maintenance of high rates of growth of production. The average annual increase in industrial output in the USSR was 7.1 percent in 1971-72 and 7.3 percent in 1973, while in the United States it was 3.2 percent, in the Federal Republic of Germany it was 2.8 percent, in England it was 1.8 percent, and in France it was 6.4 percent. The total volume of industrial output in the USSR was 75 percent of that of the United States. Our country's lead in terms of growth rate meant that in 1971-72, the absolute growth in industrial output was more than 1.6 times that of the United States.[4]

Its economic achievements have enabled the Soviet Union, within a historically relatively brief space of time, to cope successfully with a number of socioeconomic problems: the standard of living of working people has been raised notably, a developed socialist society has been created, and we are now embarked on the path toward building the material and technical base for communism.

Foreign trade has had its role to play in the growth of our economic might and the intensification in our production. Indeed, in the modern world no country, no matter how vast its scientific-technical potential, is able to efficiently explore all the avenues to scientific-technical progress, not only because of the many levels on which it takes place and the tremendous mobility it requires, but also because it involves the expenditure of considerable material and intellectual resources.

Foreign trade, therefore, should be regarded not only as a factor for increasing the market resources of the country and expanding the list of products available, but also as a source for providing the nation's economy with goods or commodities not produced domestically or whose production would involve too great an expense.

The purchase of machinery and equipment, licenses for new technological processes, and prototypes of some new technology mean a saving in capital investment and in the expenditure of labor and materials; in the long run they make it possible to organize the production of technically advanced items within a short period. For example, it was foreign trade that enabled us to set up the car factory at Togliatti for production of the Zhiguli passenger car and to equip a number of plants at the KAMA conglomerate. Japan is a striking example of how foreign trade is able to stimulate rapid economic growth. That nation has now moved into second place in the capitalist world in terms of volume of industrial production, having overtaken the economically developed nations of Western Europe, including England, the FRG, and France. The average annual rate of growth of industrial production in Japan for 1958-70 was 13.3 percent (as compared with 4.3 percent for the United States and 2.9 percent for England in these same years), while for 1971 it was 4.8 percent (2.0 percent in the FRG and 1.6 percent in England). [5]

As numerous studies have shown, this unprecedented economic growth was made possible not only by internal factors but also through the exploitation of the advantages of the international division of labor by developing foreign trade on all fronts.

Thus Japan quite astutely imported ideas by means of patent and licensing agreements. During the 1969-70 financial year Japan concluded 1,629 agreements for the importation of foreign technology. This meant a collossal saving of investment and time for putting the new technology to work; in the end it modernized its industry on the basis of imported technology and created completely new branches of industry, such as radioelectronics, petrochemicals, the manufacture of metalworking equipment, construction machinery, as well as synthetic fibers and resins. [6]

Throughout the entire existence of the Soviet state, foreign trade was and is an important factor in the growth of our country's economic potential. Its role in this respect has been guaranteed by the planned management of both the state monopoly of foreign trade and the related monopoly over foreign exchange, which, on the one hand, have effectively protected socialist production from the chaos of the world capitalist market and, on the other hand, have enabled the state to concentrate its material resources and foreign exchange reserves on solving

The Current Organization of Foreign Trade

critical problems arising at different stages in the process of building socialism.

During the first years of industrialization, foreign trade was used to equip the nation with advanced technology and to improve the skill level of the work force by engaging foreign specialists.

Now, as the scientific-technical revolution proceeds apace, the role of foreign trade as a factor in the intensification of production is growing. It is sufficient to note that during the years of the Eighth Five-Year Plan alone, the machinery construction industry obtained 800 million rubles worth of metalworking machinery from abroad, including 36,000 metal-cutting machines. During this same period our fleet was increased by 1,350 foreign-built vessels of various types.[7]

The import of equipment, especially from other socialist countries, has helped to speed up the growth of a number of branches of industry, e.g., the chemical, metallurgical, automobile, and foodstuffs industries.

As a factor in the intensification of production, foreign trade fulfills a dual role: on the one hand its aim is to acquire highly productive techniques and advanced technology, and on the other it must ensure that broad layers of the scientific community and specialists are kept abreast of the latest innovations in science and technology. It is for these reasons that technical sections have been created in all-union associations, and a Technical Administration has been set up in the Ministry of Foreign Trade.

The function of these agencies is to acquaint specialists in industry with innovations and achievements in science and technology and to ensure that intelligent choices are made in the import of machinery and technology. In other words, the study of scientific-technical achievements abroad by these technology departments should in the final analysis develop into a factor of primary importance in shaping our policy toward technology with regard to the import of machinery and equipment.

Thus foreign trade has been given a fundamentally new role to play in the present stage of our development, as Party General Secretary L. I. Brezhnev pointed out at one of his meetings with Western businessmen:

> Over the past few years we have begun to get away from old notions with regard to this important question. This is only natural, since the old forms of economic relations no longer meet the needs of time. The economies of different countries have acquired new dimensions. The scientific-technical revolution is proceeding at a rapid pace, driven onward by the great achievements of human genius and labor. There have been great accomplishments in the area of culture and education. This relentless progress has brought about a tremendous growth in the needs and demands of people and requires a wider and wider international division of labor, the development of trade, and the growth of economic, scientific-technical, and cultural ties between governments. [8]

Continuing in this line of thought, L. I. Brezhnev stressed the importance of creating harmonious, stable, and large-scale relationships based on economic cooperation between nations.

An example of such large-scale cooperation is Soviet foreign trade with other socialist countries, especially those that are members of the Council for Mutual Economic Assistance [CMEA]. This cooperation takes place on the basis of long-term trade agreements; the principal characteristic distinguishing it from trade with the capitalist countries is that it is based on increasing specialization and cooperation in production between CMEA members. As production grows in the socialist countries, they export more and more items that can be advantageously produced by the domestic economy, and they cut back on or eventually cease production of goods that cannot be manufactured efficiently, turning to imports instead. Ultimately this means that a country is able to make more efficient use of its various factors of production: the work force, natural resources, materials, and financial resources. The Comprehensive Program for the Further Deepening and Improvement of Cooperation and Development of Socialist Economic Integration of the Member Nations of CMEA has brought long-term trade agreements more closely into line with the five-year plans of the individual socialist countries and ac-

The Current Organization of Foreign Trade

cordingly has favorably enhanced the role of foreign trade in the intensification of production.

The Soviet Union is a major purchaser of machinery from the socialist countries. Its imports of such goods from CMEA nations totaled 3.4 billion rubles in 1972. CMEA nations sell about half of their machinery output on the vast Soviet market. At the same time, Soviet exports of machinery, equipment, and raw materials to the socialist countries have grown.

The development of large-scale cooperation with capitalist countries has found expression in the conclusion of major long-term business deals, involving economic cooperation between the USSR and, for example, the Federal Republic of Germany, France, Italy, Japan, the United States, and so on. One type of such business agreements is the compensation agreement, in which Western countries participate in the construction of industrial projects within the USSR, and the industrial credits are later repaid with the output of the enterprise. Industrial cooperation is also sometimes arranged. Joint projects with Italy (the Volga Automobile Factory), Austria, the FRG, and Finland (in the natural gas industry) may be cited as examples. Furthermore, there exists an agreement to build a metallurgical plant in France with Soviet participation, a large plant in the Soviet Union with the participation of FRG firms, and finally, a number of agreements with the United States and Japan. Such transactions give the partners an opportunity to serve one another to mutual advantage on a long-term guaranteed basis rather than being of a short-term, incidental nature, subject to the vicissitudes of the business cycle.

Finally, foreign trade contributes positively to the development of the economy by making it possible to more quickly and easily eliminate bottlenecks and disproportions that arise from time to time in the course of economic growth.

As of January 1, 1974, the volume of foreign trade for the Soviet Union was 32.6 billion rubles. The Soviet Union maintains trade relations with 100 countries of the world, but most of its trade volume (65 percent) is with the socialist countries[9] (see Table 1). Table 1 shows a constant increase in foreign

The USSR's Management of Foreign Trade

Table 1

Volume of Soviet Foreign Trade
(millions of rubles)

	1950	1955	1960	1965	1970	1973
Total:						
turnover	2,925	5,838	10,073	14,610	22,085	31,343
export	1,615	3,084	5,007	7,357	11,520	15,802
import	1,310	2,754	5,066	7,253	10,565	15,541
Of which, with socialist countries:						
turnover	2,373	4,630	7,371	10,050	14,410	18,331
export	1,350	2,454	3,790	5,001	7,530	9,115
import	1,023	2,176	3,581	5,049	6,880	9,216
Including, with CMEA members:						
turnover	1,679	3,109	5,343	8,472	12,284	16,922
export	900	1,613	2,806	4,211	6,261	8,311
import	779	1,496	2,537	4,261	6,023	8,611
with developed capitalist countries:						
turnover	440	904	1,917	2,816	4,694	8,339
export	236	502	913	1,346	2,154	3,750
import	204	402	1,014	1,470	2,540	4,589
with developing countries:						
turnover	112	304	785	1,744	2,982	4,672
export	29	128	304	1,010	1,836	2,937
import	83	76	481	734	1,146	1,735

trade volume, which testifies to the growing importance of foreign trade in the nation's economy and its increasing participation in the international division of labor. L. I. Brezhnev, stressing this point in his speech on West German television on May 21, 1973, observed:

> Our plans certainly do not aim at autarky. We are not pursuing a policy of isolationism with regard to the rest of the world. On the contrary, we proceed from the conviction that our country will develop and grow as our cooperation with the outside world grows over a broad front, and by this we mean not only with the other socialist countries but also with countries with an opposing social system.[10]

It should be noted that the USSR has vast unutilized possibil-

The Current Organization of Foreign Trade

ities for increasing its participation in the international division of labor. This, indeed, should be evident just from the fact that the USSR's position in world trade does not match its rank with regard to industrial production.

As the Soviet Union becomes increasingly integrated into the international division of labor, the share of industries operating at above-average production efficiency in the economy must continually increase, while industries that are only marginally profitable will be cut back or abolished and the need for their products covered by imports. But such a trend will also give rise to a number of difficulties, particularly when it comes to working out and putting into effect a rational structure for our exports. The fact is that the increasing share of imports, connected with the intensification of production, requires foreign exchange procured through exports. It follows then that guidelines concerning the nature and direction of exports over the long term must be specified without delay in order to minimize the export of goods that are relatively expensive to produce.

First, production of goods for export must be expanded, their quality and technical level must be improved, and they must be made competitive on the world market. Of course, the formation and development of an export structure is a difficult task; to cope with it successfully, not only must domestic needs be met and more capital investments made, but products must be made competitive, markets must be clearly defined, etc.

This by no means exhausts the list of problems. In reality the interrelationships between foreign trade and the economy as a whole are much richer and more complex. Sometimes they are contradictory and require a good deal of calculation and analysis before an adequate notion of the extent of the influence of foreign trade on the development of the domestic economy can be obtained.

But such an analysis is beyond the purposes of this book. We only want to outline some of the main problems attendant on the growing role of foreign trade as a factor in the growth of social production and as a major instrument for utilizing the advantages flowing from the international division of labor in order to correctly determine the role of organizational factors in solving these problems and to delimit basic ways to improve management and organization within the system of the Ministry of Foreign Trade of the USSR.

2. The Organizational Structure of the Foreign Trade System

Foreign trade is a form of social division of labor; it is a broad, multifaceted concept and includes activities on many fronts: political, economic, commercial, foreign exchange and financial, legal, industrial, technical, technological, and social. All of these types of activities are implied in the general term "foreign trade activity."

It is evident, therefore, that the organization of activities to carry out the tasks involved in foreign trade is a quite complicated problem having many aspects. The keynote in our efforts to cope with this problem was struck with the decree of the Soviet of People's Commissars of April 22, 1918, entitled "The Nationalization of Foreign Trade," in which the state was given a monopoly over foreign trade activity. The decree reads:

> I. All foreign trade is hereby nationalized. Trade transactions involving the sale and purchase of any type product (extractive, manufacturing, agricultural, etc.) with foreign governments or private commercial enterprises abroad will be done by agencies specifically authorized to do so on behalf of the Russian Republic. Apart from these agencies, any trade transactions abroad for import or for export are prohibited.
> II. The People's Commissariat for Trade and Industry shall be the agency responsible for nationalized foreign trade.
> III. A Foreign Trade Concil shall be established under the People's Commissariat of Trade and Industry to organize exports and imports.
> IV. The Foreign Trade Council will implement a plan

The Current Organization of Foreign Trade

for the exchange of goods abroad, worked out and ratified by the People's Commissariat of Trade and Industry.[11]

This decree organized foreign trade or the activity implied by it along two lines: it set up a centralized Foreign Trade Council, and it established "authorized agencies" for supervising the "sale and purchase of any type of product" abroad; these two forms of organization, seen as a system, constitute a dialectical whole, a unified, complex, and constantly changing system.

A. The organizational structure of the Ministry of Foreign Trade

As it has developed, the Ministry of Foreign Trade has undergone continual improvements in accordance with the requirements of building socialism. At the present time it is organized to cover three basic areas of activity, which may be provisionally described as follows:
— the organization of directly commercial activity;
— the organization of activity associated with the supervision, management, and regulation of foreign trade activity;
— the organization of activity concerned with promoting the development of foreign trade.

The departments established by this structure fit into four groups.

The first group (commercial and accounting activity) consists of all-union export-import associations and all-union export-import offices, which perform directly commercial operations (the preparation, conclusion, and execution of sales and purchases). It also includes a subgroup of authorized associations attached to Soviet trade missions, trade consultants attached to Soviet embassies and missions, and embassy consultants on economic affairs stationed in foreign countries to protect the rights and interests of all-union associations.

The USSR's Management of Foreign Trade

A second group (involved in the supervision, management, and regulation of foreign trade activity) is the central apparatus of the Ministry of Foreign Trade.

A third group (to promote the development of foreign trade) consists of the Scientific Research Institute on Business Cycles of the Ministry of Foreign Trade, the All-Union Academy of Foreign Trade, and the Moscow State Institute for International Relations of the Soviet Foreign Ministry, all of which are concerned with promoting the development of the Soviet Union's economic ties with foreign countries.

The fourth, quite special group within the foreign trade apparatus consists of Soviet trade missions, trade consultants attached to Soviet embassies and missions, and embassy consultants on economic affairs. They regulate and supervise foreign trade with the host countries; they are official agencies of the Union of Soviet Socialist Republics, exercising its rights attendant on the state monopoly of foreign trade.[12]

From the very beginning of Soviet power, foreign trade has been an organic part (one of the sectors) of the socialist economy by virtue of this state monopoly. All activity pertaining to foreign trade and the various organizational structures designed to deal with it have been dictated by and subject to the same economic laws of socialism as the entire system of socialist division of labor.

First of all, foreign trade develops as an organic part of the economy, i.e., export and import flows and their commodity structure are strictly determined (what, to whom, and when goods are supplied and sold to meet the social requirements of the socialist economy as a whole). The quantitative and qualitative aspects of these processes are determined in the economic plan. Organizationally this means the establishment of adequate links between the Ministry of Foreign Trade, the USSR Council of Ministers, and its functional arms (Gosplan USSR, Gossnab USSR, the State Committee of the Soviet Council of Ministers for Science and Technology, the Ministry of Finance, etc.), on the one hand, and with the ministries for particular branches of industry and the councils of minis-

The Current Organization of Foreign Trade

ters of the union republics, on the other. While in the first case these links are intended to ensure that the political and economic development of foreign trade is consonant with the interests of society as a whole, in the second case, they represent the practical embodiment of those interests.

It follows, of course, that foreign trade activity must also be organized with a view toward its bearing on both these areas, i.e., socialist production and the foreign market. Accordingly there is on the one hand the central apparatus of the Ministry of Foreign Trade, with all its various subdivisions, which have centralized ties with government agencies and determine trade policy; on the other hand there is the operational apparatus, consisting of independent, economically accountable state foreign trade all-union associations involved directly in sales and purchases and maintaining ongoing practical relations with the sectoral ministries and their enterprises for the purchase and sale of goods.

The organizational structure of the central apparatus of the Ministry of Foreign Trade includes the minister, his deputies, the Collegium, the Secretariat, the Records Section, the Inspectorate under the ministry (trade-policy administrations for Trade with the Socialist Countries of Europe, the Eastern Administration, the Administration for Western Countries, the Administration for Trade with the Americas, the Administration for Trade with Asia, the Administration for Trade with Africa, the Administration for Cooperation with the CMEA Countries, and the Administration for International Economic Organizations), the main sectoral administrations (Main Administration for the Export of Transport, Highway Construction, and Agricultural Machinery; the Main Administration for the Export of Industrial Equipment; the Main Administration for the Import of Machinery and Equipment for Socialist Countries; the Main Administration for Import of Machinery and Equipment from Capitalist Countries; the Main Administration for the Export of Manufactured and Consumer Goods; the Main Administration for the Export of Raw Materials; the Main Administration for the Import of Consumer Goods and Raw Materials for Their Production; the Main Administration for the Import of Industrial Raw Materials; and the Main Administration for Compensation Projects), and functional administrations and departments (the Administration for Legal Contracts; the Main Administration for Economic Planning; the Main Administration for Foreign Exchange; the Financial Administration; the Transport Administration; the Main Tariff Administration; the Accounting, Auditing, and Bookkeeping Administration; the Technical Administration; the Administration for the Organization of Labor and Information Systems; the State Export Quality Inspectorate; the Cadre Administration; the Affairs Administration; the Central Archives; the Central Library; and the Computer Center).

The Ministry of Foreign Trade is the central apparatus for the supervision, management, and regulation of foreign trade; its activities are defined in the 1923 "Statutes for the People's Commissariat of Foreign Trade," in the "General Statutes for Ministries of the USSR" ratified by the Council of Ministers in 1967, and in the regulations governing its various subdivisions.

What, why, when, and how the activities of any of the departments should be performed is regulated by the statutes concerning the rights and duties of departments, ratified by the leadership of the ministry.

The all-union export-import associations conduct their activities on the basis of ordinances ratified by the Ministry of Foreign Trade and ordinarily published in the journal <u>Foreign Trade</u> [Vneshniaia torgovlia]. They are not permitted to trade in goods or to perform acts not specified in the regulations.

B. <u>The present organizational structure of an all-union association</u>

The all-union export-import associations are independent state organizations operating on the principles of economic accountability and enjoying the rights of a juridical person.

The Current Organization of Foreign Trade

At the beginning of 1974 the Ministry of Foreign Trade had under it 43 all-union export-import associations and all-union export-import offices.

They are of two types, those dealing in specific goods ("Aviaeksport," "Avtoeksport," "Avtopromimport," "Litsenzintorg," "Mashpriborintorg," "Mashinoeksport," "Metallurgimport," "Mezhdunarodnaia kniga," "Medeksport," "Prodintorg," "Prommashimport," "Promsyr'eimport," "Raznoimport," "Raznoeksport," "Soiuzkhimeksport," "Sudoimport," "Traktoroeksport," "Eksportlen," "Eksportkhleb," "Eksportles," "Tekhnoproimport," "Tekhmashimport," "Zapchast'eksport," etc.) and associations servicing trade ("Soiuzvneshtrans," "Sovfrakht," "Vneshtorgreklama," "Vneshtorgizdat," etc.). A separate group is formed by regional foreign trade organizations (V/O "Vostokintorg," the all-union offices "Lenfintorg," "Dal'intorg," Vneshtorgbank SSSR). [See the glossary on pp. 238-41.]

In the organization of the activity of the all-union export-import associations, it is possible to discern a variety of different areas of activity — commercial, economic, auxiliary, and administrative — each representing a specific combination of material-technical, manpower, and financial resources. To take care of these tasks, a number of subdivisions are formed: operational, export, import, and export-import offices, departments for economic planning and for foreign exchange and financing, etc.

These various types of activities constitute an organic unity and together shape the overall foreign trade activity of an association; the activity is carried out through a vast network linking the association with the various subdivisions of the Ministry of Foreign Trade and government agencies, on the one hand, and with foreign firms on the other. Figure 3 shows the various relations maintained by a typical import association.[13]

All-union associations differ in terms of the list of goods handled and the direction of trade (export or import, or both).

For example, one group of associations deals with machinery (V/O "Aviaeksport," "Avtopromimport," "Avtoeksport,"

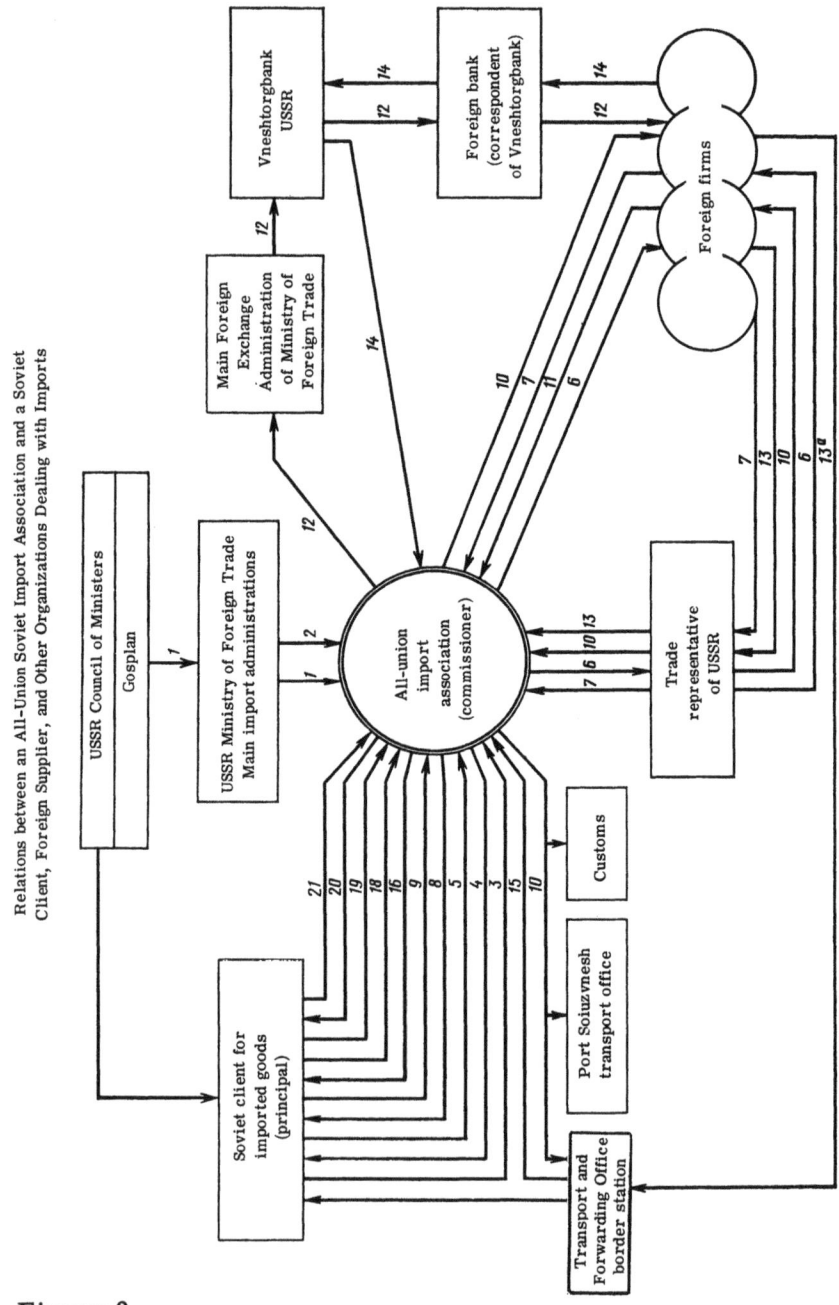

Figure 3. Relations between an All-Union Soviet Import Association and a Soviet Client, Foreign Supplier, and Other Organizations Dealing with Imports

Figure 3.

1 – import plan, plan for deliveries to the economy, particular regulations of the Council of Ministers on imports during the current plan year; 2 – import permissions; 3 – application for import or commission for import; 4 – specification of the technical terms of the order; 5 – customer's answers to the questions posed by the association; 6 – posting of bids to foreign firm; 7 – receipt of offers from the foreign firm; 8 – preparation of draft contract and its coordination with the customer; 9 – customer's confirmation of the terms of the contract; 10 – conclusion of contract with foreign firm; 11 – receipt of notification from the firm that the goods are ready for delivery; 12 – open letters of credit through Vneshtorgbank USSR; 13 – receipt of notification that the goods have been delivered; 14 – receipt of bills and other documents for receipt of payment from the firm; 15 – receipt of information that the goods have passed the country's border; 16 – presentation of bill to customer; 17 – movement of goods over the territory of the USSR; 18 – receipt of deed of provisional transfer of goods from customer; 19, 20, and 21 – communication with customer (information on how the equipment is working, etc.).

The USSR's Management of Foreign Trade

"Zapchast'eksport," "Mashinoimport," "Mashinoeksport," "Mashpriborintorg," "Prommashimport," "Stankoimport," "Sudoimport," "Tekhmashimport," "Tekhmasheksport," "Traktoroeksport," "Energomasheksport," "Elektronorgtekhnika"); another deals with raw materials (V/O "Almaziuvelirtorg," "Medeksport," "Metallurgimport," "Prodintorg," "Promsyr'eimport," "Raznoimport," "Raznoeksport," "Soiuzgazeksport," "Soiuznefteeksport," "Soiuzplodoimport," "Soiuzpromeksport," "Soiuzpushnina," "Soiuzkhimeksport," "Tekhnopromimport," "Tekhsnabeksport," "Eksportlen," "Eksportles," "Eksportkhleb"), and still others trade specific goods (V/O "Litsenzintorg," which buys and sells patents for inventions and licenses for their use; V/O "Novoeksport," which exports handcrafted items made of wood, bone, stone, and metal, ceramics, porcelain, etc.; and V/O "Vneshposyltorg," which deals in retail and small-scale sales of industrial and consumer goods).

Some associations do only exports or imports, others do both. The associations trade in an extremely large number of items, which of course makes their activity more complicated. For instance, seven machinery associations purchase imports of industrial equipment from a list covering more than 120 branch ministries and agencies, while the number of branch ministries and agencies with which associations dealing in both export and import conduct business is even greater. This, of course, is one of the reasons why associations dealing exclusively in exports or exclusively in imports were set up. But this can create problems in coordinating the two flows, since the possibilities for using imports to stimulate exports will be far from fully utilized. Furthermore, when identical lists for imported and exported goods are brought together under one association, it will have to maintain a wider network of relations, and that in the end can only complicate its activity. To deal with this problem it appears appropriate to proceed along the line of breaking up the associations, but within the framework of large, economically accountable for-

The Current Organization of Foreign Trade

eign trade associations. These latter then function as government foreign trade enterprises, operating on the principles of economic accountability and specializing in a restricted list of goods.

The bulk of the activity of foreign trade associations involves commercial operations; all its other activities are auxiliary, aimed at keeping these operations free of snags. The commercial activities of an association are organized by commodities and sectors: an association's list of goods is broken down by particular offices. Thus the entire commodity list of "Mashinoeksport," which includes a large group of electrical, power-producing, transport, oil-processing, and other equipment, is divided up among ten offices: electric, pumps and compressors, power-producing equipment, transport equipment, petroleum-processing equipment, and an office for excavators and self-powered cranes, armatures, mobile railroad stock, above-ground transport, electric transport, and high-voltage equipment. Each office conducts trade operations with all countries for the items on its list. Usually the staff of each office is divided into engineers and managerial personnel.

The pumps and compressors office of "Mashinoimport" can help illustrate the structure of an office set up according to the sectoral principle. The staff consists of two groups, one for the purchase of compressor equipment, the other for pumping equipment.

In some associations these offices are organized by region rather than by goods sector. Thus V/O "Soiuznefteeksport" has offices for trade with the West, the East, and the Far East, each office trading in all the items on the association's list. V/O "Mezhdunarodnaia kniga" has offices for disseminating Soviet literature in capitalist and socialist countries.

Thus in practice these offices are organized along a variety of different lines. The form of organization that will be the most efficient in the particular case will depend on the goods being bought or sold, the specific features of the market for these goods, and the goals and tasks of the association. All these factors must, therefore, be carefully weighed in working out or improving the organizational structure of an office, and haste should be avoided. The organization of the commercial activities of V/O "Sudoimport" is an example of the complexity of such questions. The association contains offices for the export and import of ships and offices for the export of ship equipment. Studies done by the association staff show that the work load is distributed unevenly among the office personnel. The offices for the export and import of ships bear their greatest load when orders are being moved and ships are being delivered, while the offices for the export of equipment are constantly overburdened. It would appear than under such conditions, if the export of equipment and the import of ships were combined into one office, the work load would be more evenly distributed. A merger of this sort is further favored by the fact that exported equipment goes on vessels being built to Soviet order. But there are also some negative aspects to such a structure. For example, the staff of these offices may find that they do not have enough time to process the technical and other documentation that is especially important in filling the individual orders characteristic of shipbuilding.

However, the organizational structure of an all-union association and its offices does not give us the whole picture of how commercial activities are organized. These activities include export and import transactions, price calculations, study of commodity markets and the influence of political and economic factors on them, monitoring of trends in the evolution of the structure and design of an item, its competitiveness, and finally, dealings with suppliers and clients at home and abroad.

Export and import transactions are complex processes in which many factors are involved: quantity, costs, the novelty of an item, its importance, price, and quality, whether a purchase or sale is to be with capitalist or socialist countries, whether a purchase is part of the plan, if it is mass-produced, etc.

Subjective factors are involved as well, e.g., the technical and commercial experience of the staff, customer relations,

The Current Organization of Foreign Trade

age, command of the foreign language, general erudition, etc.

For these reasons the organization of commercial activities is a process with many aspects, such as organizing the various subdivisions and providing precise descriptions of the tasks of each department and employee and of their relations and ties with other agencies and with the world at large (see Figure 3). These tasks fall under the regulations set down in the association charter, in the statutes concerning offices and departments of associations, and in official instructions ratified by the management of the association.

Since commercial operations involve a definite process, their organization, like the organization of any activity, requires the appropriate instruments for carrying them out, that is, certain procedures must be observed if export and import operations are to be carried out efficiently. To this end were issued in 1960 the "Conditions for Supplying Goods for Export," with subsequent amendments and additions, and the "Conditions to Be Observed by Foreign Trade Organizations in Filling Orders by Soviet Organizations for Imported Goods" of 1969.

Thus there are seven main steps (a total of 40 steps in all) involved in a typical import transaction involving machinery:

First step — the decision to buy (resolution by the Council of Ministers, the import plan, instructions by the leadership of the Ministry of Foreign Trade);
Second step — submission of the import application to the foreign trade association;
Third step — posting of the request to the firm;
Fourth step — receipt of bids from the firm and forwarding them to the customer;
Fifth step — receipt of the customer's decision;
Sixth step — signing of the contract;
Seventh step — delivery, installation, and putting the equipment into operation.

Each step in this sequence is defined in the individual case by a resolution from the Council of Ministers, the import plan, instructions by the leadership of the Ministry of Foreign Trade, or by the "Conditions to Be Observed by Foreign Trade

Organizations in Filling Orders by Soviet Organizations for Imported Goods." All these steps are organically interrelated, and delays in one will cause a breakdown in another. The first and second steps require considerable preparation on the part of the customer, the ministry, and the foreign trade association, and the expeditious handling of the rest of the transaction will depend on how well this preparation is carried out.

The third, fourth, and sixth steps are the strictly commercial side of an association's activities. These steps place great demands on those who work with foreign trade: they must know the market for the particular equipment, and they must be technically competent to deal with it. The fourth step involves computations and pricing and drawing up a contract for negotiations, and the sixth step involves negotiations and conclusion of the contract. Thereafter it is incumbent on the foreign trade association to ensure that the terms of the contract are observed and that settlement is made with the foreign supplier and the customer.

The dealings of V/O "Medeksport" with capitalist firms can serve as an example of the actual mechanics of an export transaction.

First, preparations are made for concluding a contract with a foreign firm. The first step is to send an offer to the prospective buyer. The offer contains the following requisite points: designation of the item, quantity, price, total cost of the purchase, time of delivery, terms of payment, and the period the offer is valid. Offers are firm and binding. If the buyer is interested in the item offered, a full or partial acceptance of the offer is made. Often correspondence ensues during which price, delivery time, transportation, and many other questions are decided. Then the actual contract is drafted, typically including the name of the firm, the object of the transaction, price, terms of payment, period of guarantee, and the firm's address.

Once the draft is approved by the pertinent functional departments and signed by the association's management, it is

The Current Organization of Foreign Trade

sent to the firm for signing. Usually the buyer keeps the first copy of the contract, and the second is signed and returned to the association. At this point the contract is considered concluded, and the foreign trade association assumes the obligation to deliver the contracted goods to the firm.

The contract, signed by both parties, is again approved by the functional departments and passed on to the accounting department, where a check is made to see if other accounts with the supplying factory and the purchasing firm are in order. The office keeps one copy of the contract for its economist and one copy for the secretary. Another copy is sent to the trade representative in the country of the buyer.

In the case of manufacture and supply of medical equipment, the export association submits an order schedule to the supplying factory, specifying the time by which the latter must have shipped the item ordered.

Thus we see that the organizational structure of the Ministry of Foreign Trade is determined by a number of factors: the scale of operations, the variety of items offered, the number of business ties within the country and abroad, etc.

The main features defining the structure of the Ministry of Foreign Trade are:

— the degree of specialization of all-union associations with regard to the nomenclature of goods which they handle, S';

— the degree of specialization of all-union associations with regard to particular types of products covered by the ministry as a whole, S'';

— the degree of specialization of all-union associations with regard to groups of products within the ministry, S''';

— the extent of cooperation between foreign trade associations;

— the degree of specialization of auxiliary and supplying services.

The variables S', S'', and S''' may be determined as follows: Let n be the number of foreign trade associations trading m types of commodities. Then the distribution of the volume of trade turnover among the different foreign trade associations and with respect to the nomenclature of goods offered can be described by the matrix:

$$\begin{matrix} b_{11}, & b_{12} & \ldots & b_{1j} & \ldots & b_{1m} \\ b_{21}, & b_{22} & \ldots & b_{2j} & \ldots & b_{2m} \\ \ldots & \ldots & b_{ij} & \ldots & \ldots & \ldots \\ b_{n1}, & b_{n2} & \ldots & b_{nj} & \ldots & b_{nm}, \end{matrix}$$

where b_{ij} is the volume of export (trade turnover) expressed in the total value of item j exported by association i.

The degree of specialization of that association with respect to item j can be calculated by the formula:

$$S' = \frac{b_{ij}}{\sum_{j=1}^{m} b_{ij}},$$

where $\sum_{j=1}^{m} b_{ij}$ is the total volume of product exported by association i.

For the ministry as a whole, the degree of specialization is:

$$S'' = \frac{b_{ij}}{\sum_{i=1}^{n} b_{ij}},$$

where $\sum_{i=1}^{n} b_{ij}$ is the total volume of item j exported by all associations n, and finally:

$$S''' = \frac{\sum_{i=1}^{n} b_{ij}}{\sum_{i=1}^{n} \sum_{j=1}^{m} b_{ij}},$$

where $\sum_{i=1}^{n} \sum_{j=1}^{m} b_{ij}$ is the volume of the total export (trade turnover) of the Ministry of Foreign Trade.

A knowledge of the degree of specialization of all-union foreign trade associations and their departments provides us not only with an idea of the internal organizational structure of

The Current Organization of Foreign Trade

the Ministry of Foreign Trade, but also helps us to determine the conditions for a rational choice of structure for the management of foreign trade as a whole and of the particular foreign trade associations. The structure of production determines the structure of management, the number of management subsystems, and their interrelationship. These questions will be dealt with in the next chapter.

CHAPTER TWO

Theoretical Foundations
of the Management of Foreign Trade

1. <u>Methodological and Practical Aspects of the Application of the General Theory of Management to Foreign Trade</u>

The term "management" has a variety of interpretations in the scientific literature, although most of them agree that management, first, is one form of labor activity within the overall system of the social division of labor and, second, is intended to achieve rational organization of the labor activity of collectives as they strive to accomplish the goals they set for themselves.

We feel that this definition describes the essence of management most fully and that it has important methodological and practical significance. In the first place, it follows from this definition that management, as a specific kind of activity within the overall system of the division of labor, has its own unique characteristics that distinguish it from other kinds of labor, and that these characteristics are always present, regardless of the sphere of application of managerial activity (i.e., whether it is economics, transportation, trade, culture, etc.). What this means, in essence, is that there exist more or less objective criteria for classifying workers according to their sphere of activity. Indeed, it is no secret that in practice, engineering-technical workers have often been classified as managerial personnel because of their education (engineer, economist, technician, etc.).

In addition, the above definition of management allows us to abstract from the many kinds of activity and to concentrate our attention on investigating the principal recurrent patterns in managerial activity.

The Theory of Managing Foreign Trade

One feature specific to the development of managerial activity is that its end result is not concrete material goods; rather, it is oriented primarily toward organizing collectives engaged in production or in the achievement of specified objectives. Management involves purposeful influence on the object of management by a subject.

This influence evolves as a continuous repetitive process, with its own characteristic stages, following one another until the specified goals have been achieved.

The first stage of this process is <u>planning</u>, which culminates in a decision concerning the goal of some collective activity and the definition of the tasks that goal imposes on the collective as a whole, as well as its separate offices. Goals and tasks are delineated, options are spelled out, and the commercial, technical, financial, and other resources instrumental to achieving these goals and tasks are enumerated.

But the mere setting of goals and formulation of tasks do not yet mean their accomplishment; the appropriate conditions must first be created for this. Hence the second essential stage is the <u>organization</u> of activity directed toward their realization; in this stage the forms and types of productive relationships between workers, various offices, etc., are determined. The end result of this stage is the creation of an organizational system in which each participant (department, office) has a specific function and knows what must be done, who is to do it and why, when it must be done, and how it must be done.

After the personnel and material means have been so organized, the stage is set for direct action aimed at accomplishing the specified task, in the process of which the constant coordination and direction of the activity of the participants is essential. This type of activity constitutes the third stage of management, which is <u>coordination</u> (guidance).

Finally, the actions of the particular system (collective) culminate in the achievement of specific results. In this stage the results obtained are compared and contrasted with the tasks and goals set down beforehand in the plan. This stage is the stage of <u>control</u>. In it the activity of the given system is evaluated with regard to the accomplishment of the goals it had set for itself, and if necessary, some adjustments or modifications are made in the specific terms of the goals or in the general direction of the collective's activity.

The actions performed by managerial personnel in each of these successive stages are the functions of management. They are essential to any process of management, regardless of whether it takes place in industry or foreign trade, at an enterprise, or in an all-union association.

In fact, each element of foreign trade activity — the object of labor, the instruments of labor, the work force, and the industrial process (in our case the foreign trade process), as well as all of these taken together — requires planning, organization, coordination and guidance, accounting, and control.

Each function of management (planning, organization, coordination and guidance, accounting, and control) is in essence a uniform managerial activity, consisting of a multitude of special kinds of work. They essentially reflect the task-functions of management, whose content is determined in each particular case by the nature and complexity of industrial processes and by the specific features of the object. Management thus has a dual nature: it consists, first, of the realization of its principal functions (planning, organization, coordination and guidance, accounting, and control), which are constant regardless of the object of management (i.e., whether it is industry or foreign trade, an enterprise or an all-union association, etc.); and second, of the task-functions whose specific content is determined by the distinctive features and characteristics of the object.

The task-functions of management may be illustrated by means of a matrix in which the functions of management are differentiated in accordance with the principal elements of the foreign trade process.

Each element in the matrix A_{nm} is a task-function of management that must be performed if a principal function of management is to be fulfilled. For example, to fulfill the managerial function of planning, it is necessary to do concrete work (task-

The Theory of Managing Foreign Trade

Table 2

Differentiation of the Principal Functions of Management
in Accordance with the Elements of the Foreign Trade Process

Elements of the foreign trade process	Principal functions of management			
	Planning	Organization	Coordination	Accounting and control
Subject of labor	a_{11}	a_{12}	a_{13}	a_{14}
Instruments of labor	a_{21}	a_{22}	a_{23}	a_{24}
Work force	a_{31}	a_{32}	a_{33}	a_{34}
Foreign trade process	a_{41}	a_{42}	a_{43}	a_{44}

functions) on planning the objects of labor a_{11}, the instruments of labor a_{21}, the work force a_{31}, and on combining them in a way necessary to carry out process a_{41}.

But it is not difficult to see that in this form the matrix is not yet adequate for defining the specific features of management for each object or process; the principal functions must first be further broken down into both the basic elements and subelements of the foreign trade process.

Table 3

Matrix for Determining the Task-Functions of Management
in Foreign Trade

Stages of the foreign trade process	Principal functions of management					
	Principal elements of the foreign trade process	Subelements of the foreign trade process	Planning	Organization	Coordination and guidance	Accounting and control
Procurement of funds						
Conclusion of contracts						
Placement of orders						
Deliveries						

This matrix brings out the specific features of the object of

39

management as reflected in the content of the managerial task-functions.

Thus, for example, the task functions of management of foreign trade activity are:

— planned direction of foreign trade activity, with attention paid to the complex and dynamic development of the nation's economy;

— continuous strengthening and deepening of foreign economic relationships with socialist countries, especially with the CMEA nations, as part of the implementation of the Comprehensive Program for Socialist Integration;

— an overall raising of the economic effectiveness of foreign trade by improving export and import structures, expanding the export of machinery and equipment and of other finished products;

— active introduction of new forms of foreign trade based on broadly conceived economic cooperation with all countries of the world.

In terms of everyday activity these task-functions of management amount to the following. Quantitative and qualitative determination of the component parts of these task-functions creates the preconditions for evaluating management work, determining its scope, and developing normative guidelines for staff size. Finally, with this as a basis, a rational structure for the management system can be constructed.

The next distinguishing feature of management is that the relationships between the subject and object of management are relationships of power, subordination, and command on the part of the subject and compliance with command and subordination on the part of the object.

These relationships are realized through specific organizational forms that serve as the framework for the relationships and interactions between the subject and object of management (channels for the implementation of managerial actions and feedbacks). Together, according to systems theory, the subject and object of management and their interactions form a complex, constantly evolving system in which the subject is the managing, and the object the managed subsystem; in most cases, moreover, subject and object are themselves complex structures characterized by their own hierarchically organized system of elements.

The concept of "system" is not essentially a new one. It has recently assumed great importance, however, in connection with the growing complexity of economic relations and social processes. In the contemporary literature a system is viewed in two aspects: as a means for organizing our knowledge about some object or process being studied or regulated from the vantage point of an observer, with the purpose of achieving an adequate reflection of its real workings in our consciousness; and as an integral structure consisting of individual elements that are interconnected by energy or information channels and that possess certain integrative characteristics not inherent in full measure in any of its elements taken separately. From the second part of the definition it follows that the whole of the real world around us consists of systems and is a kind of system in its own right.

In other words, systems can be classified according to whether they belong to the real world (real systems) or whether they are constructs of human consciousness (abstract systems).

All the various sorts of information we have about a real system can be subdivided into separate groups according to specific attributes. Thus the information and data we have about an all-union association as a real system can be broken down into information about offices, lists of goods, information media, etc. Depending on the goal of our inquiry, we may be interested only in certain bodies of information or in the entire aggregate of information available. This aggregate of information about an all-union association is a system of knowledge and is analogous to a real system. An abstract system, seen as an aggregate of information, will find expression either in a simple description or in a set of figures, mathematical equations, or graphs.

A number of graphic methods are most often used to provide fuller information about a real system (an all-union association, office, etc.).

The USSR's Management of Foreign Trade

All systems, depending on their nature, are classified in general systems theory as biological, mechanical, biochemical, and social.

Furthermore, since all systems function in time, they are called dynamic. This means in essence that the system should be viewed not only from the vantage point of its static structure or its individual properties, but as a whole, taking into account its functioning over time.

At the present level of development of science, most real systems subject to human regulation, as well as the processes taking place within them, cannot be described by a single language. Moreover, in a number of their aspects they cannot even be formalized and are at their core complex dynamic systems.

Most of the systems of management in foreign trade are such systems.

An example of such a complex dynamic system is, for instance, the management of foreign trade, which consists of a huge number of elements that in turn are complex dynamic systems in their own right. Hence, when we speak of systems of management in foreign trade, we will implicitly be extracting from this whole, from this "system of systems," as it were, that aspect of it which interests us at the particular moment in accordance with our particular purpose.

In the specific instance management may be carried out by two more independent managed subsystems. In general form a system of management can be described as follows (see Figure 4).

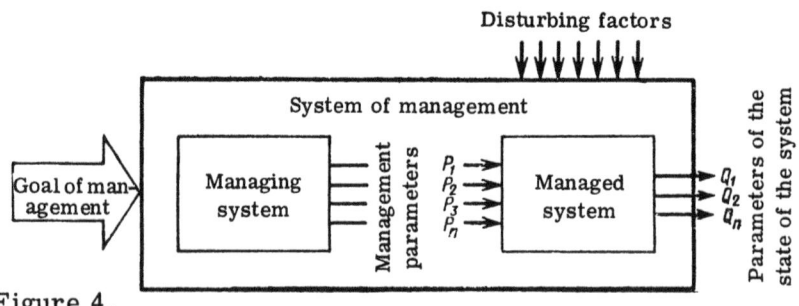

Figure 4.

The Theory of Managing Foreign Trade

We should bear in mind here that any system, in our example an all-union association, must in its functioning be held in some prescribed state or changed in some desired direction. The necessity of change derives from the fact that our system (an all-union association) functions within a determinate environment and is subject to its influence: specifically, the Ministry of Foreign Trade, clients, suppliers, etc. Hence the function of the managing subsystem (the managerial staff of the all-union association) is to act on the managed subsystem (which is the operations of all the parts of the all-union association) in such a direction as to maintain the desired state expressed in the output parameters $Q_1 \ldots Q_n$ (fulfillment of the export-import plan, etc.), which are achieved by using various methods of influence $(P_1 \ldots P_n)$ on the managed subsystem. This influence $(P_1 \ldots P_n)$ consists of material incentives for the staff, regulation of the number of employees, setting of plan targets, etc.

Obviously, and this follows from Figure 4, the more parameters there are for the influence P_n exerted on the managed subsystem, the more manageable is the entire subsystem. But it should be kept in mind that any increase in the magnitude of the parameters brings about an increase in the complexity of the process of management, and in a number of cases a decrease in its effectiveness as well, especially when there are no means to obtain a quantitative estimate of the parameters.

2. The Effectiveness of Management of Foreign Trade and Ways to Improve It

Opinions vary, of course, as to what is meant by efficient management. However, most agree that its definition should in some way or other be based on a comparison of what is aimed for and what is actually achieved in terms, for example, of the net results of foreign trade activity. Without rejecting this approach, we think that in addition, the dual nature of managerial activity should be taken into account in the definition of effective management.

Accordingly, in the first instance it is the amount of labor expended in performing purely managerial activities (handling information, preparing and making decisions, etc.) and the reliability, flexibility, and productivity of management, in a word, the degree of optimality and rationality in the way it is organized, which are of primary importance in evaluating the efficiency of management.

For instance, some helpful parameters would be the time consumed in managerial activities, the number of documents handled by one administrative employee, the level of training of the administrative staff, the extent to which managerial activities are mechanized, the stability of key personnel (personnel turnover), the number of employees in one administrative department, the number of employees of all-union associations in one administrative department, the number of all-union associations in one organizational department of the overall system, the volume of the proper flow into one administrative department of the entire system.

In the second instance efficiency would be defined in terms of a comparison with the net results of the outlay on maintaining the administrative apparatus as a system plus costs of carrying out foreign trade (salaries of workers, costs of goods, loan repayments, maintenance of buildings and equipment, and other noncommercial expenses). This would be an economic definition of managerial efficiency.

Some helpful parameters would be the cost of maintaining one administrative employee, the cost of maintaining the overall administrative apparatus per thousand rubles of foreign trade volume, the proportionate cost of maintaining the apparatus in terms of the intrinsic costs of exports and imports, the proportion of employee wages in the total wage bill, and so on.

Hence the efficiency of management can be evaluated only in terms of the whole system, not any single index. Using a set of parameters enables us to assess the efficiency of the system from several different aspects; but at the same time, it makes it more difficult to reach decisions regarding problems associated with the overall functioning of the system. A broad,

The Theory of Managing Foreign Trade

multifaceted assessment of management is necessary. In other words, the question is whether management as a whole can be evaluated on the basis of methods of mathematical economics, which reflect the logic of the foreign trade process and use the most important criteria for the effectiveness of management. When it is the management of large systems, such as the system of management of foreign trade, which is at issue, a simple approach is not sufficient for evaluating efficiency. In our opinion, in this case the problem should be dealt with in terms of how the effect of management is distributed over the different levels of management. In a number of cases it should be distributed according to types of managerial functions (planning, coordination, control, etc.). In the end this will enable one to see at once whether any operations are duplicated as a function is performed from top down within the organizational structure, and to determine the scope of work performed at each level in itself.

It also follows from what we have said that to achieve a high degree of effectiveness in management, all the above-enumerated parameters must be fulfilled to an optimal degree. To achieve this, of course, is a complex matter. Everything will depend on the existing conditions of functioning of the system, on having an optimal number of elements in the system, and on the quality of their internal relationships, which in turn determine the quality and organization of the system of management as a whole. In other words, with regard to foreign trade the problem touches on the conditions under which the functions, powers, and responsibilities of the Ministry of Foreign Trade and its departments (main administrations, all-union associations, trade missions, etc.) are realized in the process of accomplishing its goals as a managerial body. Looking at the system of management of foreign trade, the conditions for its functioning can be divided into external and internal. Furthermore, one specific feature of the management of foreign trade that must be taken into account is that it functions within two external environments which develop along fundamentally different lines. They are: the socialist economic system, which evolves on the basis of planning, and the capitalist system, which evolves spontaneously, on the basis of competition. Thus while in the first case the conditions of functioning are basically stable, in the second case they are extremely unstable, cyclical, and transient and are shaped by many factors. The conditions of functioning of the management system are manifested in different ways at different levels. Thus for an all-union association they are determined by the conditions of functioning of the Ministry of Foreign Trade as a branch of the economy in itself, by the conditions of functioning of the various other branches of the economy (industry, agriculture, plant and equipment, etc.), and finally, by the conditions of functioning of enterprises in socialist countries and capitalist firms. Taken together, the functioning of the foreign trade management system is determined: by the conditions of development of socialist production, the conditions of development of the world socialist system, and the conditions of development of the world capitalist system. It is at this level that the accumulation and use of knowledge about the laws and conditions of development of socialist production and capitalist production take place. On the basis of an informed foreign trade policy, which takes into account basic political, economic, commercial, monetary and financial, and legal developments in the world at large, the activities of the all-union associations, trade missions, and other organizations involved in foreign trade are coordinated and regulated.

All these aspects are reflected in the way management is organized; for example, administrations for trade policy were created in order to take into account the political and economic factors of world developments in formulating trade policy, while the main industrial branch (product group) administrations owe their origins to the need to regulate and coordinate the purchase and sales of specific types of products.

But in discussing the conditions determining the functional efficiency of the foreign trade management system, it should be borne in mind that it consists of complex, multifaceted structures, each of which has its own form of input into the system as a whole and at times comes into conflict with the others.

The Theory of Managing Foreign Trade

It is therefore extremely important not only to know the basic factors involved in determining the functional and organizational efficiency of the foreign trade management system but also to detect, control, and adjust them. A classification of factors in terms of the nature of their input into the system may be helpful in this respect. They may be classified as follows:

1) by temporal attributes, i.e., as long-term, short-term, and periodic influences on the management system;

2) by the forms of their activity. Here one notes such factors as internal and external, which in turn can be broken down into:

— political: consolidation of political agreements or the creation of a favorable climate for their development, strengthening of the world socialist economic system;

— economic: the state of the economy in different countries or regions, the state of our own economy, its needs, and the forms and methods of making use of the advantages of the international division of labor;

— commercial: the state of foreign trade, geographic orientation, commodity structure, conditions for conducting foreign trade, customs policy, export and import possibilities of different countries, as well as our own. Business trends on the markets for particular goods;

— currency and financial: the state of foreign exchange payments balances of different countries and the major corporations, state of different foreign currencies. Foreign exchange payments balance of our own country, our foreign exchange needs;

— organizational: the number of independent structural departments, personnel composition broken down by skill and training and by age, number and quality of relations with suppliers and clients, equipping of management with technical facilities, etc.

The factors enumerated in the first four groups belong basically to the second aspect of management, while those in the fifth group characterize direct activities. Of course, this classification is very provisional; in real life all are intertwined with one another and usually operate together as a whole.

In addition, the magnitude of their influence on the functioning of management will vary depending on the level of management.

Thus, in a number of cases it will be useful to determine factors for typical situations encountered at each level of management (main administrations, all-union associations). A factoral analysis can be used as one of the methods for determining the effectiveness of foreign trade management. In this case it would be advisable, of course, to determine factors for all the specific aspects of foreign trade: commercial, economic, internal, and their components, and to determine the size of the managerial staff, set work norms, etc.

The list of factors is therefore long. Some can be measured quantitatively, others cannot, requiring indirect assessments instead. Factors that can only be evaluated indirectly are: the stability and durability of relations with foreign suppliers and purchasers, fluctuations in supply and demand, work discipline, the smoothness of working relations between all-union associations and trade missions on the one hand and industry on the other, and many others.

Of course, in real life the cause and effect relationships between management and the level of development of foreign trade activity are much more complex; to define them, whether quantitatively or qualitatively, is a costly and laborious process. It is very important, therefore, to acquire some idea, if only on the methodological level, of the factors that reduce the efficiency of management. We have compiled a tentative list of four groups (see Table 4).

It follows, then, that the functional efficiency of a system will depend on the degree to which these parameters are taken into account and rationally regulated by the management system. The ability to take into account all these parameters will of course to a considerable extent depend on how well and precisely the management system is organized internally and on the degree of definition of its links with the entities under its control and with its external and internal environment, i.e., on the quality of its information channels.

Let us take a look at the broad features of these channels in

The Theory of Managing Foreign Trade

Table 4

Causes of a Lack of Management Coordination and
the Sphere of Their Origin

Group number	Causes of a lack of management coordination	Sphere of origin of cause
I	Unforeseen behavior of environment that is impossible to forecast (military conflicts, natural disasters, change in political structure, etc.)	High stochasticity of process. Process does not lend itself to description or theoretical accounting
II	Unexpected behavior of the environment that could have been forecast (drop in business activity, change in demand on market, etc.)	Poor formulation of situation and of information gathering
III	Imprecise functioning of the management system due to: a) low level of organization; b) inadequate level of skills; c) low performance of personnel; d) bad work procedures.	Poor organizational structure. Selection, deployment, training, and education of personnel do not meet requirements
IV	Incoming information is revised for a long time	Weak technical equipment

the process of the actual functioning of the management system, using the example of the Main Administration for the Export of Industrial Equipment. This administration, like all others in the ministry, supervises the fulfillment of export plans; sees that government resolutions and ministerial edicts bearing on the export of industrial equipment are carried out; studies the commercial conditions of export and sees to it that business trends are properly taken into account and utilized in the conclusion of transactions by all-union associations; works together with the all-union associations on drafts for export plans and assists them in fulfilling their export plans; examines orders by foreign governments for goods; negotiates with foreign delegations on export matters; keeps an eye on the export structure and looks for new items of potential export value; controls, regulates, and directs the activities of the all-union associations; issues permits for the export of equipment; takes part in preparing contract prototypes and general terms of delivery; establishes direct relations with branch ministries and Soviet agencies with regard to matters pertaining to the export of industrial equipment.

It is evident from this enumeration of responsibilities that the Main Administration for the Export of Industrial Equipment has a broad and varied range of responsibilities to perform.

Organizationally, the administration consists of a funds and planning section, offices for exports to socialist countries and to capitalist countries, respectively, and a technical office. It coordinates the work of nine all-union associations and has dealings with forty branch ministries, USSR Gosplan, and the trade policy and functional administrations of the Ministry of Foreign Trade.

The director of the main administration and his assistants constitute the management body or system, and the offices of the administration are the subsystem managed.

For the control system to function effectively, there must be a good relationship between leaders and subordinates. These relationships are the internal channels of self-administration and depend on such human characteristics as ideological conviction, willpower, consciousness of purpose, determination, intelligence, inner discipline, etc. Formal and informal relationships must be distinguished. Formal relationships are defined by the specific internal organizational structure of the administration, and the form they take will depend on job functions, instructions, and the order of importance and essential coherence of the types of problems handled by individuals in their work. Formal relationships are regulated by job instructions and legal norms.

Informal relationships are part of any group; they depend on the goals of the group and on the personal relations between workers, their personalities, likes and dislikes, preferences, etc.

To a considerable extent informal relationships determine the working atmosphere of the group. For this reason it is extremely important to take them into account and support them in every way possible. Herein lies the meaning of the expression of "group solidarity," which in our view means essentially

The Theory of Managing Foreign Trade

the creation of those informal relations that affect every aspect of the group's activity.

The system of organization of management includes not only personnel but also the technical instruments of management: i.e., equipment for handling, preparing, and reproducing documents, various kinds of office equipment, etc.

The efficiency with which managerial actions are transmitted will depend on relations between these technical instruments and the personnel, on their quality, their justified quantity, and the ability to use them.

The practical use of technical equipment in the Ministry of Foreign Trade still leaves something to be desired. The principal flaw is that in a number of cases technical equipment is used by workers who are unfamiliar with it. This means not only shoddy work, frequent breakdowns, and wasteful use but also the improper use of highly skilled workers, since they are doing work for which they have not been trained (see Table 5).

The second factor determining efficient management is, as we have said, the degree to which the ties between the administration and the all-union associations, sector ministries, and other government agencies function smoothly.

To determine this one should take a look at the number of such ties per worker, the degree to which they are sufficiently formed, the existence of intermediate links, and the existence of duplications.

In terms of the aforementioned requirements, we can say that the management of the Main Administration for the Export of Industrial Equipment is basically organized efficiently as far as such ties are concerned; but if we examine these ties from an overall standpoint, i.e., from the interests of the ministry as a whole, we will find that a large number of such ties are duplicated. For example, several main administrations will have ties with the same sectoral ministry, or one all-union association will have ties with several main administrations: with one administration for exports, with another for imports, with a third for socialist countries, with a fourth for capitalist

Table 5

Content of job	Done by	Who should do it
Processing of incoming and outgoing correspondence (registration, sorting, opening, addressing of envelopes, etc.)	Forwarding office, office secretaries, office workers of sections, offices, and management secretarial staff	Forwarding office
Transporting of documents	All technical and office personnel, managerial personnel	Courier service
Typing	Secretaries, office and section typists, foreign language correspondents, bookkeeping staff, typing pool, foreign office, office workers	Typing pool
Duplicating work	Typists, secretaries, foreign language correspondents, office workers, etc.	Duplicator pool
Accounting operations, including the receipt of bills and final invoices	Office workers, technical personnel, foreign language correspondents, management	Accounting office
Foreign translating	Office workers, foreign language correspondents, managers	Foreign office
Supervision of paperwork	Not defined	Secretarial staff of all-union association
Protocol measures	Secretarial staff, office workers, office secretaries, manager	Protocol service
Custodial work, including the carrying of heavy objects, etc.	General division, office and technical personnel	General division

countries, etc. Thus the powers of a main administration director do not extend to the all-union association as a whole, and he will have no responsibility at all for the activity of the all-union association. He directs only that part of the all-union association to which his own job pertains. Hence the requirement of management theory that the leadership of the activity of subordinate entities be fully united has not been met. The practically and methodologically important conclusion to be drawn from this is that in rating the efficiency of management of any administrative segment, it is not sufficient to look merely at its direct activities; rather one must proceed from a comprehensive position, i.e., there must be a systems approach.

A systems approach to the management of foreign trade activity

The integration and differentiation of science that has been the special mark of the scientific-technical revolution has made it necessary to further refine methods of inquiry and has given rise to the so-called systems approach to the study of complex objects and processes of management.

To manage a complex system such as foreign trade, it is important to know the patterns and trends of its development as well as the major internal relations existing among and between its various elements (offices, divisions) and subsystems (main administrations, all-union associations). Lenin's comment is apposite here: "To really know an object it must be grasped and studied from all sides, in all its connections and 'mediations.' We will never achieve this completely, but the requirement of comprehensiveness in this sense will safeguard us from mistakes and failures."[1]

These words of Lenin's essentially constitute the methodological basis of the systems approach, which, in contrast to a mechanical view of the world around us, sees phenomena complexly, in all their internal and external relationships and interconnections.

Today the systems approach is absolutely essential for dealing with the problems that arise in foreign trade; indeed, foreign trade activity has become so complex and has reached such dimensions that the overall properties and features of foreign trade as a system cannot be discerned on the basis of a study of the properties of its elements alone (main administrations, all-union associations, etc.). Applied to the analysis of foreign trade activity, a systems approach entails:

— study of the interrelated requirements of objective economic laws that determine the nature and basis of foreign trade activity and of its planning;

— definition of the goals of developing the various departments of foreign trade activity within the overall context of foreign trade activity as an integrated system;

— structural analysis to shed light on the nature of the interrelations between the various foreign trade departments and organizations and the purposes of each;

— study and determination of specifically how and to what degree the conditions of functioning of foreign trade influence its system in order to increase the reliability of its management;

— study of the decision-making process in each element of the system, taking into account its interaction with other subsystems and its place within the system as a whole.

It is not sufficient to examine the separate functions or groups of functions of management; the connections and mutual dependences existing among them must be determined and their content analyzed as well. For example, one can determine the extent to which working procedures are correlated with the use of technical means. We know, for instance, that the shortage of technical means in all-union associations has been made up for by introducing certain progressive working procedures, e.g., making copies of papers by the single-operation method, the institution of a courier service, etc. (see Chapter 4). But the introduction of technical equipment (dictaphones, computers, etc.) required changes in working procedures and in the style of work. Here is another example. The quality and flexibility of formulating and making a decision on some aspect of foreign trade activity depend on the degree of refinement of the methods and style of work of those in charge, on the availability of technical equipment, and on the extent to which foreign trade personnel have been prepared to carry out various managerial activities independently.

The systems approach entails, among other things, bringing all the functions of management together and examining them as a whole, as well as each of them from the standpoint of the whole. In this way management is subject to ongoing improvement both by determining the weak points in one aspect and compensating for them with the strong points in another, and

The Theory of Managing Foreign Trade

by predicting how changes in the types and instruments of administrative activity in one area of management will affect factors in other areas. Finally, it is very important to determine forms and methods for improving the management system.

But a systems approach requires systems analysis, which involves a set of specialized procedures, techniques, and methods (methods and procedures for studying operations to work out quantitative recommendations; methods of systems analysis used to determine tasks and select lines of action for assessing the performance of systems under conditions of indeterminacy) by means of which a system can be analyzed into its component parts from the standpoint of the interests of the whole. In practice this means that an analysis should yield perspectives on foreign trade activity from three points of view: its organization, planning, and management, while the requirements of the systems approach entail, in addition, the analysis to focus on the interrelationships between these three elements, which are organically intertwined and essentially determine how foreign trade activity will develop.

These elements are organically intertwined in two respects: namely, without organization, planning, and management, foreign trade could not exist as such; second, each one of these three elements is an organic part of the others. Indeed, is it even possible to speak of the forms of organization of any activity without also including the planning element and without delimiting methods and forms of managing that activity?

Any discussion of the planning of foreign trade must include an examination of the forms and methods whereby this planning will be managed and organized.

3. Main Principles of the Management of Foreign Trade Activities

However sophisticated a management system may be, if it is really to function as a unity, certain functional principles must be observed.

The USSR's Management of Foreign Trade

The system of management of foreign trade is an integral aspect of the management of social production in advanced socialism; as such it is based on certain principles rooted in the very nature of the socialist economic formation. These principles were first elaborated and discussed in detail by Lenin and later developed and given concrete embodiment in the resolutions and documents of the congresses and plenary sessions of the Central Committee of the CPSU. First and foremost it should be underscored that the management of foreign trade, like that of the economy as a whole, is based on the principle of democratic centralism.

This goes without saying. On the one hand, a centralized system of management of foreign trade, which is based on knowledge acquired about the objective trends on the world market and which utilizes the advantages of the international — especially the socialist — division of labor, is responsive (by means of a planned system of specific goal-oriented tasks and by concentrating foreign exchange reserves and material resources) to public needs and at the same time encourages development of creative initiative by the masses in management. It is able to ascertain what is necessary to develop particular commodity markets and, by taking into account the interests of the economy as a whole, is able to satisfy the needs of social production more fully and more effectively.

Practically, a set of centralized planned targets is obtained by the all-union associations from the main administrations, and trading partners are selected and contracts concluded independently.

The point basically is to achieve a sound and efficient balance in the distribution of powers and responsibilities between the centralized leadership and units further down the organizational ladder, particularly between the central apparatus of the Ministry of Foreign Trade and the all-union associations, so that some initiative and independence can be preserved at the base. Because of the specific features of foreign trade, particularly the fact that foreign exchange is used and that many different organizations must coordinate their efforts on foreign markets,

The Theory of Managing Foreign Trade

centralization, in accordance with the principle of democratic centralism, has long been the watchword in developing management in this area.

The consequence of this has been that many controlling bodies have sprung up in the form of different main administrations and functional sections, and that the most highly trained and specialized workers spend a good part of their time making decisions about routine matters, which means that they have less time to spend on developing strategies for foreign trade policy and for improving business relations with industry.

In the present period, with the economic changes that have been instituted within the country (the transition to the new system of planning and economic incentives in practically all sectors of the economy) and the increasingly complicated internal relationships in the management of foreign trade, the second aspect of democratic centralism is being stressed, namely, greater independence is being given to the all-union associations in their commercial and economic activities.

However, this is not as simple a matter as might appear at first glance. Although the all-union associations may be given greater independence, this must not be at the price of sacrificing the state monopoly over foreign trade. The first step, therefore, is to obtain a clearer definition of the respective powers and responsibilities of the different levels of management in the Ministry of Foreign Trade system.

We need a scientific approach to the relationship of the duties, powers, responsibilities, and their scope at each level of management. This point was taken up specifically in the Report of the Central Committee to the Twenty-fourth Congress of the CPSU:

> It is important to define the scope and interrelationships of the powers and responsibilities at all administrative levels. Broad powers with little responsibility cause administrative arbitrariness, subjectivism, and hasty, ill-conceived decisions, and this is in no way better than a lot of responsibility with few powers. In such a situation even the most diligent worker will often be powerless,

and it is difficult to demand his full engagement in a matter with which he has been charged.[2]

It should become a hard and fast rule that decisions be made where (i.e., at the level on which) the most information exists about the given question, and where one may be assured that they will be implemented most competently. In our opinion this can be achieved if there is a new approach to the concept of a "job." We must concur with Professor Kowalewski of Warsaw University, who believes that "in the metaphorical sense (and often in the literal sense) every job can be regarded as a concrete work place."[3]

In this concept of a job the work performed in it is rigorously delimited, so that any other work done may be done poorly or may be completely impossible to do.

Is this requirement met in foreign trade practice? Not always, by any means. A time study done by the Administration for the Organization of Labor and Information Systems of the Ministry of Foreign Trade shows that office workers waste 60 percent of their time doing work that has nothing to do with what they had been trained for. They must do such technical work as printing, handling incoming and outgoing correspondence, etc.

For each job, therefore, a list of functions should be drawn up. These functions are job functions. In determining the number of functions in each job, the principle should be observed that no function that can be performed more easily and better in one job should be delegated downward: i.e., in other words, a job is a work place in which certain specified types of work are performed.

A list of functions also makes it possible to check that something important is not omitted in the work that is performed. As Kowalewski points out, by comparing the list of functions with what a department head does, it should be easy to determine how much time he wastes on work that has nothing to do with his functions. We should caution here against one mistake: a list of job functions is not a list of duties.

This approach will also have an important role to play in working out a system of delegation of powers in the Ministry

The Theory of Managing Foreign Trade

of Foreign Trade, which is one of the preconditions for achieving an objective posed by the Twenty-fourth Congress of the CPSU, namely, that "each link in the managerial system should do its own work, so that higher levels are not overburdened with a mass of routine matters that will distract them from more important problems, while the lower levels are able to deal efficiently and promptly with matters within the domain cut out for them."[4] If this is not the case, it is of no use to talk about the combination of centralization and decentralization in management.

The delegation of powers (from one department or department head to another) should become an organizational rule of thumb in the practical task of improving the efficiency of foreign trade management. It is necessary for a variety of reasons, but primarily because of the steadily increasing burdens on department heads, which can simply become too much to deal with. In practice a number of workers are extremely overburdened. Thus in the study referred to above, it is observed that most of the heads of main administrations and all-union association directors are directly responsible for eleven to seventeen organizational divisions and employees, the end result of which is that they become overburdened with routine, current problems and thus have no time to deal with more important long-range issues.

On the other hand, their deputies are directly in charge of two or three departments, which makes them interfere inordinately with the department heads under them, from time to time replacing them on the job and smothering initiative. It also obliges them to perform operations that do not belong to their jobs. Yet it is obvious that one person, no matter how capable, can only do so much work and no more, that he has his limits. Hence if a department head refrains from delegating some of his powers, he may gradually find himself submerged in a sea of trivial problems and he will be obliged to resort to snap judgments, even about questions that should be given careful thought and examination. The outcome is inefficient and even wrong decisions. In addition, it should be borne in mind that the impulse to deal with all questions by oneself is detrimental to the development of independence and initiative among one's subordinates, the end result of which is that employees find themselves forced to turn to their superior for instructions on how to do every single trivial task, which of course means that the manager wastes time uselessly.

This is why the delegation of some powers to lower levels is an efficient method at the present time, when foreign trade relations are becoming increasingly complicated, to operatively manage foreign trade activity. In this situation the manager will still have the job of coordinating the work of his staff on major questions, but he delegates the authority to make decisions on less essential matters to others. A manager should operate on the principle that the more people authorized to make decisions in his name, the more work he himself will be able to do. In other words, by delegating authority a manager widens the sphere of his activity, since without such delegation his activity is limited by his own physical capacities. A manager's strength lies specifically in his ability to utilize the creative capacities of others. Another advantage of the delegation of authority is that by placing more free time at a manager's disposal, it enables him to use this time for creative work on long-range questions.

Moreover, it is not just the manager who is able to work more efficiently as a result of the delegation of authority; the work of everyone is improved. Nonetheless, its net advantage will be reduced to zero if a manager does not support those under him and does not bear in mind that they too may make mistakes. He should always be prepared to step in to correct these mistakes and, where possible, to prevent them.

Despite the clear advantages and benefits that derive from delegation of authority, it has been somewhat neglected in the Ministry of Foreign Trade. The reasons for this vary, but they are for the most part psychological. In a number of instances it is claimed that there is no one available as capable as the manager to make effective decisions. In other cases the reason given is a manager's fear of rivalry from his subordinates or his fear of losing his reputation or authority. A number of managers explain that they do not have the time needed to explain to their staff their powers and duties.

The overcoming of this psychological barrier is an urgent problem. But a good point to start from is the rule, spelled out by A. Carnegie, the American management expert, that a good manager is a person who tries to gather around himself people who are more competent than himself. By doing this a manager gives himself more time to deal with more important problems and in the process prepares himself, as it were, for a higher-level job, while at the same time training someone else to take his place. In other words, the refusal to delegate some of one's own authority actually hinders the personal progress of a manager himself.

But just to recognize that some of one's authority should be delegated to others does not solve the problem. Indeed, here is where the problem first starts. For instance, how broad an authority can be delegated, on what basis, and how should it be organized?

One should not think, however, that the partial delegation of powers is a purely formal, administrative measure. Its effectiveness is contingent on whether it is preceded by a careful analysis of all activities and a precise determination of the full scope or detailed specification of all the tasks necessary for a smoothly functioning department. Then to such a list should be added tasks or jobs a manager should do himself but does not because he has no time. In compiling such a list of duties and tasks a manager should perform and handle himself without enlisting the aid of his superiors, a breakdown into the following groups will be useful:

— tasks not requiring supervision;
— tasks requiring ordinary supervision;
— tasks requiring special supervision;
— tasks requiring thorough supervision.

In other words, the tasks performed by a manager are classified according to their importance, and on the basis of this list a manager decides which of the tasks of lesser importance can be delegated to others to give himself more time to deal with more important matters. Then it would be advisable to draw up in written form a program of how to do those jobs that are to be delegated. It is important that a manager always be sure that the performance of the work will not be impaired if it is delegated, assuming of course that the employee assigned the work has been properly trained and that there has been an appropriate communication of experience and consultations.

Finally, it is important that after he has delegated his authority, a manager does not meddle in what his subordinate does. Theodore Roosevelt had something interesting to say apropos of this, namely, that the best manager is one who has enough intuition to choose the best people to do what he wants, and who has enough restraint not to meddle in their work.

In delegating some of his work a manager should understand that it is he who bears the responsibility for the quality of the delegated work. Therefore a manager should require his subordinates to fill him in on anything that goes wrong.

The effectiveness of delegation of authority depends on the ability of the manager to guide the activity of those under him in the direction needed, and this in turn requires a strict coordination of powers and duties. One cannot require responsibility from a subordinate if he has not been given the powers corresponding to it.

An important aspect in the development of delegation of authority is to intensify collective principles in management while maintaining personal responsibility. At present the definition of goals, working out of decisions, and supervision of their implementation could be more effectively handled with the involvement of many people. But for this it is necessary to ensure equality among all those participating in a collective decision, which means that an evaluation of proposals must be based on their real utility and that there must be no material, moral, or administrative pressure put on the workers taking part in such decisions. Practice has shown that coercion of any sort prevents most participants in a meeting from productive work.

Second, the concept of "responsibility" must be redefined.

The Theory of Managing Foreign Trade

Currently a worker is responsible for what he has done, i.e., for how "well" or how "poorly" he has done his job. Accordingly, an enterprising worker who has done a lot may be criticized more often than a person who has done little and hence makes fewer mistakes.

A system of employee responsibility must include responsibility for what has been done, which will signify the level of accomplishment, and for what has not been done, which shows the level of practical initiative.

"When a decision is made," said L. I. Brezhnev at the Twenty-fourth Congress of the CPSU, "it should be quite clear who bears the responsibility for it, just as it also should be clear who is responsible if an urgent decision is not made or is delayed."[5]

Of course, we should bear in mind that while this second criterion is more difficult to measure, it can be expressed indirectly, for example, in the criterion "missed opportunity." If, for instance, an all-union association tries only to meet equipment delivery times without taking into account the scheduled term for getting a project going, missed opportunity may be measured as either the total funds diverted from circulation because of storage or as the business opportunities lost by a firm because of the delay in deliveries.

In this context, it should be more important that newly opened opportunities were given more weight than the pedantic following of directives handed down from above. On this account it has been aptly observed that a manager who tries at any price to avoid risk also avoids success.

An important principle followed in the foreign trade management system is unity of political and economic leadership. This principle was developed most fully and consistently after the Twenty-fourth Congress of the CPSU. The development of foreign trade and economic cooperation with capitalist countries was preceded by political decisions. But at the same time, sound political decisions would be inconceivable without stable, mutually advantageous foreign trade and economic relationships. This unity is clearly evident in the acceptance of the Comprehensive Program for the Further Development and Improvement

The USSR's Management of Foreign Trade

of Cooperation and Development of Socialist Economic Integration of the CMEA Member Nations.

The principle of planned control of the economy is the core of the organizational management of the foreign trade monopoly. The practical implementation of the advantages of socialism in conducting foreign trade is achieved through planning, thereby ensuring stable and enduring economic relations for our country.

The major principles guiding our foreign trade management system are a scientific approach, material and moral incentives, the correct selection and deployment of personnel, etc.

Finally, scientific management is impossible without setting up suitable organizational structures adequate to it. The principles of scientific management, a harmonious functioning of all the elements of the system in one unified whole, a rational delimitation of powers and responsibilities of the different levels in the managerial hierarchy, and the possibility of using computers and organizational-technical measures must become part of the reality of the organizational structure of management, and this in turn means that all the principles of management must be taken into account.

CHAPTER THREE

The Current Organization of the Management
of Foreign Trade and Ways to Improve It

1. The Existing Structure of Foreign Trade Management

Foreign trade can neither function nor grow if it has no clear-cut system of management. In practice this means creating efficient channels of control between the steering system and that which is to be steered, defining the forms and methods for steering the various aspects of foreign trade activity, and establishing rational and efficient quantitative and qualitative links between the various elements of the system.

Most importantly, an optimal structure for management must be found, one that realistically reflects the integral process of management, with all its discrete parts, as described in Chapter 2.

The literature on problems of management provides a variety of definitions of its structure. Some see it as "an ordered aggregate of interconnected elements existing in more or less stable relationships with regard to one another and hence functioning or evolving (changing) as a single, integral whole."[1] Others propose that structure is "a way of distributing the functions and powers of decision-making among individuals and groups of individuals (structural divisions) who together constitute an administrative whole."[2] Finally, other scholars[3] subscribe to the view that the structure of management consists of the elements of a system and all the relations between them. We feel that this last definition of structure most completely captures the essence of management in that it gets directly to the division of managerial labor, rather than just touching on its external aspects.

Thus our conception of the structure of management must from the very outset presume to cover a whole range of particular managerial divisions, the characteristics of each of them with regard to its capacity to fulfill certain specific functions, and the interaction among them and with the external world in the course of the system's functioning.

In other words, the organizational structure reflects the degree of division of labor and cooperation, the technology of operational processes, and the management, disposition, and use of manpower and material resources. It also reflects the formal definition and distribution of duties and defines the responsibilities of the various levels of management for the system, the purpose of which is to coordinate the activities of all the different structural subdivisions and to ensure a reliable link between the various working parts.

It follows, then, that the structure of management reflects the process of management as a whole, as well as all its particular functions. It should ensure an efficient division of labor in matters of management, provide for specialization and cooperation, and in this way create conditions enabling management to function smoothly and efficiently. The structure of management must be seen from two aspects: a static aspect, reflecting the way managerial functions are distributed and overlap among the various subdivisions of a system, and a dynamic aspect, which changes depending on various external and internal factors. The stability or variability of the organizational structure of management is determined by a number of factors:

— the variability of the external environment in which a foreign trade department or association must operate;

— the need to create conditions ensuring continuity in the organization's activity.

In practice the variety of organizational structures for management is quite large. They may be classified conveniently into three groups, in accordance with the way in which the actions of management are put into effect, namely, linear, functional, and combined structures.

Improving the Management of Foreign Trade

1. <u>The linear (hierarchical) structure of management.</u> In this type of structure each level of management is strictly subordinated to the one above it. Its merit lies in the fact that the decisions of management are unambiguously and directly translated into action. Varying interpretations of orders are impossible, since there are no intermediate links between a manager and those under him.

A negative aspect of this structure is that it requires the manager to shoulder a large burden of responsibilities: planning of production, the organization and coordination of many individuals or departments, supervision, etc.

In the case of large-scale production or organization, such a structure will place excessive burdens on the managerial staff, and certain aspects of production or other activities will necessarily fall into neglect. Such a structure is inefficient for large dynamic systems.

2. <u>The functional structure of management</u> entails the dividing up of the overall process of management into different functions. This type of structure ensures a more highly qualified leadership for each function (planning, supervision, coordination, etc.). Compared with the linear structure, it is more susceptible to changes and new ideas. In it the importance of each particular element is enhanced at the expense of the organization of the whole. Some negative features are that many functional departments exercise influence on managerial action and that it is difficult to coordinate the activities of the various functional departments, etc. In large dynamic systems these difficulties are magnified, since the same managerial personnel bear the responsibility for day-to-day decisions as well as those of a more strategic nature.

3. <u>Combined structures of management</u> use aspects of both the linear and functional types. In practice there are two varieties: the linear-staffed and with limited functionalism.

The <u>linear-staff structure</u> combines the linear principle of management with the constructive principle. Its advantage over the purely linear type lies in the fact that the manager, while retaining for himself executive and administrative powers, enjoys the possibility of receiving qualified recommendations from specialists in various types of activity. However, this type of structure is basically inert, since it already entails a lag in decision-making.

A <u>structure with limited functionalism</u> combines a linear system of management with a functional structure, assigning limited powers to the functional departments of the system. In other words, a system of limited functionalism combines specialization of managerial functions with a unitary management. Some of the shortcomings of this system are the multiplicity of relationships in the management system, difficulties in coordinating the activities of functional services, and the fact that no one is responsible for the activities of subordinate organizations.

Thus these combined structures blend the advantages of linear and functional structures, but in turn they are cumbersome, inflexible, and difficult to control. In order, therefore, to make these structures more flexible, new features must be introduced.

One of these is <u>management by project</u>, which has come into wide use in the United States and a number of countries in Western Europe. In this form a general strategy is worked out at the corporation level, while strategies for the planning of individual projects, control strategies, and a strategy for day-to-day management are the responsibility of ad hoc groups formed in the process of carrying out the project.

One merit of this organizational form of management is that it allows for strategic, structural, and production maneuverability. It is quite flexible, since it can be quickly reshuffled. A shortcoming is that the areas within which it can be used are relatively limited, namely, only for organizations in which the range of products manufactured changes frequently, and in which a broad maneuverability in matters of production and strategy are necessary. In its pristine form it is used widely in scientific research institutes.

This management-by-project structure has a near relative in a <u>structure oriented to the quest for innovation</u>. As foreign economists affirm, this structure has features that meet all the basic criteria: efficiency in coping with static problems, a high degree of maneuverability, and flexibility with regard to strategy and organizational forms. In this structure new types of products are developed by research teams that study, plan, and test the feasibility of producing new types of goods. They are responsible for a project until the profitability of production of the new item reaches a stable level, after which it is handed over to a current production team. A structure of this type can be used in our scientific-technical production associations, as well as in all-union offices engaged in exports. Perhaps special departments should be set up in these offices which, together with production, would be concerned with the development of new products and the search for markets for them.

Recently a number of firms have appeared that have built up their management structure on the marketing principle, as a result of intensified competition and sales difficulties.

Formerly, ten to fifteen years ago to be exact, firms concentrated primarily on production and for the sale of their products set up a separate sales and marketing section within their administrative structure. At that time this was entirely sufficient. Now, however, that it has become increasingly harder to dispose of goods and competition has grown sharper, the main stress is placed on the study of supply and demand, on finding new products and new markets, and only secondarily on the organization of production and on the technology of manufacturing the needed goods. It is understandable, then, if firms are demonstrating interest in reorganizing management, in expanding the role of sales and marketing sections, and in modifying their functions by giving them a broader range of rights and responsibilities. In many instances these sections are also engaged in product research, finding new markets, and new sales methods and procedures. In other words, the structure of management is based on the marketing principle, i.e., essentially to meet market demands (see Figure 5).

From the chart we see that the head of the marketing section is responsible for thinking up new products and for the range

Structure of the Management of a Firm Oriented toward Marketing

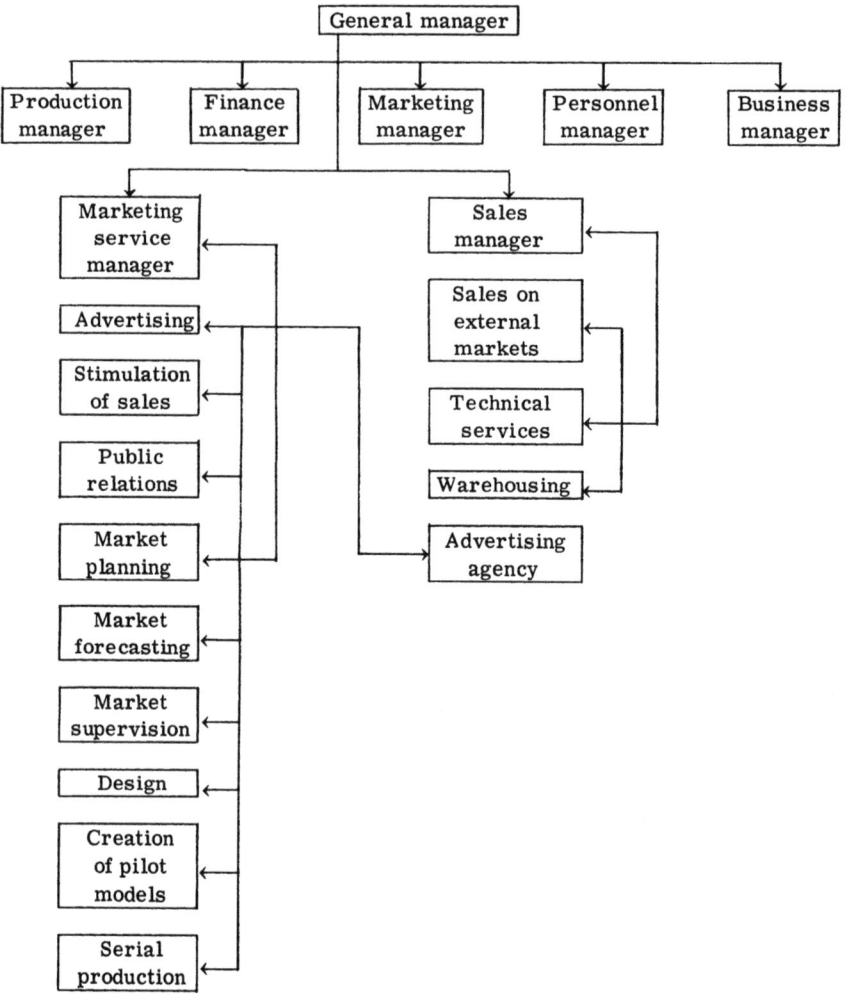

Figure 5.

of products offered. Formerly these functions were in the hands of the production manager, who in the new managerial structure is now responsible only for the organization of production, i.e., its technical aspects.

But we also see from the chart that marketing is one of the functions of management. The recent trend has been to give an increasingly greater role to marketing in the structure of management, indeed, so much so that it is becoming its principal function (see Figure 6).

Structure of the Management of a Firm

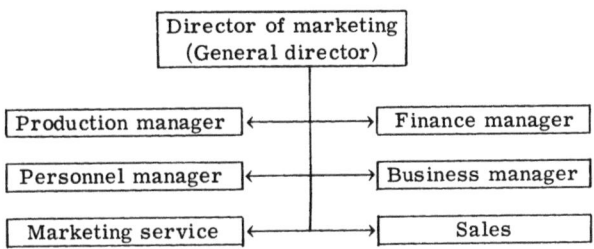

Figure 6.

All the technical, economic, and financial sections are under the marketing director, who has become the general manager. In experiments with this new structure of management, it was found to be most efficient in firms manufacturing a relatively small range of products. In large conglomerates this system is used in a somewhat modified form, which has been given the name of management by product (see Figure 7).

In management by product strategic questions are resolved at the top, while all current and tactical problems related to concrete production are dealt with on the spot by the various departments of the firm.

Diversification of production has also given rise to its own system of management, called management by territory, in which independent branches are set up and invested with the powers and responsibility for territorial sales.

One especially interesting type of management, we think, is customer-oriented management. This form is based on the needs and changing demands of specified groups of customer in one or several regions (see Figure 8).

Given this variety of different systems of management, it is

The USSR's Management of Foreign Trade

The Structure of Management by Product

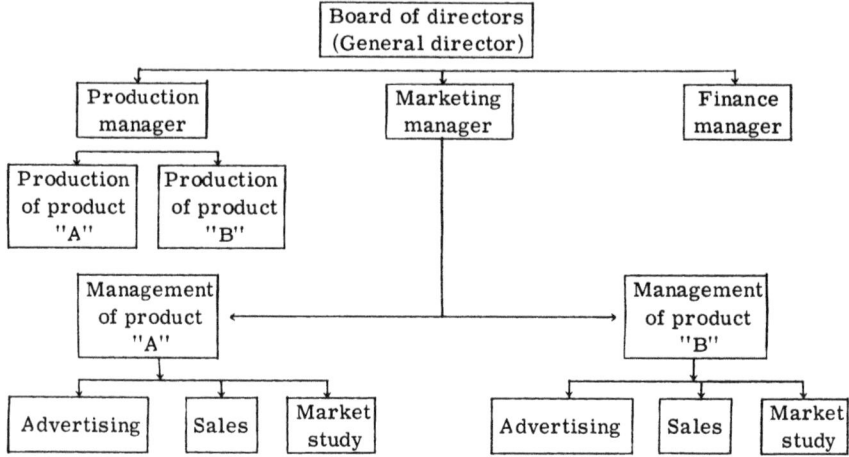

Figure 7.

The Structure of Customer-Oriented Management

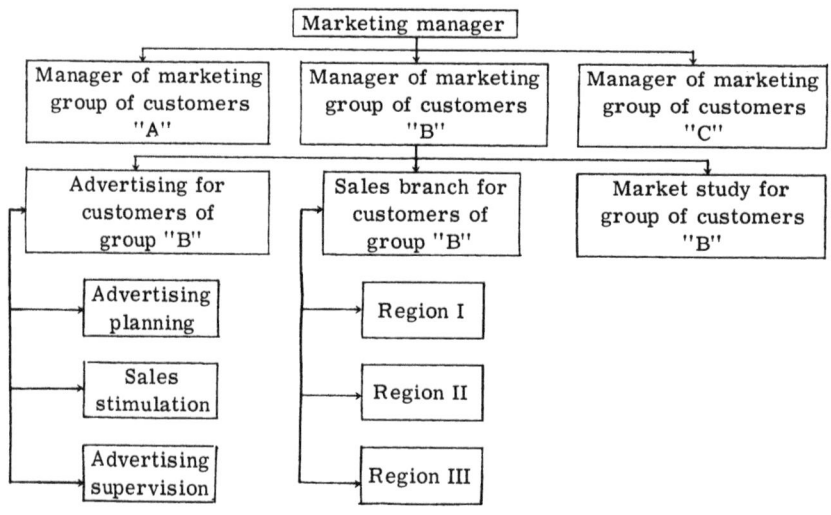

Figure 8.

Improving the Management of Foreign Trade

clear that a number of factors are at work to influence the choice of one particular system: for example, there is the nature of a firm's activities, the scale of production, administrative flexibility, and many others, whose relative importance will be examined in later chapters. But in general the main principles governing the organization of management in capitalist firms are:

— thorough centralization of the firm's general functions within special departments;

— an increased stress on decentralized decision-making on current questions within centrally established guidelines for the firm's activities.

The management structure of the Ministry of Foreign Trade

How is the management of the Ministry of Foreign Trade organized at present? Does it satisfy the requirements of scientific management?

The management structure of the foreign trade branch of the nation's economy has been shaped under the influence of processes characteristic of socialist production.

If we imagine the entire economy as a complex machine, the various sectoral ministries will function, as it were, as individual units within the whole, and the pace of their operations and how and at what points they intermesh with each other are quite precisely defined and are fixed by directives in the central economic plan.

Organizationally, this means that identical functional bodies will be found in most ministries; these bodies maintain ties with the administrative bodies of party and state (Central Committee of the Communist Party, Presidium of the Supreme Soviet, Council of Ministers, Gosplan, and other ministries and agencies). For instance, the Ministry of Foreign Trade contains the following departments: the Main Economic Planning Administration, the Financial Administration, the Main Foreign Exchange Administration, the Transport Administration, etc. But in contrast to the industrial ministries, the organizational structure of management in the Ministry of Foreign Trade has also been influenced by the outside world and the foreign markets, as evidenced by the formation of such specialized departments as the Main Foreign Exchange Administration, the Main Tariff Administration, administrations and sections for trade policy, and by the kinds of ties and relations that have evolved among these various departments.

The present management structure of foreign trade, which functions as a single dynamic whole, is shown in Figure 9.

The organizational structure of the management of foreign trade reflects both a number of elements (subdivisions) and the hierarchy of their subordination. Each of its structural elements is considered a subdivision empowered to make decisions within the area of its competence and in accordance with its organizationally prescribed goals. Basically, the management of foreign trade is structured according to the principle of limited functionalism. The commodity, functional, and political-geographic principles form the basis for this structure.

For instance, while departments such as the Main Economic Planning Administration, the Financial Administration, and the Main Foreign Exchange Administration are managed according to the functional principle (i.e., specific functions such as planning, finances, foreign exchange operations, etc.), the main commodity (sectoral) administrations operate according to the commodity principle, and the administrations dealing with trade policy operate according to political and geographic criteria. Of course, these criteria often do not function in pure form but are combined in various ways. For instance, several main commodity (sectoral) administrations are specialized not only for a particular list of goods but also by country, i.e., both the commodity and geographic criteria are operative (the Main Administration for Import of Industrial Equipment from Socialist Countries, the Main Administration for Compensation Projects and Import of Industrial Equipment from Capitalist Countries).

One can conveniently distinguish twelve autonomous vertical levels or subsystems in the foreign trade management struc-

Structural Chart of the USSR Ministry of Foreign Trade

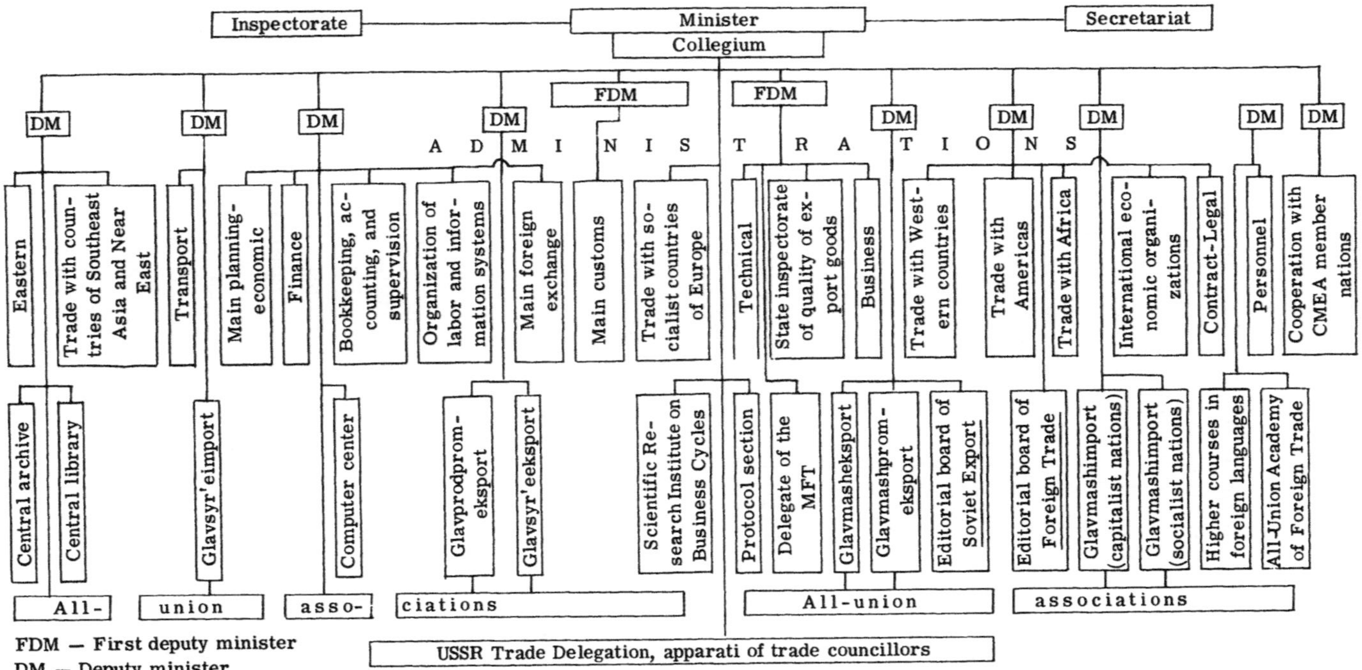

Figure 9.

FDM — First deputy minister
DM — Deputy minister

ture (see Figure 9). These include four levels of management built on the functional principle (economic planning, foreign exchange, financial, bookkeeping and accounting, the Main Tariff Administration, the State Export Quality Control Administration, the Technical Administration, the Business Administration, the delegates of the Ministry of Foreign Trade, the Personnel Administration); four levels organized by commodity and geographic criteria (export and import of industrial raw materials, consumer goods, and finished products; export of industrial equipment and export of transport, highway, and agricultural machinery; import of machinery and equipment from socialist countries; and import of machinery from capitalist countries, etc.); three levels structured in accordance with principles of political geography (Administration for Trade with Western Countries, Administration for Trade with the Americas, Administration for Trade with Africa, Administration for International Economic Organizations, the Eastern Administration, Administration for Trade with the Countries of Asia, the Central Archives, and the Central Library); and finally, one level designed on the industrial goods principle (Transportation Administration and Main Administration for the Export of Raw Materials).

The management structure of foreign trade is also hierarchically organized on four horizontal levels.

At the <u>first level</u> (minister and the Collegium of the ministry) all the various kinds of foreign trade activity are integrated. Duties are assigned, the extent of responsibility of ministerial officials, heads of administrations and committees, and directors of all-union associations is defined, and strategies are developed for foreign trade operations and more general questions of foreign trade policy.

At the <u>second level</u> (first deputy and deputy ministers) the day-to-day overseeing of the activities of the all-union associations and other foreign trade organizations takes place. The first deputy ministers are in charge of coordinating and integrating the activities of the ministerial deputies.

At the <u>third level</u> (main commodity administrations, functional administrations, trade policy administrations, etc.) the activities of the all-union associations are coordinated. This level displays certain features not found at the other levels. For example, not all the departments operating at this level have the same powers. For instance, while the main commodity administrations perform the functions of planning, supervision, and day-to-day management of the activities of the all-union associations, the functional boards are not concerned with the day-to-day operations of the latter but instead oversee them only with regard to each administration's designated functions. Finally, the trade policy administrations coordinate and monitor the trade activities of the associations, as well as each administration's designated group of countries.

At the <u>fourth level</u> direct management of foreign trade operations is exercised.

Thus we see that the higher the level of management, the wider the range of questions with which the agencies at that level must deal, and hence the more varied will be the methods used in addressing these questions.

There are two discrete systems distinguishable in this managerial structure: the ministry's central administration (the management system) and the all-union associations, trade missions, and other foreign trade organizations (the managed system).

The primary task of the central administration is to deal with the strategic questions of foreign trade, e.g., protecting its monopoly, determining the volume and structure of trade, setting its direction, and choosing the appropriate trading procedures and methods.

On the one hand, the activities of the various departments in the system must be integrated, and on the other, duties, powers, and responsibilities must be delegated over the various horizontal and vertical levels of management. A significant feature of this process is that the degree of integration will vary for the different levels. Integration is greatest at the ministerial level, where problems associated with economic planning, foreign exchange and financing, customs, transport, and a number of other activities are dealt with.

On the other hand, problems associated with export and import of particular goods are dealt with departmentally. For instance, the export of machinery and technical goods is handled by two main administrations, while two others handle the imports of the same items. Integration of these tasks takes place at the level of the appropriate ministerial deputies and in the Collegium.

The administrative structure of the main commodity, functional, and trade policy administrations is determined by the tasks they are assigned. Usually there is a main administration head, two or three deputies, and administration heads and deputies.

In some cases (e.g., the Main Administration for the Export of Transport, Highway Construction, and Agricultural Machinery) the head of the finance section is responsible to the head of the main administration, while the experts are responsible to the head of the administration and the deputy of the head of the main administration.

Since the chief commodity (sectoral) administrations manage according to commodity and geographic principles, and since in many cases their list of products is narrower than that traded by all-union associations, the latter find themselves responsible to several main commodity administrations at the same time (see Figure 10).

Figure 10 shows that 26 of 41 all-union associations are answerable to two, six are answerable to three, eight are answerable to one, and one is answerable to four main commodity administrations.

The organizational structure of the foreign trade administrative apparatus is obviously quite complex. For example, there are a large number of departments in operation, and management is organized according to several principles. The result of all this has been the emergence of a complex system of formal and informal interrelationships. For example, V/O "Tekhsnabeksport" is answerable to four main administrations (for the export of raw materials, for the import of industrial raw

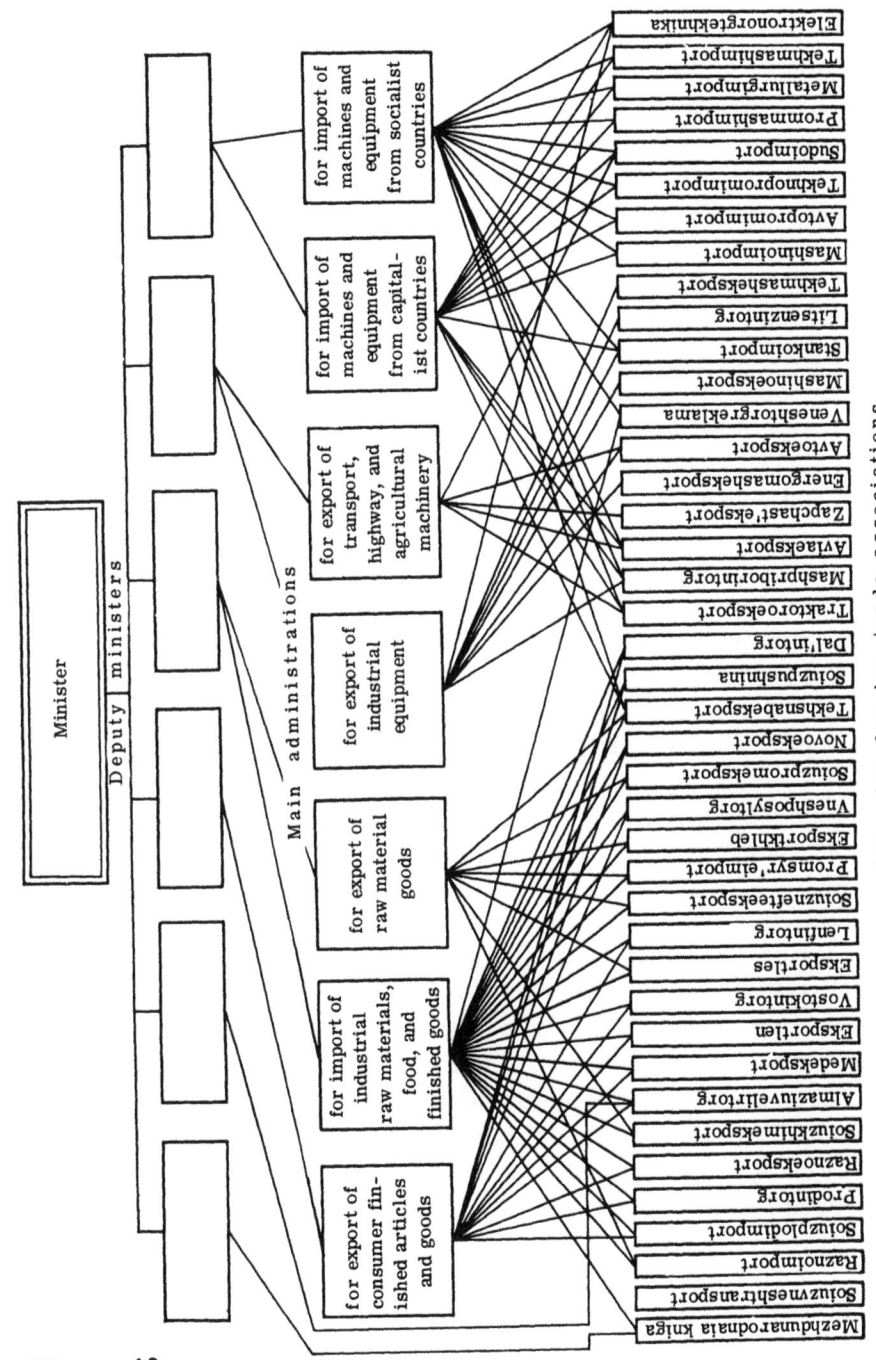

Figure 10. Organizational Structure of Operational Management of Foreign Trade

materials, for the import of machinery and equipment from socialist countries, and for the import of machinery and equipment from capitalist countries), which in turn are accountable to two deputy ministers. V/O "Traktoroeksport" is accountable to three main administrations, which in turn are accountable to two different deputy ministers. V/O "Mashpriborintorg" and V/O "Aviaeksport" are in analogous situations.

And then there are nine all-union associations that are accountable for exports to the Main Administration for Exports of Raw Materials, while at the same time they are accountable for imports to the Main Administration for the Import of Raw Materials and the Main Administration for the Import of Manufactured Goods; yet for foreign exchange transactions and financial operations, they report to the Main Foreign Exchange Administration and the Financial Administration. In addition, matters bearing on transport must be coordinated with the Transport Administration, since the main administrations in charge of current operations do not have the appropriate departments. But if one also takes into account the informal relations with trade policy administrations and the individual functional administrations, the interconnections between the different departments become even more complex.

The result is that the channels of accountability among the all-union associations, the main commodity administrations, and the functional administrations are many and at times are duplicated. Thus an all-union association sends the same statistical report to the relevant main commodity administration and to the main economic planning administration.

Second, because of this organizational structure, the day-to-day operations of the various departments and of all-union associations dealing with exports and imports are not sufficiently coordinated.

There are at present four main administrations for export and three main administrations for import, but there is no department to analyze export and import trends as a whole. The Main Economic Planning Administration, in collaboration with the main commodity administrations, is engaged mainly in drawing up the export and import plans for the all-union associations, coordinating them with national planning, and maintaining a balance between exports and imports. The main import administrations usually have no way to make use of imports as they should to move our products onto the world market. They usually do not make purchases abroad contingent on the supplier's agreement to purchase Soviet goods in return.

These circumstances have led to a situation in which tasks that go hand in hand with the promotion of imports and exports, such as the creation of export sectors, the organization of technical servicing abroad, etc., are solved in isolation.

Third, since the administrative structure is rigidly compartmentalized, many questions of a day-to-day nature are dealt with by the deputy minister or by the heads of departments. The result is that the most qualified personnel at the higher managerial levels spend a large part of their time dealing with routine problems. Coordination of activities at different levels and decision-making concerning the proposals of numerous departments take place at a high level (deputy minister). As tasks become more complicated, so too does coordination, until finally the burden on top-level personnel becomes excessive. Some data[4] on the distribution of working time of the managerial staff of an average capitalist company may therefore not be without interest (see Table 6, page 82).

As we see from Table 6, top-level managers budget their time as follows: 40 percent is devoted to problems three, five, and ten years in the future, and only 18 percent to current questions (two years).

Fourth, with so many links and interrelationships between departments and all-union associations, it becomes very difficult to follow the chain of responsibility from the bottom up through the organizational hierarchy. In practice the directors of all-union associations are accountable for all their current commercial and economic activities to the first deputy minister and to the minister. Thus the managers of the central apparatus do not bear the primary responsibility for the activities of the all-union associations.

The USSR's Management of Foreign Trade

Table 6

Distribution of Managers' Work Time
in the Average Capitalist Company

Job \ Planning time	Planning of activities, in %							
	1 day	1 week	1 month	3-6 months	1 year	2 years	3-4 years	5-10 years
President	1	2	5	10	15	27	30	10
Executive vice-president	2	4	10	29	20	18	13	4
Vice-president for operations	4	8	15	35	20	10	5	3
General director of basic administration	2	5	15	30	20	12	12	4
Branch manager	10	10	24	39	10	5	1	1
Section manager	15	20	25	37	3			
Group manager	38	40	15	5	2			

2. The Existing Managerial Structure of an All-Union Association

The all-union export-import associations, as we have shown, are the main production units of the Ministry of Foreign Trade and are directly engaged in foreign trade activity. Since they represent a particular organization (combination) of material-technical resources, financial resources, and manpower, they must be managed like any other organization and hence have their own management structure.

As of October 1, 1974, in most all-union associations duties were typically assigned among the managerial personnel in accordance with product group and geographic criteria. In most cases the factors determining the managerial structure were selected on the basis of experience; in others they were influenced by personal relationships. Ultimately this has meant that there has been a certain amount of diversity in the way all-union associations' management has been organized. One characteristic feature of their organizational structure is the distribution of duties among the managerial personnel in ac-

Improving the Management of Foreign Trade

cordance with commodity and geographic criteria.

This structure is quite complicated. First, there are two or even three chains of command. In V/O "Stankoimport," for instance, six offices have dual subordination, and one even has triple.

A second problem is that it is difficult to evenly distribute the various departments among the managerial personnel. For example, in addition to being responsible for the activity of the association as a whole, the director has twelve different departments (and sometimes even more) under him, and his deputies have from three to ten. In some associations there are cases where a director's deputy has only one department under him (V/O "Eksportkhleb").

Third, in such a system the managers, particularly the director's deputies, become almost jacks-of-all trades, performing all the functions related to the association's activities. This reduces the efficiency of management, especially in those cases in which profound knowledge of some specialized area of activity (commercial, economic, administrative, etc.) is required; and this, of course, means specialization, i.e., the learning perhaps of several functions but by no means all. This is why since 1973 the all-union associations have begun adopting a managerial structure based on a functional approach, in which director's deputies for administrative and for economic and commercial activities were added.

In this model the interrelationships are clearly delineated, and hence the distribution of responsibility among the managerial personnel is well defined. Moreover, with such a distribution of responsibilities the problem of how to replace managers when they are absent (military call-up, illness) is dealt with in a new way. Instead of a horizontal line of replacement, as formerly existed, vertical replacement has been introduced. The result is that an all-union association has at its disposal at any moment a number of managers on permanent call and thus meets the requirements of scientific management; on the other hand, it can check on how the staff filling in for management are coping with their new duties; thus there is always a reserve ready for promotion to managerial posts.

It should be noted that this management model is essentially a functional structure with limited functionalism.

The functional sections of all-union associations (economic planning, the business cycle, foreign exchange and finance, technical, advertising) are linked to the operational offices through multiple chains of command. They are meant to assist the operational offices in maintaining ties with industry and with the central administrative apparatus of the Ministry of Foreign Trade, to supply the offices with needed information, etc. However, in practice feedback is becoming increasingly important: regular reports are demanded from offices concerning commercial operations, and checks are made to determine whether instructions and recommendations from the corresponding ministerial administrations are being carried out. As studies have shown, in most of these relationships directives from functional departments carry imperative force.

Functional departments are structured linearly. The organizational structure of management of the business cycle department is a good example; it is typical for the majority of all-union associations. In it the experts and senior engineers are directly accountable to the department head.

The tasks of the staff of the business cycle department, as of all routine staff of the various offices of an association, are to study the business trends on the world markets, to put the results of such studies into efficient practical use, and to carry on a day-to-day struggle to improve the efficiency of commercial operations.

The responsibilities of a <u>department head</u> include the organization and general overseeing of the whole of the activities of the business cycle department; he must review competitive lists and price calculations, and he must keep management and the office staff informed about the commercial activities of business offices as well as of the association as a whole.

The responsibilities of the <u>experts and senior engineers</u> include overseeing and monitoring of competitive lists, price calculations, and contracts for product lists compiled by the business offices; they must: prepare reports on the prices of equipment handled by the association; keep files on prices for the product lists of each business office and assist business engineers of the offices in moving orders for equipment to aggregate factories; study and assess business trends on world markets for equipment; accumulate economic data and indices for different countries and equipment markets; select data for the indicators used to compute equipment prices and prepare manuals for calculating prices on equipment and spare parts; and take part in price discussions with firms on behalf of the department head. In addition it is incumbent on the experts to consult the engineers of the department and business offices on questions concerning their commercial activities and to disseminate the commercial statistics of the association.

The principal commercial unit in the system of the Ministry of Foreign Trade is the operational office. It is headed by an office manager who usually has one or two assistants in charge of different aspects of the day-to-day commercial activities handled by the office staff. In some cases, for example, in V/O "Raznoeksport," separate business teams, consisting of a senior engineer, engineers, one or two foreign correspondents, and one economist, are set up to handle specific products.

The office manager oversees foreign trade operations, endeavors to improve their efficiency, and organizes the study of markets and customers, both potential and existing, along both direct and indirect channels.

In some all-union associations the office staffs are directly under the office manager or his assistant. This is usually the case in offices handling trade for a small product list. The V/O "Prodintorg" offices are a good example: there the entire business office staff is under the office manager (e.g., as in the sugar office).

Comparing the different administrative charts, we see that in V/O "Raznoeksport" the administrative structure enables the office manager to devote a good deal of his attention to broader questions affecting the operating efficiency of the office as a whole. In the management structure for the sugar office, on the other hand, the office manager does not have this opportunity, since he must spend his whole time dealing with current problems. Also, this structure does not allow the members of the staff to take over one another's jobs in case of absence due to military call-up, illness, etc.

In some cases offices engage in both export and import operations. Then, in addition to being responsible for the activities of the office as a whole, the office manager must also take charge of the export or import team. The export and import office of V/O "Novoeksport" is an office of this type.

We see, then, that the existing structure of foreign trade as a whole, as well as of the all-union associations, is quite complex. The diversity of goals and interests of the foreign trade divisions and organizations and the complexity of their interrelationships make top-level management difficult — not only for the minister and his deputies but also for the various main administrations.

In the final analysis all this bespeaks the need for constant improvements of the organizational structure of management.

3. Methodological and Practical Aspects of Rationalizing the Structure of Management of Foreign Trade

In the preceding section we examined the static aspect of the managerial structure of foreign trade, i.e., the distribution of powers and responsibilities among the various levels of management at any given moment. But since foreign trade is complex and constantly evolving, its managerial structure should also be analyzed dynamically, i.e., as it changes over time.

This approach is of both theoretical and practical value, since any effort to improve management must be seen as an ongoing process and not as a single, discrete measure. In other words, a change in any of the particular elements of the managerial structure or in the relationships existing between them must conform not only to present exigencies but also to the requirements of the presumed future development of foreign

Improving the Management of Foreign Trade

trade as well. But this in turn means that from the outset one must have a clear idea, on the one hand, of one's objectives defined in terms of the prospective development of foreign trade, and, on the other hand, guidelines for improving the organizational structure.

The original objective may be the creation of a managerial structure of optimal form, i.e., one which at any given moment would ensure a maximum correspondence between organizational structure and the actual nature of foreign trade processes as they take place and, at the same time, would provide for smooth decision-making and reliable and efficient functioning of the system as a whole.

To achieve this is a complex problem, with many facets, in which many factors must be considered together and not separately and at random. The approach, therefore, must cover a broad front. After all, the Ministry of Foreign Trade and all its constituent elements is a complex entity in which commercial (offers, negotiations, conclusion of contracts, etc.), economic (type of cost accounting, material incentive system, arrangements with suppliers, etc.), technical (quality of equipment, performance, etc.), organizational (modes and procedures for managing foreign trade, organization of labor), sociopsychological (staff seen as a whole, interpersonnel relations, conflict situations, individual interests), and physiological (working conditions, fatigue, work schedule) aspects are subtly intermeshed.

It is not enough simply to enumerate these factors; they must be approached as a complex whole. The task cannot be broken down into simpler parts to rationalize particular structures, to be solved in isolation, divorced from the overall organization of foreign trade and its managerial structure. For instance, the problem of streamlining the structure and process of management cannot be tackled adequately by taking one all-union association and dealing with it separately if the same questions have not already been resolved at higher levels, i.e., the main administrations or the ministry as a whole; nor, indeed, can the economic aspects be solved in isolation from commercial activities.

The experience of numerous organizations and ministries in the Soviet Union and of major capitalist firms in dealing with these same problems, namely, the rationalization of management, has shown that they can be effectively resolved only if organizational changes are carried out, first, administratively, i.e., by special divisions directly accountable to the top-level management and invested with the appropriate powers. These powers involve not only the assignment of functions and the redistribution of responsibilities, powers, and duties but also the reshuffling of staffs and the implementation of broad programs for retraining personnel in accordance with structural changes in foreign trade operations related to information processing. There exist such special divisions in firms in France (Renault, Sopad, Electricité de France, Air France), Holland (Stamicarbon, Unilever), Italy (Olivetti, Fiat), and other Western European countries. Second, such measures must be carried out on the basis of a unified concept that allows one to see foreign trade management as a whole. This concept should serve as a monistic reference point in defining new subsystems, outlining their main objectives, and assigning fundamental powers and responsibilities to the various levels and divisions of management.

"In this giant administrative machine, each mechanism, each gear, so to speak, was within the purview not only of the controlling bodies but of all the workers as well."[5] This, of course, would be impossible if an administrative apparatus were built up according to one set of principles and the all-union associations according to another; if that were the case, we would be faced with a plethora of parameters and indices that often conceal the system of responsibilities. (An example is the system of responsibilities and command existing between the various commodity administrations and the all-union associations.)

Third, changes in the structure of management should be undertaken only in accordance with the recommendations of managerial science. Indeed, because of the continuous growth of foreign trade, the complexity of foreign trade processes, and the high degree of indeterminacy about them, many questions cannot be resolved by old, traditional methods. A scientific approach is needed.

There are several reasons for this: the great variability of the environment, which adversely affects the functioning of the foreign trade system as a whole (delays in meeting contractual obligations, the ups and downs of supply and demand, insufficient export funds, etc.); the multitude of external ties both with foreign clients, domestic suppliers, and other organizations and agencies whose activities are supervised and regulated by the Ministry of Foreign Trade. The result of all this is that the number of managerial tasks that must be tackled also approaches the indeterminate.

One of the central problems in working out an administrative structure for foreign trade as a whole, as well as for the particular all-union associations, is to delimit clearly the respective tasks and functions of the various divisions of management while maintaining a single line of authority. One approach to this problem is to build matrix models for the distribution of tasks and functions among the units (divisions of management) in the organizational structure.

Table 7

Management functions \ Management subdivisions	Performers of tasks			
	1	2	...	i
1	A_{11}	A_{21}	...	A_{1i}
2	A_{12}	A_{22}	...	A_{2i}
—	—	—	—	—
j	...	A_{ij}	...	...
m	A_{1m}	A_{2m}	...	A_{nm}

---

n is the quantity of management subdivisions formed in the management structure;
m is the number of assumed management functions;
i is the designation of the subdivision;
j is the designation of the management function.

The matrix element A_{ij} represents an aggregate of administrative tasks performed by the administrative subdivision handling function j within a particular group of tasks.

If each operation in the aggregate A_{ij} is designated by a, then all the operations that must be performed in each administrative function can also be represented in matrix form (see Table 7).

$$A = \begin{vmatrix} a_{ij}^{11}, & a_{ij}^{21} \ldots & a_{ij}^{P1} \\ a_{ji}^{12}, & a_{ij}^{22} \ldots & a_{ij}^{P2} \\ \ldots & \ldots & \ldots \\ a_{ij}^{1Kj}, & a_{ij}^{2Kj} \ldots & a_{ij}^{P_iKj} \end{vmatrix},$$

where:

K_j is the number of administrative operations carried out in fulfilling each task required by function j;

$P_1, P_2 \ldots P_i \ldots P_n$ are the different kinds of tasks for which each administrative subdivision is responsible;

$a_{ii}^{11} \ldots a_{ij}^{Pi}$ are the operations that must be performed to accomplish a task of the P_i-th type.

Thus to accomplish a task of the P_i-th type (e.g., planning of equipment deliveries to capitalist countries), K_{pi} operations must be performed, where:

$$K_{P_i} = \sum_{j=1}^{n} K_j$$

(in our example, $j = 1$ designates the function "planning").

In any administrative subdivision i, K_i operations must be performed, i.e.,

$$K_i = \sum_{P_i=1}^{P_i} K_{P_i},$$

while for the entire administrative apparatus as a whole

Improving the Management of Foreign Trade

$$K_{c6} = \sum_{i=1}^{n} K_j.$$

Constructing such matrices provides a graphic picture for the distribution of tasks and functions by administrative subdivision. But it still does not directly define the shape and nature of the managerial structure. For this we must know a number of other factors, including:

— the number of practical workers under one department head (managerial norm);
— the number of managerial levels;
— the degree of specialization of an administrative subdivision ("horizontal" delimitation of services);
— the degree of centralization of management ("vertical" delimitation of services);
— the degree of devolution of powers within the managerial system.

Yet even when we have determined all the factors defining the specific structural features of the managerial system, the way in which administrative processes and measures are effected, and the relationships between the various administrative divisions, we still have not solved the entire problem. The rationalization of the existing administrative structure of the ministry as a whole, as well as of the individual all-union associations, must also ensure that goals are effectively fulfilled and that decisions are not only made but also implemented smoothly and reliably.

This condition is especially important in the area of foreign trade, where there are always a wide range of variable factors and conditions that must be taken into account. For this reason it is essential that the goals of an expanding foreign trade be clearly defined.

A. Defining the goals of expanding foreign trade and their effect on the organizational structure of management

Defining and setting goals is one of the most crucial, yet at the same time most complex and least studied, problems of management. Indeed, management begins with a definition of its objectives, so much so that it is difficult to conceive of effective management of any type without well-defined objectives. The more precisely stated and defined goals are, the easier it is to select the means to achieve them. A goal serves as a yardstick for development against which the effectiveness of management over time can be measured (it would be difficult to affirm that what we think is a good result of our activity actually is so if we have no clearly defined goal for determining the extent of our achievement); but it is also a criterion we apply in selecting the best means from a range of options for attaining that goal.

Defining goals is complicated; it requires us to assess a vast number of facts and tendencies and the various forms in which they are manifested in social life, even though these facts and tendencies in most cases resist quantification and sometimes even appear to be contradictory.

The definition of goals, therefore, is a complicated and dynamic process, with its own specific features and its own form of organization. In the science of management this activity is called "management by objectives." In terms of systems theory, "management by objectives" signifies a dynamic process (system) that includes the definition of goals, the setting of a time limit on their validity, their arrangement in order of importance, and finally, supervision of their attainment.

In defining goals one must state

<u>what</u> the goal is;

<u>how</u> it should be defined in detail;

<u>how long</u> it should operate.

In practice it is useful to distinguish among fundamental, strategic, tactical, and day-to-day goals. In terms of content, goals are political, economic, commercial, social, technical, research and scientific, cultural, etc.

All goals can be classified as macroeconomic or microeconomic, depending on the level for which they are set.

This classification can be broken down further: for example, at the microeconomic level, in all-union associations there are commercial, social, informational, financial, and research goals, etc.

In defining goals one should bear in mind that there is an essential difference between fundamental goals and those of a strategic, tactical, or day-to-day nature.

The fundamental goal of a system is understood to be the state or situation whose attainment is the system's subjective interest; but often it is quite difficult to ascertain just what that goal is. It may, for example, be at the association level and consist in the endeavor to make maximum economic impact on the market or to attain maximum technical-scientific prestige among competitors, maximum stability in product turnover, etc. In other words, a goal is something wanted or desired and need not depend on the existing situation.

<u>Strategic goals</u> determine how the system will act over a protracted period of time in the future. They should contain the best possible solutions with regard to achieving the basic goals of the system. In practical terms this means that they must be logically consistent with the basic goals and create the means to exert an influence on how the system is behaving with regard to achieving its set goals. In the vast majority of cases, strategic goals are qualitative, not quantitative.

<u>Tactical goals</u> are defined in quantitative terms, unlike strategic goals. They determine the behavior of the system over relatively short time intervals. For example, in an all-union association they may reflect impending price changes on the market or in the sales situation, etc.

<u>Day-to-day goals</u> are short-term. They usually describe in detail how the system functions and are the principal reference points in exercising control.

Actually, day-to-day goals are instruments for the supervision and coordination of ongoing activities and of information intended for analysis; they are necessary for the operative management and supervision of current results.

How and in what terms goals are defined will depend on the managerial level for which they were set. For instance, the methods and approach used to define goals for the economy as a whole will differ from those used for particular branches of the economy, for associations, or for enterprises.

In a socialist society the goals for the economy as a whole are determined in the light of theoretical conceptions, which find concrete reflection in the resolutions of party congresses, the plenary sessions of the Central Committee of the Communist Party, and the decrees of the central state administrative agencies.

In formulating the goals of a developing socialist society, the Communist Party of the Soviet Union refers consciously to the economic laws of socialism, which express the stable and recurrent relationships inherent in economic phenomena and processes. It is this <u>stability</u> and this <u>recurrence</u> that make it possible not only to give genuine consideration to the real needs, capacities, and interests of society at each stage in its development, but also to predict with some degree of accuracy how the society is likely to develop and thereby to control that process. The report of the Central Committee of the Communist Party to the Twenty-fourth Party Congress puts it in these terms: "A theoretical formulation of the phenomena characterizing the life of our society and its principal trends enables the party to predict the course of social processes, to work out a correct political course of action, and to avoid mistakes and subjective solutions."[6]

This can be illustrated by how goals are defined for the economic life of a socialist society as a whole. Proceeding from the higher goal of social production under socialism, which is to provide the fullest gratification of the material and cultural needs of the people, the party set a course for socialist industrialization of the country and collectivization of agriculture as a fundamental goal in the first stage of the construction of socialism in the USSR. In the Ninth Five-Year Plan the primary task spelled out by the Twenty-fourth Party Congress provided for a substantial rise in the well-being of working people, keeping in mind that this course would not only shape our activity for the five-year period ahead but would also set the general course of economic development for a long time to come.

The first step in defining goals is to ascertain society's real needs within the given plan period (both the needs of production and other needs are meant here). This stage culminates when a list of control indicators for the plan has been worked out and submitted to the various sectoral ministries. To ensure that the formulated goals are realistic, the described social needs are measured against the available material resources and work force, in order to determine what means the society has at its disposal for gratifying the indicated needs. In practice this is done by assessing the available quantities of each resource (material and cost balances, balances of labor resources, and a total balance for the economy as a whole are drawn up). But under the conditions of the scientific-technical revolution, which is causing profound changes in production and technology, this is not enough. Not only must several alternative solutions be worked out, but the best one must be chosen. Forecasts and the methods of mathematic economics are widely used for this purpose.

As we have said, foreign trade is an important factor in the growth of the nation's economy. It is a way for our economy to participate in the international division of labor; for instance, our domestic economy obtains goods that are relatively costly to produce in the USSR or that are not produced at all. Accordingly, one of the features of defining the goals of foreign trade is that <u>a proper balance be struck</u> between the volume of <u>own</u> production and <u>imports</u> of specific types of products. This is a laborious and multileveled task, since its solution requires the determination of a whole series of economic costs involved in producing a certain product with the imported item and without it. Another important aspect of the definition of the goals of foreign trade is that export and import operations create various economic relationships, and this requires planning of foreign trade in two basic areas: first, foreign trade operations (exports and imports, the transporting of shipments, insurance, foreign exchange accounts for foreign trade, credit operations in foreign exchange, financial or clearing operations in Soviet rubles), and second, organizations to carry out these various functions. Finally, a third factor involved in defining the goals of foreign trade is that the impact of the growth of foreign trade on trade policy and foreign policy must be assessed.

The targets for the growth of foreign trade are given in the annual state economic plan and are called the "plan for the import and export of goods" for the following year. The plan has three parts.

The first part contains export and import indicators compiled by country, with commodities designated for export to each country and import from it; the total value of imports and exports (in foreign trade plan prices), with a breakdown according to the clearing procedure used; and export and import volumes (expressed in terms of value) broken down by groups of countries:
1. Socialist countries,
    including:
        CMEA countries;
        non-CMEA countries.
2. Capitalist countries,
    including:
        countries settling in freely convertible currency;
        countries clearing with free conversion;
        countries with restricted clearing and restricted currency.

The second part contains figures for planned deliveries of goods for export by ministries and agencies of the USSR and the union republics.

The third part contains a plan for deliveries of goods to the domestic economy through imports. This part has two subsections:
1. Machinery and equipment (broken down into socialist and capitalist countries).
2. Raw materials, materials, and goods for mass consumption.

Improving the Management of Foreign Trade

Long-range plans for the growth of foreign trade contain a considerably more narrow range of parameters than annual plans.

Finally, a summary foreign exchange plan for the country is compiled annually and contains sections and indices such as:

1. Trading operations (export and import of goods and related receipts and payments).
2. Services (export and import of services and transport, communications, technical services, tourism, etc.).
3. Nontrade operations (payments to international organizations, etc.).
4. Credits and property (movement of financial capital and property).
5. Nonremunerative aid.

Thus, defining of foreign trade growth targets is a quite complicated, dynamic process requiring, first, consideration of the balance-sheet relations between foreign trade and other branches of the economy and the material, financial, and foreign exchange resources used in foreign trade; second, determination of the economic effect derived from the country's participation in the international division of labor; and third, consideration of political and commercial results of the growth of foreign trade.

Management with targets (goals) takes place at the level of the Ministry of Foreign Trade and USSR Gosplan. But since, as we have pointed out above, the Ministry of Foreign Trade is a complex developing system consisting of a large number of subsystems and elements, a second and no less important task of management with targets is the distribution of these targets and their coordination among the different management levels, divisions, and organizations.

All these targets for the activity of foreign trade divisions and organizations are based on general targets for foreign trade growth and constitute an internally coherent, top-down unified system of targets for the entire branch.

In practical terms this means that at the level of the Ministry of Foreign Trade, targets are derived from the needs of the society at large and express the interests both of the particular sector of the economy, i.e., foreign trade, as well as the interests of the all-union associations, which are themselves based on the interests of the overall development of foreign trade. In other words, there is a hierarchy of goals in which they are ranked according to their relative importance and their direction. Schematically this may be described as a "goal chart," the apex of which is interpreted as a final goal, and all the branches and arcs as relationships between intermediate goals in accordance with their order and rank. The apex represents the highest goal of foreign trade as a branch of the economy; under it is the level of general goals, which flow directly from the highest goal and are directly subordinate to it; and then follow the level of secondary, tertiary, etc., goals.

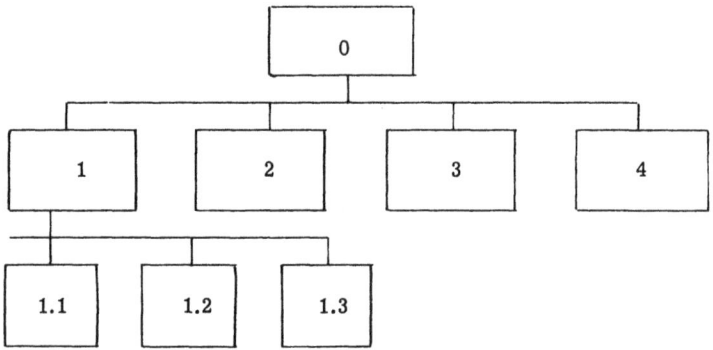

Figure 11.

    Where 0 is the highest goal of the foreign trade system, which consists of satisfying the needs of socialist society on the basis of efficient utilization of the advantages deriving from the international division of labor, and particularly the socialist international division of labor;
1, 2, 3, 4 are general goals of the development of foreign trade:
    1 is constant growth of exports;
    2 is meeting the needs of society with efficient import goods;
    3 is securing an active balance in the conduct of foreign trade;
    4 is securing a stable financial status for the system.

In Figure 11 each lower-level goal is a means to achieve a higher goal. For instance, goal 1 derives from the general goal 0 of foreign trade as a system and, second, represents the integration of three second-level goals, to wit: 1.1. Expansion of the list of export goods; 1.2. Expansion of markets; 1.3. Increasing the efficiency of export.

In its turn the goal "expansion of markets" is implemented at the third level of goals: improvement in the quality of export goods, improvement in old and introduction of new forms of organization and procedure in foreign trade, reduction of the delivery times for export, improvement in competitiveness of export goods. These goals are then specified at the fourth, fifth, etc., levels.

The other general goals of foreign trade development are specified in a similar way. A characteristic feature of the hierarchy is the fact that in going from the higher levels to the lower levels, the goals become increasingly more specific and more and more quantitatively definable.

Each unit — an all-union association or a division — tries to achieve its own local goals, which derive from the higher ones.

One of the most important tasks of foreign trade management is to coordinate these local goals and interests of particular socioeconomic and industrial units with the general goals and interests of the society as a whole. Such a problem first appears under socialism. Under capitalism, because of irreconcilable class contradictions, there can be no coordination of particular goals at the level of the whole socioeconomic organism. The objective possibility of such coordination first becomes possible under socialism, which is governed by the maxim: what is good for the society must be good for each producer. This principle is inherent in each aspect of the life of a socialist society.

However, this problem is most difficult and complicated to solve in the economic domain. It is not always possible to successfully combine concrete local goals and goals of a higher order (e.g., the goals of an all-union association and sectoral goals and the goal of social production). Economically, the practical meaning of this is that the unity of higher- and lower-order goals breaks down. This occurs when an enterprise finds, for some internal reasons associated with the economic interests of its collectivity, that it is not expedient to use all its capacities for increasing exports. Consequently, one of the leading tasks of foreign trade management is the creation of an economic mechanism of management that will ensure the transformation of goals from higher levels to lower levels and the coordination of actions at different levels.

In the narrow sense of the term, foreign trade management by means of central state planning is such an economic mechanism; it creates an optimal structure for managing different types of foreign trade activity in separate divisions and in all-union associations, as well as by means of economic levers.

From the foregoing it follows that this multifaceted character of foreign trade gives rise to multiple goals, representing an interconnected single system of goals ranked according to their social importance. The degree of fulfillment of these goals at any given moment is characterized by the qualitative and quantitative state of foreign trade as a system, on the one hand, and the effectiveness of management — in particular, the degree of perfection of its organizational structure — on the other. The second aspect may be elucidated by determining the degree of correspondence between the chief elements of the structure and the goals set, determination of the intrastructural disproportions between large divisions and within them, and on the basis of a study of the competence of leadership in making managerial decisions and of the degree of centralization and decentralization of decision-making. In practice this means that it is necessary to determine: the number of elements at different levels of the organizational structure; the significance of the elements within the system as a whole and at each level; specialization of the elements and the degree of this specialization. Then one must ascertain the major (quantitative) interactions between elements on each level and between levels, the types of interaction between elements and their quantitative distribution, the correlation between contiguous elements in the process of achieving a set goal; it is also necessary to estimate the disproportions and bottlenecks in the structure. If an organizational structure is simple, there are no special difficulties in analyzing its effectiveness; that is not, however, the case for complicated organizational structures such as the Ministry of Foreign Trade.

In our opinion this case may be dealt with in two ways: on the basis of logical reasoning, by comparing goal charts with the existing organizational structure for management of the system or its divisions, the integration of identical functions of management, and the establishment of divisions to take care of them; or on the basis of methods of mathematic economics, which will enable us to construct simulation models of the organizational structure of management.

B. <u>Methods of logical analysis of the organizational structure of management</u>

As a means for achieving generally established goals, the organizational structure of foreign trade management — as a whole, or in its separate elements (subdivisions, all-union associations, and so on) — consists of a specific number of elements (subdivisions), intended for the fulfillment of subgoals at the $n-1$ level, which in turn are distributed among a specific number of elements at the $n-2$ level, and so on.

In a simple variant the number of elements of the organizational structure of management can be equal to the number of goals (see Figure 11), that is, we are considering a variant which fulfills the requirement of congruence between goals and structural links.

However, such an ideal model does not exist in real life; usually the number of units in an organizational structure will be larger or smaller than the number of goals. Everything will depend on the degree of integration of goals, to what extent they are detailed, on the amount of work required to fulfill them, etc. But in all cases the achievement of a goal is contingent on certain basic functions of management (planning, organization, coordination, leadership, supervision, and control), which presume the fulfillment of certain functional tasks.

The first step, then, in drawing up a goal chart for the entire system or any of its divisions is to develop the managerial function-tasks that determine the content and direction of managerial efforts to achieve the established goals of the particular division (all-union association, office, etc.).

This can be done by breaking down the basic functions of management with regard to the basic elements and subelements of foreign trade activity.

In Table 8 the symbols A, a_{11} ... a_{24}; B, $в_{11}$ ... $в_{24}$; C ..., etc., are the function-tasks of management determined by the need to ensure that the basic functions of management are carried out (planning, organization, leadership, coordination, accounting, supervision, and control) with regard to the basic elements of the foreign trade process. For example, $в_{11}$ designates a function-task whose content is the control of import planning; $PЭ_{13}$ is a function-task defined by the necessity of realizing the basic managerial function (coordination and leadership) associated with incorporating the export plan into the plans of ministries and agencies.

Of course, the breakdown of foreign trade activity into subelements may go on ad infinitum, with longer and longer lists of the jobs that must be done, until all the managerial tasks required to fulfill managerial functions are listed.

If we group similar tasks together, we can form special divisions for getting them done. There are two basic ways to group tasks:

— according to similarity of the subelement of foreign trade activity performed (grouping done horizontally). For example, the function-tasks a_{11}, a_{12}, a_{13} and a_{14} may be grouped together under the heading "political aspects"; in so doing we create a division whose activities extend over all the basic functions of management. In our example this activity pertains to trade-political administrations;

— according to similarity of one or several basic managerial functions (vertical grouping). For example, if we group the function-tasks A_{11}, B_{11}, C_{11}, $CД_{11}$, etc., for the "planning" function, we obtain a division concerned with planning, i.e., in our

Improving the Management of Foreign Trade

Table 8

Matrix for Defining the Function-Tasks of Foreign Trade Management

Basic elements	Basic subelements of foreign trade activity	Basic functions of management			
		Planning	Organization	Coordination and guidance	Accounting and control
I. Defining foreign trade policy	By content: political aspects, trade-economic aspects, national economic needs, export opportunities, business cycle	A_{11} a_{11} a_{21} a_{31} —	A_{12} a_{12} a_{22} a_{32} —	A_{13} a_{13} a_{23} a_{33} —	A_{14} a_{14} a_{24} a_{34} —
	By socioeconomic direction: socialist countries CMEA members capitalist countries developing countries	A_{21}	A_{22}	A_{23}	A_{24}
II. Setting goals	Long-range: import plan export plan plan for deliveries to the national economy	B_{11} B_{11} B_{21}	B_{12} B_{12} B_{22}	B_{13} B_{13} B_{23}	B_{14} B_{14} B_{24}
	Current: import plan export plan	B_{21}	B_{22}	B_{23}	B_{24}
III. Concluding agreements	By countries: by types (trade contracts, trade-payment agreements, trade protocols, etc.) by form of deliveries (accounts in transferable rubles, commercial credit, credit-clearing)	C_{11} CT_{11} $C\Phi_{11}$	C_{12} CT_{12} $C\Phi_{12}$	C_{13} CT_{13} $C\Phi_{13}$	C_{14} CT_{14} $C\Phi_{14}$
IV. Transactions	By commodities: by types (commodities, purchase-sale, compensational, services, licenses, rent, etc.) by contractors (firms, state organizations, etc.)	$CД_{11}$ CB_{11} CK_{11}	$CД_{12}$ CB_{12} CK_{12}	$CД_{13}$ CB_{13} CK_{13}	$CД_{14}$ CB_{14} CK_{14}

The USSR's Management of Foreign Trade

Basic elements	Basic subelements of foreign trade activity / Basic functions of management	Planning	Organization	Coordination and guidance	Accounting and control
V. Work with industry and other branches of the economy	Inclusion of the export plan in the plans of ministries, departments, and enterprises	$PЭ_{11}$	$PЭ_{12}$	$PЭ_{13}$	$PЭ_{14}$
	Production (supervision of periods for preparation and fulfillment of technical conditions, etc.)	$PП_{11}$	$PП_{12}$	$PП_{13}$	$PП_{14}$
	Shipping (supervision of shipping deadlines, etc.)	PO_{11}	PO_{12}	PO_{13}	PO_{14}
	Accounts with enterprises	PP_{11}	PP_{12}	PP_{13}	PP_{14}
VI. Accounts	Deliveries of goods	PT_{11}	PT_{12}	PT_{13}	PT_{14}
	Accounts with foreign buyers	PH_{11}	PH_{12}	PH_{13}	PH_{14}

case this will be the main planning-economic administrations, the main trade-political administrations, and so on.

So by defining the functional tasks of management and grouping them either vertically or horizontally, we are able to get a more objective idea of the number of elements in a management system necessary for the organization to function smoothly. However, the matrix in Table 8 does not give us any idea of the relationships and responsibilities existing between different divisions, and hence levels of management.

A description of these relationships on the basis of job instructions and division regulations does not provide a full picture of the organizational structure in all its complexity. A functional diagram in the form of a matrix can do so.

The merit of this way of depicting managerial tasks and the individuals performing them, as compared with the one described in the foregoing, lies in the fact that it is simple, easy to interpret, unambiguous, and time saving as compared with the usual way of description; moreover, it reflects both vertical and horizontal relationships.

Improving the Management of Foreign Trade

Table 9

Functional Diagram

Tasks	Performers of tasks					
	$R_s \atop K$	P	$R_j V$	P_p		
	$I, R_s \atop K$	$P_1 N$	N	PR		
	Z_p	N_s				

Along the vertical stand departments and other subdivisions of the Ministry of Foreign Trade; along the horizontal appear management tasks that must be done. The intersection of horizontals and verticals, that is, the cells of the matrix, represent forms of action (functions) performed by departments to carry out tasks set:

P is the planning function;
R_j is decisions in various circumstances;
K_s is the control function;
R_p is the right to cooperate in a decision;
N is the commercial function;
P is the right to command;
I is initiative, stimuli;
PR is preparation of decisions;
Z_p is development of plans;
V is delegation of rights.

C. Use of the methods of mathematical economics to analyze the organizational structures of management

Modeling of the structure of management consists of two successive stages:
— modeling the goal order of the elements;
— modeling the goal interaction of the elements.

The first stage involves use of the theory of graphs and information theory. The primary concept here is a partially ordered set, which is defined as a system X (in our case, the Ministry of Foreign Trade) with the binary relationship $X\ Y$ fulfilling the conditions:

if $X \leqslant Y$ and $Y \leqslant X$, then $X = Y$ (asymmetry), i.e., one equation of two is operative;

if $X \leqslant Y$ and $Y \leqslant Z$, then $X \leqslant Z$ (transitence).

The hierarchy of the organizational structure of foreign trade management (coefficient of order in a partially ordered set) is defined by the number of elements included in it (in its structure).

Let us suppose we have the normal organizational structure of an all-union association, with its two-level system of management (the director and his deputies and the heads of functional sections, offices, and groups).

We shall use the following designations: P — the all-union association; P_1 — office No. 1; P_2 — office No. 2; S_{11} — group 1 of office No. 1; S_{12} — group 2 of office No. 1; S_{21} — group 1 of office No. 2; S_{22} — group 2 of office No. 2. The organizational structure of the all-union association will then be written in the form:

$$P = f(P_i), \quad P_i = f(S_{ij}),$$

where: $i - 1, 2 \ldots$ offices, and $j - 1, 2 \ldots$ groups.

General algebraic principles are used to construct a model for the goal interaction of the structural elements. Let us assume that an organizational element P_i (in our example an office) interacts with element P_j (in our example a group in the first or second office), then q_{ij} will be the weight coefficient characterizing the closeness of the tie between P_i and P_j, and q_{ji} will be the weight coefficient characterizing the closeness of the tie between P_j and P_i. If we take the purposeful functioning of the Ministry of Foreign Trade whose structure is $P = (P_1; P_2 \ldots P_n), n(n-1)$ magnitudes are fixed. Then the quantitative estimates of the interrelationships (closeness of ties) or weight coefficients of intersections may be described in matrix form:

$$Q(q_{ij}) = \begin{vmatrix} q_{11} & q_{12} & q_{13} & \cdots & q_{1n} \\ q_{21} & q_{22} & q_{23} & \cdots & q_{2n} \\ q_{31} & q_{32} & q_{33} & \cdots & q_{3n} \\ q_{n1} & q_{n2} & q_{n3} & \cdots & q_{nn} \end{vmatrix}$$

Expert evaluation and prognosis of the development of the organizational structure of management. Expert evaluations amount to a generalization and statistical assessment of the opinions of highly qualified specialists in some area of knowledge about foreign trade (day-to-day work; planning, financial activity; business trends, etc.) with regard to questions bearing on an evaluation of the existing structure and possible ways it might be rationalized. Experts present their conclusions concerning the problems posed to them anonymously (under a code).

The effectiveness of this method depends on the competence of the experts, whether the questions are formulated correctly, the rules for conducting inquiries by the experts, etc. To improve the productivity of using expert surveys, their opinions are processed by statistical methods. The most widespread method of expert evaluations is the Delphi method, which uses statistical processing of expert opinions.

The following sequence and list of measures are recommended for evaluating the organizational structure of management: defining the goals of the expert opinion; formulating questions for the experts; laying down the rules for surveying the experts; determining a way to evaluate the competence of the experts; formulation of the rules and methods for processing the opinions of the experts; the survey itself; processing and evaluating the results of the survey of experts; proposals on improving the organizational structure of management.

The main objectives in obtaining an expert evaluation of the structure of foreign trade management or the management of its individual elements (all-union associations, main administrations, administrations, offices, etc.) are to evaluate the existing structure of management from the standpoint of how efficiently the tasks of the Ministry of Foreign Trade and its divisions and organizations are carried out, as well as to present proposals for its improvement.

The number of questions posed to the experts and their general orientation should therefore yield an evaluation of its structure and provide some idea of how it can be improved. The principal lines along which questions should be formulated are as follows:

1. Determination of the basic factors involved in setting up the existing structural ties;

2. Probability of changing these factors within the next five to ten years, etc.;

3. Probability of new factors appearing that make improvement in the organizational structure necessary;

4. Determination of the strength of the ties between the different divisions and organizations at the same level in the administrative hierarchy and at different levels;

5. Determination of the relative importance of particular elements in the management structure, etc.

After all questions are formulated, rules for conducting the survey of experts and for selecting the experts can easily be worked out. For example, several experts can be called on to deal with the same problem, or different experts can be called on to deal with different aspects of a problem. The number of experts called on should be large enough so that statements by any of them will not carry inordinate weight. In other words, the number of experts is an important factor in achieving the desired accuracy.

Calculations made by different authors show that the accuracy of experts' evaluations decreases sharply if their number is less than ten, and it increases negligibly when their number is increased from ten to thirty. In examining their answers to the questions, it should be borne in mind that not all the experts will have the same degree of competence with regard to any one aspect of the problem. Hence it is advisable to evaluate their competence before doing the survey. This may be done by self-evaluation, i.e., each expert can rate himself on the basis of a scale furnished him. In the particular case a ten-point scale is used, with the rating 0 corresponding to total ignorance of the question involved; 0.5 means that the expert is well acquainted with the problem but does not specialize in it. A rating of 1 means that the expert is competent to deal with the given question. On the basis of these self-evaluations, all experts can be classified according to the level of their knowledge about particular questions, i.e., subgroups can be

Improving the Management of Foreign Trade

created consisting of qualified specialists on some narrowly defined question.

The expert evaluation should later be refined depending on the number and magnitude of the mistakes made by any expert in evaluating an event. For example, if a group consists of n_j (where: $j = 1, 2, 3 \ldots$ is the number of experts) experts and each of them has made N_i ($i = 1, 2 \ldots$ is the number of an evaluation) evaluations, the relative error of the i-th evaluation of the j-th expert will be:

$$S_{ij} = \frac{\hat{x}_i - x_{ij}}{\hat{x}_i} \, 100,$$

where: x_{ij} is the i-th evaluation given by the j-th expert;
$\hat{x}_i$ is the actual significance of the i-th evaluation.

To show the degree of competence of the expert or the weight of his evaluations, one can adopt the quantity

$$a_j = \frac{\sum_{j=1}^{n} MS_j}{MS^i},$$

where: j is $1, 2, 3 \ldots n$,
M is the sign of mathematical expectation.

$$MS_j = \frac{1}{N_j} \sum_{i=1}^{N_j} S_{ij}.$$

To define the degree of agreement of n experts, one takes into consideration the so-called coefficient of agreement:

$$W = \frac{\sum_{i=1}^{m} \left\{ \sum_{j=1}^{n} X_{ij} - \frac{1}{2} n(m+1) \right\}^2}{\frac{1}{12} mn^2 (m^2 - 1)},$$

where: $j = 1, 2, 3 \ldots n$ is the total of experts and the number assigned each expert;

$i = 1, 2, 3 \ldots n$ is the total and ordinal number of the evaluated events or parameters;

X_{ij} is the evaluation given by the j-th expert to the i-th event.

The coefficient W varies within the limits 0 to 1, so that when $W = 1$, one observes total agreement.

The efficiency of evaluation of proposed measures for improving the organizational structure of management is fundamentally determined by the measures adopted to analyze the experts' opinions. In particular, this relates to uncovering the most important factors that influence the development of organizational structure, to determining their interrelationships, and so on. Thus, to determine the most important factors the method of event ranking is used; the factor whose importance is noted by the majority of experts is ranked in first place, followed by factors receiving fewer "votes," and so on. It is important here to determine the interrelationship of these factors and of elements in the organizational structure. This can be expressed in the form of the matrix in Table 10.

Table 10

Matrix of the Interrelationship between Factors with Structural Subdivisions

Basic factors in their importance	Performers of the interrelationship	Elements (subdivisions) of the organizational structure				
		1	2	3	......	n
1		P_{11}	.	.	....	P_{in}
2		.	.	.	....	.
3		.	.	.	....	.
....		.	.	.	....	.
....		.	.	.	....	.
....		.	.	.	....	.
i		R_{i1}	.	.	....	P_{in}

i — number of factors.

P_{in} — degree of influence of the i-th factor on n structural subdivisions.

Improving the Management of Foreign Trade

The experts rate the strength of the interrelationship on the basis of the following scale:

0 — no interrelationship between factors and a structural division exists;
0.5 — weak interrelationship;
0.8 — strong interrelationship;
1.0 — very strong interrelationship.

Intermediate ratings are also possible. Once a set of factors has been ranked according to their relative importance and their influence on some element of the organizational structure has been determined, the organizational structure of management of foreign trade as a whole and of its different divisions may be constructed.

With matrices and models the correlation of the organizational structure of management with the goals governing the function of the system or its elements, as well as the volume of work involved in performing the functions incumbent on the different divisions, can be analyzed. But such an analysis will not necessarily yield the best structure, i.e., the most flexible, reliable, and smoothly running as far as decision-making is concerned. For this a systematic approach is required such that all the work and effort expended in achieving goals are regarded from the standpoint of solving problems rather than from the standpoint of a hierarchy. The focus should be on improving interactions and integrating all types of managerial activity.

It is important to have an accurate idea of the real relation between specialization and cooperation in managerial work (managerial duties carried out at the various levels). Specialization of management according to kinds of activity unquestionably improves its efficiency, but it also sometimes causes indifference toward responsibility in coping with problems crucial to the development of the system as a whole. This is especially apparent when a management system is built up by function. For example, the creation of specialized main commodity administrations in the central apparatus of the Ministry of Foreign Trade has made possible more qualified decisions with regard to various problems of foreign trade activity; but on the other hand, it has diluted the sense of responsibility toward the activities of the all-union associations as a whole, since there are so many links in the chain of command; at the same time all-union associations are subordinate to several main administrations and ministerial offices. In addition, in a situation where staff and the wage fund are apportioned among the various divisions in a centralized order, each functional division (main administrations, trade-political administrations, etc.) tries to delimit its activities in such a way as to obtain a large wage fund and staff, which is not always necessarily consonant with the interests of the system. These conflict situations are resolved at the top managerial level (minister and his deputies on the collegium). The upshot is that top-level management is obliged to deal with both long-term and current problems.

Cooperation in management is an important way to reduce the number of administrative staff; but in complex systems it also reduces the quality and smooth functioning of management, since the same worker (or division) will have to cope with several managerial problems at once.

In our opinion the quest for a proper and realistic balance between specialization and cooperation in management should proceed along the lines of creating a more clear-cut integration of the horizontal and vertical ties in the management structure. Such an integration should be achieved by unifying specific kinds of activity, not by a mere trading of information between different divisions of equal standing (e.g., as occurs in relationships between the main economic plan administration and the main commodity administrations when the plan for the development of foreign trade is compiled or when current reports are drawn up).

One way to deal with this problem is to use the so-called matrix organizational structure of management. Such a structure uses the existing (traditional) functional structure of management, which is built up on particular tasks. But in addition to the permanent functional divisions (main administrations and administrations), temporary ad hoc groups are also set up to deal with particular problems. These groups consist of specialists from different main administrations and administrations at the same level in the hierarchy (horizontal). In each case the specialists are subordinate to two higher authorities: organizationally to their main administration or administration director, and second, to the leader of their group (at the level of the job at hand).

This structure helps overcome intra-organizational barriers between different divisions in the Ministry of Foreign Trade and also integrates their work in dealing with problems of a general nature affecting the system as a whole. It also makes for a more flexible distribution of manpower in dealing with particular problems.

The horizontal integration of activity covers strategic problems dealt with at the ministerial level, while everyday operations are managed vertically on the linear or functional principle. The institution of such a structure presupposes a clear definition and delimitation of the powers and responsibilities of the different group leaders and functional divisions, on the one hand, and the specialists on the other. The statement of the vice-president of TRW is very illuminating in this respect: "A matrix is a very fragile thing. If people don't want it to work, they can easily make it break down."[7]

In other words, psychological factors play a very important role in determining if measures to improve a management structure are going to be effective. This means that the building up and improving of an organizational structure for management is a complex, multifaceted process, requiring the conscientious efforts of many specialists.

4. Main Directions in Improving the Organizational Structure of Foreign Trade Management

As we have seen, improvement in the organizational structure of foreign trade management is an ongoing process, and its effectiveness will depend on the availability of sufficiently well-developed methods that can integrate synthesis and analysis and ensure correct choice of measures within a long-term perspective. There must, of course, exist an intelligent overall concept on the basis of which rationalization measures and changes in the existing structure can be carried out.

In fact, the Ministry of Foreign Trade and all its various agencies and divisions are currently experiencing a ferment of activity directed toward the simplification of the structure of management, improving the division of labor, making cooperation more effective, and eliminating superfluous links and stages in the system. All this is undoubtedly important and necessary. But to what extent are all these efforts coordinated with one another and with the future development of foreign trade and the demands made by the modern scientific-technical revolution? This question can only be answered if there is a general, overall, scientifically sound concept of the objectives of such improvements.

In our opinion any overall concept must proceed from:
— how the organization of foreign trade looks now and how it has evolved;
— the specific facts, trends, and circumstances that determined its development in the past and will retain their importance in the future;
— the internal and external limitations on and potential of its development;
— the characteristic features of foreign trade activity, which it would be either impossible or undesirable to change;
— the choice and distribution of foreign trade tasks according to the time available to complete them;
— the possible consequences of allocating the resources at hand by different sets of problems;
— the choice of preferred directions for improvement in foreign trade activity.

The first thing in working out an overall concept is to decide on what basis all the above-listed features are to be coordinated. We think that such a basis should be the introduction of

Improving the Management of Foreign Trade

automatic control systems (ACSs) in the Ministry of Foreign Trade and in the all-union associations. Indeed, if the streamlining of management is not based on the introduction of automatic control systems, and primarily on the consequences this entails, the effectiveness of any measures will only be brief and in some cases may cause material losses.

The acceptance of ACSs by the Ministry of Foreign Trade and the all-union associations as a necessary premise for developing an overall concept of how to improve management is also dictated by the fact that a great deal has already been done in this direction in the Ministry of Foreign Trade. For example, the first stage of staff counting has been introduced; the first generations of ACSs have been introduced in six all-union associations; and ACSs are already functioning and growing in V/O "Zapchast'eksport," making it possible to:

— analyze the structure of exports of spare parts;
— determine shortages;
— ensure the most effective policy for export of spare parts, providing a continuous flow at a maximum saving;
— optimize the export plan and project spare-part production for several years, hence taking into account demand and the outlook for expanding exports to foreign countries;
— create technologically and economically warranted stocks of parts in warehouses in the USSR and abroad, with ongoing control of their depletion and prompt replenishment of stocks, etc.

Studies have shown, for example, that the introduction of an ACS into V/O "Zapchast'eksport" has enabled it to export spare parts for 435 models and 169 modified versions of machinery, to process 440 tons of items for 4,140 orders from different purchasers, to supervise the delivery of 587 notes of consignment, and to send out bills promptly to foreign firms. It would be impossible to handle such a volume of information by the old "manual" methods.

ACSs embrace almost every aspect of foreign trade activity. But it should be borne in mind that to develop an overall concept of how to improve management, it is not so much their installation and area of use which are important, as the changes they cause in the nature of managerial activity. It is important to know what problems a specialist should handle and what problems can be handed over to machines in the dialogue "man — machine."

The installation of ACSs in the Ministry of Foreign Trade and the all-union associations requires huge sums of capital investments, which are sometimes beyond the resources of the associations themselves. We must therefore begin to think about creating large economically accountable export-import enterprises formed by the merger of several all-union associations. This is possible if the list of goods handled is standardized. For example, the all-union associations "Sudoimport," "Traktoroeksport," "Avtoeksport," "Zapchast'eksport," and "Energomasheksport" could be merged into a large economically accountable export-import foreign trade enterprise, which might be called "Vneshtorgtransport," with its own centralized funds for development and economic incentive. Such export-import enterprises can be formed in one of two ways:

— first, on the basis of a broad list of goods similar with regard to their consumer uses;

— second, on the basis of a narrow group of specialized goods. In other words, export-import enterprises can be either narrowly specialized or have a wide range of goods; their overall organization would be similar. Which way is chosen depends on a number of factors, and one should proceed by comparing the situations created using both approaches; in this way decisions can be made on a sounder basis, management will be effective and smooth, and the efficiency of foreign trade will be increased.

In all cases organizational integration can be carried out in several ways:

— on the basis of creating a separate specialized management apparatus;

— on the basis of one of the all-union associations, by raising it to the status of a principal foreign trade enterprise;

— on the basis of the main commodity administrations, by

Improving the Management of Foreign Trade

removing them from the control of the central apparatus of the ministry and placing them on a cost-accounting economic basis.

True, not all the main administrations in the Ministry of Foreign Trade could serve as a basis for creating such export-import enterprises. Many of them, especially those dealing in machinery and technical goods, control either only exports or only imports or are responsible for organizing foreign trade with capitalist or socialist countries.

Of course, to create an optimal management system for foreign trade, the specific features of the activity of the existing all-union associations must be taken into account. Hence the way that is chosen to create larger foreign trade entities must be based on practical experience. In pointing out the importance of this, A. N. Kosygin, speaking at the Fourteenth Party Congress, noted that "the choice of new systems of management, adapted to the properties of each branch of industry, must be preceded by a careful study of practical experience and scientific findings."[8]

The creation of large specialized export-import enterprises is destined to play in the future a central role in improving the organizational structure of management of foreign trade, not only because it is necessary to concentrate human, material, and financial resources within the main lines of development of foreign trade in order to make Soviet goods as competitive as possible on an increasingly competitive world market, but also because of the demands for flexibility in the management of all-union associations — to be achieved by simplifying the structure of management and cutting down on the number of different agencies having a hand in decision-making.

The creation of large export-import economically accountable foreign trade enterprises will weed out unnecessary links in the management system; instead of dual or triple accountability, which is what we have now, the enlarged associations will have only one chain of command.

The creation of large export-import enterprises in the central apparatus of the Ministry of Foreign Trade will make it possible to devote more attention to long-range questions and to the solution of the concrete, fundamental problems of the development of foreign trade. In addition, the concentration of export and import operations in the same hands for the major groups of goods will enable a more effective trade policy to be developed for each group of goods, improve ties with industry, have an active influence on production, and provide a basis for a sound import policy. The latter is especially important given the narrow bureaucratic approach of the industrial ministries toward covering their own needs for goods through import procurements, at the same time as their concern about covering their imports through exports of their own goods leaves something to be desired.

The creation of export-import enterprises should also help to foster a mutual interest in the development of ties between the industrial ministries and the Ministry of Foreign Trade for the purpose of stimulating import by means of exports exceeding the plan quota for export goods and searching for new goods for export.

Another argument for the creation of export-import divisions is that it would make it possible to coordinate exports with imports more accurately on the foreign markets. For example, the all-union associations in most cases have large monopolies as their customers; these monopolies not only sell semifinished products and finished products, they also buy them in considerable volume in other countries. Naturally, this circumstance must be utilized properly to the advantage of the state by coordinating our exports with our imports, and this of course can be done most effectively when exports and imports of the same goods are in the same hands.

It should also be borne in mind that the creation of export-import organizations should be done in parallel with the reorganization of the structure of management in the central administrative apparatus of the ministry. The basic structural changes in management should involve the creation of main export-import administrations with uniform lists of goods, without dividing up their activities by country. These enterprises should take over all the functions of managing the on-

Improving the Management of Foreign Trade

going activity of the all-union associations. The following, for example, is the way the main raw materials administrations might be reorganized.

At present (Figure 10) the main raw materials administrations have under them nine raw materials all-union associations ("Soiuznefteeksport," "Soiuzgazeksport," "Soiuzpromeksport," "Soiuzkhimeksport," "Raznoimport," "Promsyr'eimport," "Tekhsnabeksport," "Eksportles," and "Eksportkhleb"). There are over 3,000 items on the lists of these associations, the main ones of which are: oil and petroleum products, natural gas, coal, industrial ores, some kinds of building materials, nonferrous metals, ferrous metal sheet, cast iron, steel scrap, wood pulp, wood chips, cellulose, paper, cardboard, and other goods.

The raw materials export and import administrations conduct business with more than twenty industrial ministries. A number of practical workers in the Ministry of Foreign Trade have expressed the opinion (and the author agrees with them) that there should be one unified enterprise created for the export and import of fuels and chemical products, and it should have under it the "Soiuznefteeksport," "Soiuzgazeksport," "Soiuzkhimeksport," and "Soiuzpromeksport" all-union associations. Such goods as asbestos and assorted commodities should be handed over to V/O "Raznoimport," and ferrous and nonferrous metal ores to V/O "Promsyr'eimport." The other four all-union associations ("Eksportles," "Promsyr'eimport," "Raznoimport," and "Tekhsnabeksport") should be placed under the main export-import administration for wood and metal products.

These structural changes should favorably reduce the number of administrative links. For example, the Main Administration for Trade in Fuels and Chemical Products will have relationships with only twelve industrial ministries instead of twenty, as is now the case. The number of ministries with which the Main Administration for Trade in Wood and Metal Products will have to deal will be reduced to fourteen.

The need to create export-import enterprises also results

from the fact that the structure of management of foreign trade, which is an integral part of the nation's economy, should correspond to the model of functioning of socialist production. The general direction of our economy is already mapped out: for example, the principles of economic reform must be consistently and continuously applied, and there must be a transition to a two-tiered and three-tiered system.

The introduction of ACSs into export-import enterprises will make it possible to centralize functional and support services and to relieve the associations that make up an enterprise of all tasks except the direct carrying out of foreign trade transactions. This, in the final analysis, should make the system of management more flexible and more effective.

The Czechoslovak foreign trade enterprise A/O "Stroiimport" can serve as an example. In it all functional and subsidiary services have been centralized. The enterprise itself was created in 1969 on the basis of an agreement between the former foreign trade association "Stroiimport" and enterprises producing metal-cutters and presses and cutting and measuring instruments. It employs more than 1,000 persons.

The organizational structure of "Stroiimport" is strictly functional. Its activities are broken down into four types:
— administrative-organizational;
— commercial;
— economic;
— trade policy.

It is noteworthy that all activities concerning long-range questions are centralized, while all day-to-day activities are decentralized. For example, on the one hand, the planning section, which numbers thirty people, is engaged in compiling long-range plans and the analysis and coordination of plan fulfillment by the operations offices; there are ties with the central apparatus of the Ministry of Foreign Trade of the CSSR and with other relevant ministries and agencies. On the other hand, the planning teams in the offices, e.g., the import office, which numbers seventeen people (a total of eighty people work in the office), prepares statistical data in accordance with the existing forms of recording and reporting, preparing and processing charts for each work team, and it coordinates and supervises all the work involved in compiling plans for both the office as a whole and for each particular work team.

The organizational structure of operational offices is also of interest (the A/O "Stroiimport" offices have as many staff as three or four offices in Soviet all-union associations). Each office (e.g., the import office, which employs eighty people) is headed by a director, with two assistants, a secretary, and a person responsible for secretarial work. There is a planning team in the office consisting of seventeen people (it has ties with the ACS of A/O "Stroiimport" and compiles all the output records and reports), a technical team consisting of eleven persons, and six operations teams consisting of nine people each: the team leader, four engineers, two foreign correspondents, an economist, and a records secretary.

The team leader supervises the carrying out of tasks, the coordination of problems with foreign trade bodies, ties with other divisions, and the preparation of data for computers (together with the economist); he also takes part in talks with foreign firms. The engineer takes care of all the routine work having to do with foreign trade transactions, including clearing accounts, a task that is completely computerized. The foreign correspondent takes care of translating and typing the necessary foreign trade correspondence, as well as some of the correspondence with foreign firms. The economist keeps a clearing file and receives and processes tabulated material for the group as a whole and for each engineer. The economist distributes the computer printouts. The records secretary takes care of the office work.

The work of the office as a whole and of its teams is reflected in tables and charts — basic documents from which one can assess the state of contracts, deliveries, payments, etc. They also usually include lists of equipment, prices, quantities, the sum and state of orders (from receipt of the import declaration to payment). A chart is compiled for each team every month, with a breakdown for each engineer. Each engineer has his own code number in the chart. The team leader can see how much work there is, how things are running, where the bottlenecks are, etc., from the charts.

Comrades from the German Democratic Republic also favor creating export-import enterprises; they feel that under the present conditions, a necessary prerequisite for performing well on the market is the combining of exports and imports into one enterprise, which should take care of the foreign trade of products from one or several branches of industry (e.g., electric appliances and apparatus, various kinds of transport, lathes and instruments, computers, etc.). The enterprise "Elektroteknik, Export-Import" is an example; it deals with the export and import of precision industrial electrical equipment, electronic equipment, and measuring instruments. It is mainly an export firm, with exports making up 70 percent of its total business volume. The staff consists of about 1,000 people. At the head is the general director, who has nine assistants, four of whom head, respectively, one of the following divisions:

1. General problems (first assistant);
2. Planning and economics;
3. Problems of trade policy;
4. Central accounts.

The other five take care of daily tasks; each has a specific group of goods to deal with. Each assistant also manages business offices dealing with a specific list of goods as well as an economic section. There are five such sections in the enterprise, one for each product group. The general director also has a special team of five persons (a leader, two reporters, and two secretaries) to help him in handling routine matters and other questions. There is also an information bureau.

The director of the business office has two or three assistants. There are thirty or forty employees in each office. Commercial workers in the offices handle dealings with one or several countries for the entire product list of a particular office. This setup enables them to make decisions on every type of equipment on their business trips, to study a country,

Improving the Management of Foreign Trade

its language, its business practices, etc. Each commercial worker has one or two office workers among whom he distributes the work.

The creation of economically accountable export-import foreign trade enterprises should be accompanied by the reorganization of the management of the all-union associations. A systems-functional approach should be taken to the improvement of the organizational structure of management; this means that each aspect of an all-union association's foreign trade activity should be examined from the standpoint of the interests of the whole, i.e., from the standpoint of the functioning of the export-import enterprise (in our example, "Vneshtorgtransport"). Only if this is done will it be possible to avoid purely mechanical linkings among the all-union associations, with all the related consequences.

The first step here should be to clearly delimit the different types of foreign trade management: there are in fact five basic types of foreign trade activity: commercial, economic planning, personnel, subsidiary, and internal.

Proceeding on the basis of these functions, a systemic approach to drafting a new structure of management would mean that most of the services should be decentralized, with the exception of the commercial service, where political trade questions should remain in the hands of the central management; the others should be decentralized. An example of this sort of organizational structure is furnished by the Czechoslovak A/O "Stroiimport" mentioned above. Thus the principal tasks of the central apparatus of an export-import enterprise should be:

— planning the main directions of development of trade in a product group featuring some common consumer feature, taking into account the needs of the economy as a whole;

— ensuring efficiency in foreign trade, making maximum use of internal resources, determining effective export goods;

— effecting a unified foreign trade and technical policy based on the latest achievements of science and technology and on the most progressive experience, with regard to factory suppliers;

— improving the organizational structure of the export-import system;

— creating the necessary conditions for effective use of the new system of planning and economic incentives.

For more effective management of commercial and everyday activities, the management apparatus of an export-import enterprise should be allotted a centralized fund for the development of foreign trade, a centralized fund for material incentives, a fund for scientific research, a reserve for providing financial assistance to its all-union associations.

Thus the managerial apparatus of an economically accountable export-import enterprise is not only an administrative center; it is equally a foreign trade center, a closed system, as it were. Hence its decisions will have a direct impact on the size of the reserves and funds it has at its disposal, on the magnitude of the material incentives for its workers, and on the financial state of the enterprise as a whole.

The creation of independent export-import enterprises is one of the general directions to be taken in improving the organizational structure of foreign trade management; it requires a number of experiments to develop a sound basis for it and to choose from among the best alternatives.

This does not mean, however, that work to rationalize the existing structure and its elements should be stopped. On the contrary, such an effort should be continued on a broad front, on the basis of an overall concept. Let us look at some of the possible ways that the organizational structure of an all-union association can be rationalized.

5. Improving the Organizational Structure of Management of an All-Union Association

There are two approaches that can be taken to improving the organizational structure of management of an all-union association: one would be to improve the system of management in the Ministry of Foreign Trade; the other (local) would

Improving the Management of Foreign Trade

be to improve the management structure of the association itself, wholly or partly independent of the more general changes.

Let us consider the second variant in a bit more detail.

A number of practical proposals worked out by professionals under the direction of the author are of interest here. The organizational structure of management of an export-import association was based on an analysis of the existing organizational structures of associations with a large list of goods ("Mashpriborintorg," "Medeksport," etc.). Before the organizational structure was designed, the general goal of the association was defined, secondary goals were formulated, and their interconnections were determined.

This approach yielded our goal chart. The overall goal of the activity of an all-union association was set as the maximum satisfaction of the needs of society for vital goods and procuring the required amount of foreign exchange; the secondary goals, instrumental in achieving the overall goal, were expansion of markets, increasing the competitiveness of goods, determining and promoting new and efficient export products, etc. These subgoals were in turn further broken down into a sequence of levels, e.g., studying demand and supply on foreign markets, study of the forms and methods of trade used by foreign competitors, organization of advertising, improving the quality of export goods, study of the conditions under which needs are shaped in our country and of the feasibility of meeting these needs through imports, etc.

A goal chart compiled on this basis helps to visualize the way goals are shaped, the way they determine one another and their interrelationships, and accordingly, to define all the problems that must be solved and, on this basis, to determine the structural elements best suited to perform these tasks.

The distribution of goals among the different management levels and the links between the structural elements of the organization of an all-union association can be represented schematically (see Figure 12).

The proposed organizational structure of management can arbitrarily be split into three levels. On the first level

The Structure of Management of an All-Union Export-Import Association

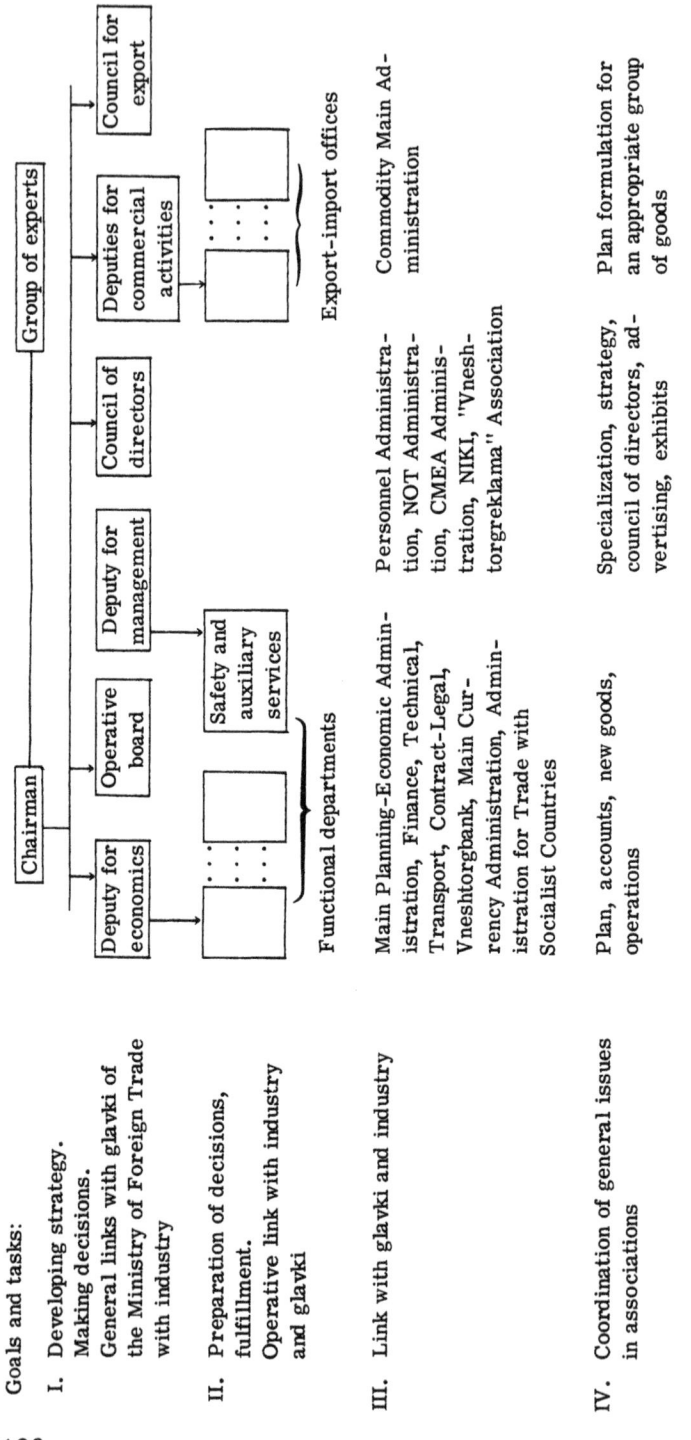

Figure 12.

decision-making, strategy formulation, and general control of the daily activity of an association are performed; problems are resolved in the area of general communications with the main administrations of the Ministry of Foreign Trade and the industrial ministries.

On the second level options and strategies are worked out, plan assignments are fulfilled, and questions involving operating relations with Ministry of Foreign Trade main administrations and the industrial ministries are handled.

The third level performs the supportive functions of supplying everything that is needed for the association to function normally.

One of the main distinguishing features of this organizational structure is that it tends to assign powers and duties more evenly among the different managerial units. For example, particular importance was attached to relieving the director of having to deal with operating issues. This organizational structure provides the director, who as before is responsible for the fulfillment of the current export-import plan, with the conditions necessary for dealing with the long-range problems of the association and for participating when necessary in the handling of some current questions. In accordance with the principle of delegation of powers, the task of supervising the fulfillment of the export-import plan as a whole has been placed in the hands of the deputy director for economic affairs. To strengthen collective habits in the management of the association, the proposed organizational structure provides for the creation of a council of directors, to function as an advisory body to the director of the association.

This council deals with the most important questions concerning the activity of the association and gives its recommendations to the management. The recommendations become binding administrative orders after they have been approved and ratified by the management.

In rough outline the functions of the council of directors include: examination of the tactics of entry into foreign markets (what must be sold and where, and the coordination of exports with imports), questions concerning the effectiveness and curtailing of the costs of running the association, working out of recommendations for new forms of export, generalization and adoption of progressive experience in the association, reports of directors of offices and sections, etc. The council of directors controls the performance of current tasks and works out recommendations on strategic questions. It may meet once per month (or two times every three months); and in contrast to current-operations meetings, which deal strictly with current problems, it deals primarily with long-range problems.

Representatives of Ministry of Foreign Trade main administrations participate in the work of the council of directors, which helps to improve coordination between the association and the main administrations.

The export council is the main advisory body in the association. Its chief task is to establish closer contacts and improve existing ties with the industrial ministries — the suppliers of goods for export. This body coordinates all questions of a general nature and acts as a mediator in resolving problems arising between the association and the industrial ministries.

The export council also deals with long-range questions of quality improvement of goods, draws up technical specifications for exported goods in conformity with market needs, helps to improve servicing, etc.

The export council meets two times each quarter (one meeting per quarter in each ministry). It works out joint measures for expanding the export of the product list of each ministry.

The deputy director in charge of exports is responsible for the export council's activities.

Thus there are three permanently functioning forms of collective management in the association:

1) the council of directors, which deals mainly with strategic questions and the most important current questions;

2) current advisory bodies, which are involved mainly in the purely technical aspects of carrying out current tasks (the deputy director in charge of economic questions is responsible for them);

Improving the Management of Foreign Trade

3) the export council, whose job is to coordinate and improve the forms and methods of working with industry.

Another important feature of the proposed organizational structure is the creation of an institute of experts. The institute of experts operates under the direction of the association and consists of three to five persons with considerable practical experience, a broad outlook, and a thorough understanding of the interests of the association. They are mainly consultants (to a lesser extent, managers) and may also perform inspector functions and disseminate information; but their principal task is to work out options and recommendations with regard to various questions for the managerial staff of the association.

In most cases it is the task of one or another of the offices or sections to implement these recommendations. In some instances joint (advisory) groups may be formed to put some document in final form, in the preparation of which an expert served as an executor or advisor.

The greatest advantage of the institute of experts is the fact that the advisory experts are not burdened with day-to-day responsibilities of the divisions and have more time to study general problems and hence arrive at a more objective assessment of the facts.

The functions of the institute of experts should include the following:

1) formulation of general questions for the director and his deputies;

2) preparation of documents issued by the association for main administrations and board meetings, and of all matters pertaining to the documents, which bring together information from several divisions of the association;

3) preparation of questions for discussion at meetings of the council of directors and the export council, participation in marketing work and other matters determined by the director;

4) participation of the experts in handling incoming documents.

This enables them to keep abreast of the main problems of

the association and to sift from among the incoming documents those with which it is important and necessary for the association and its business offices to be acquainted.

In practical terms this means that the experts take turns every day in perusing the mail, except for those mail items that concern the current activities of offices and sections.

After familiarizing themselves with the incoming mail, the experts send the correspondence around and determine on the basis of its content who shall act on each item (including office engineers). This ensures that correspondence quickly gets to the person who is to act on it and is swiftly handled; on the other hand, the management of offices and the association as a whole are able to keep abreast of the association's correspondence and the completed replies at the same time.

How the functions of the deputy director in the proposed organizational structure are assigned is determined in terms of distribution of duties in accordance with the commodity principle of courier service, the participation of each of them in the coordination of general questions, and the ensuring of steady and reliable ties with Ministry of Foreign Trade main administrations and the industrial ministries, as well as within the association.

The deputy director for economic affairs is the first deputy director; he is responsible for drawing up plan assignments and their fulfillment with regard to all indices, as well as for the general financial report of the association; he coordinates general matters of trade with the socialist countries and organizes the ad hoc meetings on problems that arise in fulfilling the plan on the basis of the materials furnished by the economic planning section.

The deputy director for economic affairs supervises optimal planning and the foreign exchange and financial and bookkeeping activities of the association, organizes the search for new goods for export, directs the activities of the legal section, and takes care of the association's ties with the Administration for Trade with the Socialist Countries of Europe, with the Main Economic, Financial, Transport, Legal-Contractual, and Technical administrations, with the Office for Accounting, Bookkeeping, and Control, with the Main Foreign Exchange Administration, and with the Foreign Trade Bank.

His responsibilities in the vertical hierarchy are borne by the head of the economic planning section.

Thus the deputy director for economic affairs is in large measure relieved of the responsibility for directly carrying out the practical aspects of the association's commercial activities and exercises continuous supervision over plan fulfillment.

The deputy director for management organizes the work of the council of directors, supervises the work on business cycle in the association and the work on cooperation and specialization with CMEA members, and coordinates export-import operations in accordance with the instructions of the Administration for Trade Policy with Capitalist Countries.

His duties include ensuring optimal organization of labor and management in the association, constant improvement of the organizational structure and expansion of the use of automatic control systems, and preparation of proposals (for the association director) on the deployment of personnel and the organization of their training.

The deputy director for management superintends work on:
— control of price calculations and market trends;
— the advertising section;
— the scientific organization of labor section;
— the personnel section;
— the chancellery.

He takes care of the association's ties with the Main Foreign Exchange Administration, the Administration for Cooperation with CMEA Countries, the administrations for trade policy with capitalist countries, the Personnel Administration, the Administration for the Organization of Labor and Information Systems, and the Scientific Research Institute on Business Cycles, the All-Union Academy of Foreign Trade, the All-Union Chamber of Commerce, and V/O "Vneshtorgreklama."

The Scientific Organization of Labor group, under the supervision of the deputy director, could, along with its normal functions, create a library of charts, i.e., it could compile charts on various relatively rare nonstandard work. These would be practical instructions for the office staff of the association.

Thus the work of the deputy director for managerial matters is basically concerned with strategic questions and with the improvement of the overall activities of the association, in addition to his work with prices and other current issues.

This structure for the management of foreign trade activity of an all-union association should make it possible to delimit the powers and duties of each of the different levels of management and thus to ensure a good working relationship with the different divisions of the Ministry of Foreign Trade and with industry, and to eliminate repetitions and duplications in this relationship.

For example, while general matters concerning the development of the export-import plan and its coordination with the different administrations of the Ministry of Foreign Trade and with industry are entirely the responsibility of the deputy director for economic affairs and his offices, the deputy director for commercial affairs directs only a portion of the goods to which these matters pertain.

This organizational structure, therefore, does away with the shortcomings of existing structures of export-import associations:

— it improves the association's ties with administrations within the Ministry of Foreign Trade and with the industrial ministries;

— it relieves the association director of routine matters by delegating authority and reducing the information flow through the director's office, and creates a group of expert assistants;

— it makes it possible to develop a strategy for the association in which the directors of offices, the deputy directors, the council of directors, and the association director all have a hand.

This list of responsibilities shows that the office staff does perform truly important commercial functions (preparing and conducting negotiations, study of markets and business trends, calculation of prices, etc.) requiring special handling, purely technical functions (preparation and drawing up of contracts, supervision of orders and the paperwork for orders) requiring less qualified skills, as well as final work that requires only a knowledge of the products.

Therefore the organizational structure should be based on a more precise delimitation of the functions of different workers; in this respect the proposal of the staff of V/O "Radioeksport" regarding changes in the organizational structure of offices is of practical interest.

This proposal suggests that independent teams, dealing with specific categories of commodities and carrying out all the above-enumerated functions, be created within each office, with the functions of each team member being strictly defined. The groups should be headed by a senior engineer with higher education in foreign trade matters (economics) and at least five years' experience in commercial work. He would be wholly responsible for the commercial aspects of the work: he would prepare material for talks with foreign firms; study market trends, firms, and delivery terms for goods and the export possibilities of trading partners; keep an eye on prices and make price proposals; participate in negotiations with foreign firms both domestically and abroad to coordinate all the commercial conditions for a transaction; and regularly update and systematize information in the commodity and firm files. The team head participates in compiling plan drafts and supervises the fulfillment of the import plan, domestic sales plan, and payments to the state budget from sales of its goods. The fulfillment of contracts concluded with foreign suppliers is under constant and strict supervision; and if deliveries are delayed, he takes the appropriate measures through his direct ties with the foreign supplier (personal or through correspondence) and through trade agencies. He is also in charge of seeing that shipments of substandard or defective goods do not get through, and he takes part in arbitrations in the Trade and Industry Chamber and the State Arbitration Board.

The engineer (or commodity expert) maintains ties with purchasers (industry) on matters having to do with improving the technical specifications of goods, import declarations, and transport dispositions; he prepares the technical aspects of documents (contracts, transport instructions), takes care of business correspondence with suppliers and purchasers, prepares material for the legal section in arbitration matters, supervises the movement of stocks of imports at ports and border points, and takes measures to help prevent pileups; he maintains relations with functional sections of the association on billing and transport matters, organizes sample demonstrations and coordinates specifications, keeps track of quality requirements, and takes part in compiling draft plans for imports. The engineer's job can be described as that of a worker who has had some experience in commercial work (especially people who have finished technical and foreign trade colleges) or who has reentered the system after completing a college course or after having worked in other agencies.

Working under the direction of the senior engineer, he gradually acquires experience in commercial work, quickly enters the mainstream of business in his section, and hence will be capable of effectively and flawlessly taking over for the senior engineer during the latter's absence. Accordingly, the proposed organizational structure for an office provides two posts of correspondence secretaries for whom a secondary technical education and typing skills are sufficient training. These persons are to do all the subsidiary work involved in typing documents, doing the paperwork for each group, etc. They will also prepare documents for the archives, proofread and correct typed material, and prepare and screen statistical and economic data for the senior engineers and engineers (commodity experts). One such worker should be sufficient for three teams.

These proposals were made on the basis of the actual situation in the office for import of electrical appliances. In other offices the proportions may be different, but the basic division of offices into working teams of this type and their approximate composition should be adhered to. If the volume of operations in any team should change appreciably, the director can review its structure and redistribute job loads by shuffling the personnel and revising the list of goods.

The stenographer would take care of the general paperwork in the office, do the typing, and do the paperwork of the deputy directors, who are in charge of commercial operations in certain goods. She also helps the director in the organization of meetings with representatives of foreign firms, sees that all daily records are kept correctly (comings and goings, discussions, business trips), records the meetings and conversations of the director, organizes office supplies, conducts and supervises correspondence (records incoming mail and sees that it is answered promptly), and looks after the filing of documents. When the director instructs her, the secretary takes care of simple form-letter correspondence with purchasers and other organizations, carries out other errands, answers telephone queries, and sends and receives telegrams.

This division of functions in the office has definite advantages. Earlier practice showed that technical and subsidiary work was usually done very poorly by the workers on account of their lack of skill.

A study done in five all-union associations, which included questionnaire surveys, showed that the business staff of the associations spent almost 17 percent of their working time performing purely technical operations, which took time away from their own main work because of an absence or inadequacy of technical personnel and poor definition of the functions of the different categories of workers.

The broad field of activities in the business office covers improvements in accounting for deliveries, in fulfillment, doing errands, filling orders, etc. At this imperfect stage in its development, too much time is wasted by office workers. Moreover, this accounting is duplicated later (of course, with some delay) by the planning section. Since the business office is obliged to submit draft plans with explanatory comments and calculations, business reports for the quarter and year (also with commentary), drafts for foreign exchange and finance plans, and monthly figures on purchases to the economic planning section, it would be expedient to concentrate all this work in the hands of one worker (or group of workers depending on the volume) — the office economist; this would relieve the business workers of these functions.

The new structure also gives the senior engineers somewhat broader powers to sign documents and carry out negotiations on their own. For example, they might be given the power to sign letters and telegrams within the country on accords concerning the technical specifications of goods, dispositions, and other transport questions, the course of contracted shipments, the quality and quantity of goods, delivery prices, accounts, and payments.

The senior engineer should also be authorized (together with the engineer or a representative of industry) to carry out negotiations with representatives of other countries (if, of course, the rank of the other party permits it) on accords determining quantitative and qualitative specifications and other terms of shipments. The senior engineer should also be given the authority to take part in meetings called at the Ministry of Foreign Trade and other ministries and agencies on questions that pertain to his domain of responsibilities.

A primary focus of the proposed structural reform in office organization is centered on increasing the role and importance of middle-level management and on permitting decisions on business problems and any other problems that may arise to be made on the spot by the people who are most knowledgeable in dealing with them.

The devolution of the authority to sign much of the office correspondence of a purely informational character on the senior engineers encourages their initiative and increases their responsibility and weight both within and outside the association, while the office management will be relieved of dealing with unessential questions of a subsidiary nature, on which they now often spend a considerable amount of time.

It should also be borne in mind that a tightening of the chain of command in management does not solve the entire problem of increasing management efficiency if it is not complemented by a clear delimitation of managerial operations among managers, specialists, office workers, and technical workers, i.e., among workers having different levels of skills. Clearly, personal efficiency decreases if a worker with a great deal of training, e.g., a deputy director or office director, is obliged to do things that could perfectly well be done by middle-level or low-level management. There should therefore be a strict correspondence between the number of workers in each category and the volume of basic and auxiliary operations in each division, i.e., the division of labor should be consistent with the level of skill. This is very important, although it is by no means a very simple matter. It is closely linked to setting standards for work which presuppose that the labor done by foreign trade workers be clearly classified into basic, subsidiary, and technical.

The introduction of automatic control systems and the computerization of routine work should facilitate the solution of this problem. But it then will become all the more important to establish the correct balance between the different categories of workers and to economize management even more (since with such expensive technology, a surplus of any category would cut down the efficiency of the system as a whole).

The division of labor and effective cooperation should be based on a scientific organization of managerial work, which is what we shall be discussing in the next chapter.

CHAPTER FOUR

Some Aspects of Introducing the Scientific
Organization of Labor in the Ministry of Foreign Trade
and Problems of Training and
Advanced Training of Managerial Personnel

1. Major Aspects of Introducing the Scientific Organization of Labor in the Ministry of Foreign Trade

However much the organizational structure of management may be refined, the desired effect will not be achieved if at the same time scientific forms and methods of organizing labor are not also introduced and foreign trade activity in general streamlined. There is a dialectic relationship here, whereby, for example, the introduction of modern management structures requires that a series of measures be carried out to apply scientific forms and methods of the organization of labor; the introduction of the latter, in turn, requires rationalization of the organizational structures of management.

If, indeed, the work of management is organized scientifically, the objective principles in terms of which management structures, and indeed managerial activity as a whole, are defined, will have a solid foundation on which to develop. What are these principles? For example, department functions and the rights and responsibilities of personnel must be defined clearly and correctly, the volume of work performed in different jobs must be determined, and workers must be correctly deployed. This is not to deny that the introduction of scientific forms and methods of organizing labor is an independent domain of activities in its own right, although it is a part of the overall set of measures taken to improve the organization of labor and management. Its main focus is to improve the productiveness of personnel working in foreign trade by deploying them more rationally, by a more rational definition of jobs and areas of cooperation, by simplifying the flow and processing of informa-

Labor Organization and Personnel Training

tion, by creating a good atmosphere for encouraging workers' constructive initiative, and by establishing the proper balance between creative work and subsidiary routines.

In this area the as yet unrealized possibilities for improving the effectiveness (productivity) of workers in foreign trade are even greater. For example, studies made by scholars and practical workers have shown that operatives spend a large amount of their time on technical operations such as obtaining information (40-50 percent), passing it on (10-15 percent), and doing calculations (20 percent); they spend only 5-10 percent on truly creative or innovative work. This has given rise to a situation in which highly trained personnel are actually doing work that could be performed adequately by persons with less training. One of the prime tasks, therefore, of the scientific organization of labor is to develop and put into use simpler and more effective work methods.

We should bear in mind, however, that this can be done only on the basis of some consistency in making efforts to apply the scientific organization of labor (SOL).[1]

Before 1966 research on the organization of labor in the Ministry of Foreign Trade had been sporadic and disjointed; but in that year a separate section for the organization of labor was created, which in 1971 became the Administration for the Organization of Labor and Information Systems, which contains three departments: one for the organization of labor, a second for documents and records, and a third for information systems.

In all-union associations and in the central administration of the Ministry of Foreign Trade, this work is carried out by SOL experts, while the V/O's "Radioeksport," "Zapchast'eksport," "Avtoeksport," "Promysyr'eimport," and "Traktoroeksport" have their own separate SOL departments.

With the creation of departments devoted specifically to SOL, the Ministry of Foreign Trade was finally able to introduce some order into this work, i.e., to plan, coordinate, steer, and supervise it.

Every year, on the basis of the five-year plan, the Administration for the Organization of Labor and Information Systems compiles an annual plan for improving the organization of labor and management in the Ministry of Foreign Trade. This plan is ratified by the top level of the ministry and sent to the all-union associations to use as a basis for working out their own plans. The annual plan contains a list of measures to be implemented either by the administration itself or by other organizations.

The principal lines along which SOL is being introduced in the Ministry of Foreign Trade are as follows:
— improvement in the organization of management;
— rationalization of paperwork and secretarial work;
— mechanization and automation of working procedures and labor;
— organization of work places and working conditions and regimens.

The chart on page 141 will serve as an illustration.

2. Rationalization of Secretarial and Paperwork

A. In the central apparatus

A good deal of administrative work consists of paperwork. In processing the information contained in all these documents and papers, the personnel of the various administrative offices perform a vast number of technical operations on the same data and statistics, within a specified period of time and according to a preset program that defines the elementary technical operations involved (i.e., recording, distribution, classification, transporting, typewriting, calculation, screening, selecting, collating, etc.). Clerical work makes up about 20 to 30 percent of all managerial activity; and as the turnover and scale of foreign trade activities grow, the amount of paperwork may be expected to increase more rapidly. Suffice it to mention that in 1972 the volume of documents and papers flowing in and out of the various subdivisions of the central apparatus of the Ministry of Foreign Trade alone was 613,000. The yearly increment is about 7 percent. It is obvious then that

Basic Modes of Introducing SOL in the Ministry of Foreign Trade

Improving the organization of the apparatus of management	Rationalization of secretarial and paperwork	Mechanization and automation of work processes	Organization of the work place, conditions, and regimen of labor
Improving the organizational structure	Rationalization of the secretarial system	Mechanization of information gathering	Improvement in the organization of the work place
Improving the forms of division and cooperation of labor	Rationalization of secretarial agencies	Mechanization of information processing	Improvement in the conditions of labor
Improving work with cadres	Standardization and unification of documents	Mechanization of information copying	Improvement in the regimen of labor and leisure
Improving labor methods		Mechanization of information storage	
Improving labor norms			

some basic steps are necessary if paperwork within the ministry and its departments is going to be organized efficiently.

But it is also obvious that a smoothly and efficiently functioning management depends to a large extent on how well work with all the different types of documents having to do with foreign trade is organized and on how swiftly and expeditiously they can be processed. An analysis done by the Administration for the Organization of Labor and Information Systems has brought to light a number of possibilities still waiting to be tried, particularly as far as expediting the paper flow is concerned. For example, as things stand with clerical work, which is carried out as per the instructions of July 31, 1969, documents addressed to the minister and his deputies are received by the forwarding department and sent on under signature to the general office of the ministry secretariat. All other correspondence is sent to the secretaries of these departments. The receipt of each piece of correspondence is recorded on the same day in the files of the general office, after which correspondence addressed to the minister or to the ministry in general with no department specified is sent to the chief of the secretariat, while correspondence addressed to the deputy ministers is recorded on a file card and passed on to the secretary of the deputy minister in the general office.

After correspondence is read by top-level Ministry of Foreign Trade officials, it is sent back to the general office, where the officials' instructions on how it is to be handled are recorded in the files.

A rough breakdown of the routing of documents in the Ministry of Foreign Trade, with total time required, is as follows:

1) the central forwarding department — general office — chief of secretariat — general office: at least 1 or 2 days;

2) general office — secretariat of deputy minister — deputy minister — secretariat of deputy minister — general office: at least 2 to 4 days;

3) general office — main administration (administration) — all-union association: at least 2 to 4 days.

Thus a piece of correspondence passing through the general

Labor Organization and Personnel Training

office and the various departments of the central administration does not reach the all-union associations and other sections of the ministry to be acted on until, at the earliest, the fifth day after its receipt. The principal reasons it takes so long for a document to pass through the administrative machinery are as follows:

— the same document must be recorded in different departments of the ministry. A piece of correspondence will have been recorded three times by the time it reaches an all-union association after passing through the central administration: once in the general office, once in the secretariats of the main administrations (administration), and once in the secretariat of the all-union associations. In some cases it will also be recorded in the secretariats of the deputy ministers;

— a piece of incoming correspondence is returned several times to the general office and to the secretariats of the main administrations and the all-union associations for notation (recording of the top-level action instructions on filing cards). Specifically, a piece of correspondence returns twice to the general office and up to three times to the main administration secretariats;

— the number of departments and offices examining a document is unnecessarily large;

— considerable time is spent in annotating a document in the secretariats of ministerial officials (deputy ministers, heads of main administrations and administrations). It is not unlikely that more than any other factor, delays of this sort are to blame for the slowness of paper flow. In terms of the time consumed in recording, annotating, and delivering correspondence, it sometimes takes a number of days before a piece of correspondence has been taken care of;

— in a number of departments of the central administration there is no clear-cut distinction between correspondence that must be recorded and that which need not.

As the experience of several ministries, agencies, and even all-union associations has shown, the time required for a document to pass through the machinery can be reduced by introducing a card-filing system for recording and monitoring the discharging of a document on its journey through the central administration.

Introducing such a system makes it possible:

— to do away with duplicate recording of incoming correspondence in different departments (a document would be recorded only once in the general office, instead of three times, as is currently the case);

— to centralize supervision of the handling of paperwork, for example, in the general office.

It should be borne in mind, however, that efficiency in this area can only be achieved if all the departments of the central administration introduce a card-filing system. Another important possible way to cut time is to reduce the amount of correspondence requiring recording. This means, of course, that a classification must be worked out for defining what kinds of correspondence requires recording and which kinds do not.

If such lists are drawn up and continually refined as experience is accumulated, and if they are conscientiously observed, the volume of recordable correspondence can be reduced to a reasonable minimum.

Finally, another important way in which it may be possible to speed up paper flow is to systematize routing procedures. At present a document goes from the top level down to the person who carries out the required action. The procedure is further drawn out by the fact that a document must return to the secretariat several times for filing notes and passing it on to the next person. In other words, the same document is handled twice by managerial staff: the first time when they receive an incoming document for perusal and further disposition, and the second time when they prepare a response.

It would be more efficient if a particular official handled a document only once. This could be done by passing a letter, for example, immediately on to an assistant who takes care of it and submits both a query and a reply, already written out in letter form, to the official. In addition to the time such a procedure would save, it would also provide an opportunity to evaluate the abilities of the assistant.

Labor Organization and Personnel Training

B. In an all-union association

In all-union associations clerical work is handled by the forwarding office and the secretariat; and in a number of associations, such as "Raznoeksport," "Avtoeksport," "Zapchast'-eksport," and "Eksportplen," central secretarial offices combining the activities of the forwarding office, the typing office, the teletype service, and a number of other facilities, have been set up and are functioning effectively, demonstrating that the centralization of these functions was organizationally just what was needed to streamline the routine clerical work of foreign trade.

At present the Instructions on the Conducting of Clerical Work in the All-Union Associations of the Ministry of Foreign Trade, which came into force on July 1, 1970, serve as the guidelines for clerical work in all-union associations. These instructions provide for the installation of a unified card-filing system for recording and monitoring all paperwork.

Filing cards are used to record and keep track of correspondence. The face of these cards is for recording incoming correspondence; the back is for recording outgoing correspondence. The filing cards are stored in file cabinets divided into compartments with different headings. Each set of cards is separated by dividers, with tabs on which the headings and subheadings are written. A file has the following sections: for decision; for familiarization; checking; expired; reference.

The "for decision" section contains file cards for documents in the hands of association management or some department for examination. The "for familiarization" section is for documents that have been passed on to some department by the secretary for familiarization. The "checking" section contains cards for documents undergoing some correction.

The "checking" section is further divided into two subsections: daily check and long-term check. The daily check section has 31 compartments numbered for the days of the month; the long-term check section contains cards for documents requiring more than one month to handle. The "expired" section contains cards for documents whose period of handling has lapsed. The "reference" section contains reference copies of filing cards. In some cases it may be useful to keep the reference section in a separate drawer.

Cards are always filed chronologically, although they may also be further classified according to subject matter or the correspondent's identifying symbol.

Experience in working with these instructions has shown that it has considerably improved the organization of paperwork. For example, documents are recorded only one time; document search is easier; the handling of documents is supervised effectively; and it is easier to analyze the status, structure, and volume of business correspondence for the purpose of further improving and systematizing it.

A positive aspect of the above filing system is that the filing card for each incoming document destined for some department is made in two copies (one for the department, the other remaining in the forwarding office), while for documents that must be brought to the attention of the top-level management, three filing card copies are made. With this system a document and the person or office that handled it can always be quickly found.

The delivery of correspondence to the right business office or section has also been considerably improved by introducing an in-house courier service.

Although the above-described organization of paperwork has reduced the time required for a document to make the rounds through the administrative machinery and has created a reliable feedback mechanism necessary for efficient management of routine business, it does not do anything to reduce the time spent in preparing and writing up documents, which, of course, is very important, since the paper flow is growing continuously.

The mechanization and automation of the operations involved in preparing documents is a major step in the right direction. Spot mechanization has improved productivity of administrative work by 10-15 percent, while across-the-board mechanization has improved labor productivity by almost twofold.

Labor Organization and Personnel Training

A quite wide range of technical facilities is now in use in the Ministry of Foreign Trade for mechanizing the preparing, processing, storage, and retrieval of documents.

Electric typewriters are now in general use in the Ministry of Foreign Trade for doing paperwork. A more recent innovation has been the introduction on a broad scale of composers that can compile documents on the basis of standardized texts preprogrammed on special media (perforated tape, punchcards, magnetic tape, magnetic cards, etc.), make alterations in a text that has already been composed, write standardized form letters automatically, copy tapes, punchcards, etc., and retrieve coded materials automatically.

Thus preparing documents has been mechanized and automated through the use of more typewriters and by introducing composers. The latter, however, are the most effective, saving both time and labor. However, it should be borne in mind that composers and other such technology will do the job desired of them only if documents have been formalized and standardized. If they have not, automation is a costly means of writing letters. Associations that have prepared standardized documents, therefore, for their composers have done the right thing.

When foreign trade transactions are effected between the all-union foreign trade associations and foreign export and import firms, a variety of documents must be drawn up in compliance with the laws and decrees of the Soviet government, the specifications of administrative and legislative acts of foreign governments, the general terms of delivery, trade customs in the foreign country, and any contracts that may be involved in the particular case. These documents include commercial documents, transport documents, insurance documents, customs documents, and technical documentation.

The commercial documents include: the invoice, the specifications, the invoice list, the certificate of quality, an affidavit of authenticity, a packing list, and the replacement sheet.

The transport documents include: bill of lading, railroad waybill, waybill for water or air transport, and a way sheet.

The schedule-order and schedule of allocations are transport and shipping documents.

The insurance documents include an insurance policy and insurance certificate. The insurance policy is issued by the insurer to the insuree and contains the terms and conditions of the insurance agreement.

The customs documents are: customs declaration, a certificate of origin, a consul's invoice, import and export licenses, etc.

The technical documentation consists of: passport, instructions on installation and use, diagrams, assembly blueprints, basic drawings, specifications of reserve parts, etc.

An examination of all these documents reveals that much of the information they contain is repeated on each document. However, since each document differs considerably in size and form from the others, each blank must be filled out separately, which means that the same data must be written down several times, involving a great deal of time and a considerable risk of error. This situation could be avoided if all the routine operations were done with machine; but for this to be possible, documents of standard form, with the particular items positioned uniformly, are necessary.

The advantages of such standardization over the way documents are done now are obvious. In the first place, only one document rather than a whole series would need to be printed. Second, the original, typed on a stencil, could be reproduced on a duplicator in as many copies as necessary.

The duplication of documents in this way is known as the single-operation method, and its efficiency can best be illustrated by the following comparative figures (on the example of V/O "Sudoimport"; Table 11).

Preparing documents in the ordinary way requires 80 minutes, while with the single-operation method only 40 minutes are required, i.e., half as much time with the same number of workers. In addition operatives gain back time lost doing routine operations.

In V/O "Mashinoeksport" the single-operation method is

Table 11

Comparative Expenditures of Labor on Preparing Documents
(minutes)

	Making a draft	Typing	Proofreading	Correction	Copying	Total	Including		
							engineer, correspondent	typist	operator
2	3	4	5	6	7	8	9	10	11
Manually									
1 Contract	10	10× 2 = 20	3	0.5× 7 = 3.5	—	36.5	13	23.5	—
2 Order	12	12× 2 = 24	3	0.5× 7 = 3.5	—	43.5	15	28.5	—
3 Notice of conclusion of a contract	4	—	—	—	—	4	4	—	—
TOTAL	26	44	6	7	—	84	32	52	—
Single-operation method									
1 Matrix	15	15	4	2	—	36	19	17	—
2 Contract	—	—	—	—	1.4	1.4	—	—	1.4
3 Order	—	—	—	—	1.6	1.6	—	—	1.6
4 Notice of conclusion of a contract	—	—	—	—	0.2	0.2	—	—	0.2
TOTAL	15	15	4	2	3.2	39.2	19	17	3.2

used to prepare a set of documents, including the schedule-order, contract, notification, and order for a bill extract. The time and money saved amounts to 1,771 workdays or 10,487 rubles per year.

All-union associations make extensive use of computers and copying machines in preparing appendices to contracts, schedule-orders, and order specifications.

The measures we have been discussing deal mainly with improving the efficiency of routine paperwork. As regards the procurement of the information necessary for efficient management, technology is being put to work to ensure rapid retrieval and processing of pertinent information, and the Ministry of Foreign Trade and the all-union associations are gradually being computerized.

3. Improvement of the Organization of Labor of Office Workers

The scientific organization of the labor of office workers depends very intimately on the nature of foreign trade activity, on the way this activity is organized, and on the technology used to perform it. Work methods must be improved, work places better organized, the work itself should have some incentive (moral and material), and finally, the level of skill of the workers must be raised if foreign trade is to proceed smoothly and effectively. The experience of the progressive departments of the Ministry of Foreign Trade and experience in other countries have shown that the above-described measures can be effective only if applied on a broad scale, with proper planning, and if the planned measures are implemented consistently and effectively. All of this, in turn, presupposes a scientifically sound system for studying labor, which in our opinion should include:

— the study of the entire production situation in which foreign trade activity takes place;

— the working out of different options for effecting an optimum

Labor Organization and Personnel Training

organization of foreign trade activity and general work processes;
— the testing and practical implementation of the best proposals;
— the setting of scientific norms for quantities, amount of work expended, and other indices.

A person in charge will be able to determine what specific measure or measures should be given the most stress by analyzing the findings of work studies. For example, as a result of a comprehensive analysis of the existing situation in the "Avtoeksport" Association, it was found that the most important measure for introducing SOL, with the aim of improving the firm's efficiency, was to relieve the workers of routine operations and to reorganize the distribution of work among them and among the different offices. To do this, however, modern computer technology was necessary. Hence the management concentrated its efforts on creating the organizational and technological conditions necessary for introducing an automated control system, which radically changed the performance of the association.

The installation of such a costly system cannot be effective if the level of technological competence of the workers is not raised, i.e., if they are not taught the habits of precision and accuracy; in addition standardized foreign trade documents must be designed, problems must be correctly posed, and the kinds of interrelationships in the "man—machine" system must be defined properly.

The work on compilation of programs has been largely completed, and the association is now going through a breaking-in period in which all business offices and functional sections are taking part.

Other all-union associations are doing similar things ("Radioeksport," "Promsyr'eimport," "Mashinoeksport," etc.). All associations are devoting increasing attention to defining more precisely the set of duties and responsibilities of an operative engineer. An analysis of the work load of an engineer in several all-union associations ("Mashpriborintorg," "Energomasheksport," "Avtoeksport," etc.) shows that he now spends most of his time on work with industry and the funds allocator, not on commercial work, and especially not on creative work (see Table 12).

There are a number of reasons for this: the functional decision-making chart is very complex, it takes a long time to obtain funds, and the industry is not very interested in exporting its products.

Another important factor in rationalizing the work of office workers is the creation of an innovative atmosphere in which all the workers should be encouraged to participate. This is an important task for scientific organization of labor. For instance, tasks must be pinpointed and defined correctly, and the staff must be kept abreast of the latest achievements in science and technology. It is very important that not only the management but also the majority of the workers have a certain amount of time to themselves to think about their work. In this respect the experiments of V/O "Avtoeksport" deserve our commendation: in its program for the organization of labor, job discipline, and control of performance, a certain amount of time is set aside daily for independent individual study of the most pressing problems in all areas of activities. During this time the staff — and this includes the heads of departments and the firm management as a whole — must not distract one another from the work at hand unless it is specifically necessary.

Planning is an important factor in the efficient use of time. It is crucial that a department head be able to allocate his time over a relatively long period. Of course, it is very difficult for a manager to set exact dates and times for discussing important commercial questions, for meetings with the staff, etc. For this reason it is important that he plan regular routines that are followed from day to day. For example, review of the progress of plan fulfillment and performance of department duties could be scheduled on Monday; Wednesday could be the day for dealing with the problem of improving relations with the industry; and Friday could be the day for reviewing efforts to increase exports.

Practical experience and studies of foreign trade activity

Labor Organization and Personnel Training

Table 12

Distribution of Work Time of an Engineer in an Operative Office
(%)

	Actual	Desired
Work in an association	40	30
Of which:		
Calculating prices	5	0.5
Preparing and sending offers and price lists	8	10
Developing statements		
Advertising		
Preparing contracts	15	10
Issuing orders		
Supervising shipments		
Exhibition work	5	
Analysis of commercial activity	0	5
Control of acceptances		
Control of models	2	1
Control of consignments		
Problems of technical services	5	0.1
Problems of penalties and arbitration		
Other		
Industry (including business trips)	15	25
Of which:		
Constant study of factory product lists		
Constant study of charts of factory production plans	0.5	10
Regular knowledge of supply of export technical documentation (including in specific language)		
Search for new items for export	0.5	5
Control of optimal prices		
Work on "Quality Emblem" (testimonials)		
Work on ads	10	5
Work on spare parts		
Other		
Fund manager	30	5
Supply of funds for annual plan		
Supply of funds for specific projects in contracts (positional)		
Clearing and transferring unused funds for each quarter		
Other		
Contractors and external market (including business trips abroad)	15	40
Including:		
Agreements on prices		
Agreement on terms of deliveries and accounts (for capitalist countries)		
Study of markets and technical level of production of competitor firms	1	30
Study of typical terms for deliveries of an item by competitors		

have shown that however urgent and essential these questions may be, they can only be resolved in any sound way if the workday of the person in charge is organized properly. Powers should be delegated to lower levels, and collective forms of management must be introduced. In addition the role of collective bodies, like the directors' council, should be broadened.

The function of the directors' council should not only lie in providing a qualified assessment of the importance of measures for the conducting of foreign trade activities. Of equal importance is its role in putting forth concrete recommendations on how to implement these measures, as well as methods for disseminating progressive experience and working procedures.

The administrative competence of the director of an all-union association may to a certain degree be rated in terms of his capacity to activate each member of the council and his ability to give personal attention to even the most trivial suggestion.

These abilities determine how much weight a director's decisions, which, if these conditions are met, assume the form of collective decisions, will carry. Lenin is a good case in point: he was able to bring his own opinion into line with the opinion of the collective.

In his memoirs V. V. Vorovskii writes that Lenin "never made a decision, never took a step, without first making sure that what he was doing was not merely the expression of his personal opinion but that of the opinions of many of his comrades as well."[2]

Another major way to improve efficiency is to properly organize work places and supply them with up-to-date equipment. The Ministry of Foreign Trade is very sensitive to this and acts accordingly. It now has an extensive inventory of technical equipment to facilitate and speed up administrative processes. This includes:
  1. Equipment for drawing up and writing up documents.
  2. Equipment for processing paperwork.

Labor Organization and Personnel Training

3. Copying and duplicating equipment.
4. Microfilming equipment.
5. Equipment for storage and retrieval of documents.
6. Communications equipment.
7. Computer technology.
8. Small computer units.

It should be borne in mind, however, that given the wide variety of technical equipment, its use will pay off only if based on sound policy. For example, it should be a policy to employ only technical office equipment that can in some measure be used generally.

Marx wrote that "a complex machine is more perfect the more unbroken is the process it accomplishes, i.e., the fewer interruptions there are in the journey of the material from the first to the last phase of the process, and hence the more it is the machinery itself rather than the hand of man that moves the material from one phase of production to the next."[3]

As regards foreign trade, this means that the same machine should be used to perform any series of consecutive as well as parallel processes if they have to do with the same aspect of management. For example, printing and duplicating machines can be combined. In the end the use of such general-purpose or multipurpose technical equipment resolves a number of problems: it broadens the range of operations a worker performs, and it makes his work more interesting and diminishes monotony, i.e., it improves the social aspect of work and helps reduce the social costs of management of foreign trade.

Foreign trade firms in the socialist countries have accumulated a considerable amount of useful experience in the use of technical office equipment. For example, the GDR foreign trade firm "Elektroteknik, Export-Import" makes wide use of "Asmann" dictaphones to prepare documents for telexes, telegrams, correspondence, bills, records, and other texts.

The dictaphones are kept in a special dictaphone bureau and are serviced by one operator. He listens to the beginning of the recording on each disc with a playback device, writes the number of the office and name of the speaker and length of the recording on a paper tape, and keeps a daily record. The dictaphone discs with the attached tape are passed on to the typing bureau: telexes in red envelopes, urgent letters in green, and ordinary texts in yellow envelopes. To avoid accidental erasures, each disc can be used only by one person once he has begun recording on it.

The recorded discs are kept for 24 hours. During this time the typing office can be informed of mistakes. Then the recording is erased. The workers dictate letters and other documents in final form, i.e., without a draft, which in the final analysis increases their productivity. Additional efficiency-promoting factors are the fact that a large portion of correspondence is signed by the office workers themselves, and only in very specially important cases are letters dictated according to a plan coordinated with their immediate supervisor. If a problem does not require a long and elaborate treatment, the supervisor himself dictates the reply over the central communications system or with his own private dictaphone.

Storage and retrieval of documents is another important area where technical equipment can be used, saving work for the office workers and allowing them more time to spend on items requiring creative ingenuity instead of on tracking down information. Small computer units, etc., are used for these purposes.

Another purely organizational means to improve efficiency of foreign trade workers is to reduce the amount of time wasted by workers, including administrative workers, in doing jobs for which they have not been trained. For example, a survey of five all-union associations conducted by the Administration for the Organization of Labor and Information Systems in the Ministry of Foreign Trade showed that because of the shortage or lack of qualified office personnel and inefficient job-definitions for different categories of workers, the office staff had to waste 16.8 percent of its working time on purely technical operations. The amount of work time lost each month was 16 percent by managerial personnel, 21 percent by engineers and commodity experts, 14 percent by economists, 6 percent by accountants and bookkeepers, and 18 percent by foreign language secretaries. Hardly an inspiring situation. Suffice it to mention that translated into money terms, this amounts to the labor of 1,035 trained workers with an annual wage bill of 1.7 million rubles.

If one considers that the labor productivity of technical personnel is twice as high as that of office personnel, to do all the technical work on hand 515 technical workers (earning an average of 80 rubles) with an annual wage bill of 496,000 rubles (1.204 million less than that actually spent) would be sufficient to take care of all the technical work on hand.

4. Socialist Competition and Its Further Development in the Ministry of Foreign Trade — An Important Means to Improve the Efficiency of Foreign Trade Management

Competition in its various forms is extensively used in the management of foreign trade. It is organized according to Leninist principles: voluntariness, the comparability of results, and emulation of the most advanced workers.

In the all-union associations socialist competition follows the guidelines set down in a resolution entitled "Conditions for All-Union Socialist Competition of Collectives in All-Union Foreign Trade Associations," issued on January 13, 1962, by the Presidium of the Central Committee of the Trade Union for Government Employees and the Board of the Ministry of Foreign Trade.

The Central Committee of the CPSU resolution "On the Further Improvement of the Organization of Socialist Competition," published on September 5, 1971, and the decision of the Board, Party Committee, and Joint Committee of Trade Union Organizations of the Ministry of Foreign Trade, published on October 5, 1971, raised socialist competition in all-union associations and other foreign trade units to a qualitatively new level.

The socialist duties of the staffs of associations and other foreign trade departments are quite specific and practically oriented; they include:

— fulfilling the annual plan for export and import deliveries ahead of time by a specified date;

— deliveries spread out evenly over three-month periods;

— the search for new exports and export deliveries above the plan targets;

— improving export and import efficiency;

— efficient use of export funds;

— prompt signing of contracts for goods deliveries, especially with long-term agreements in accordance with decisions of the CPSU and the Soviet government and with the delivery plan;

— fulfillment of the delivery plan for the domestic economy;

— fulfillment of the foreign exchange plans;

— coordination of import purchases with the prepurchase of Soviet goods for export;

— prevention of wasteful spending;

— on-time delivery of imported equipment for turnkey projects;

— fulfillment of all tasks involved in the purchase and early delivery of machinery, equipment, and other goods for agriculture;

— fulfillment of all tasks involved in the purchase and delivery of consumer goods and raw materials for their production;

— measures to improve the quality of delivered equipment and improvement of indicators over the previous year;

— stimulation of competition in the professions ("best engineer," "best economist," "best foreign language secretary," etc.);

— expansion of the movement for communist labor;

— increasing labor productivity; active introduction of scientific organization of labor; introduction and adoption of a number of efficiency-improving proposals;

— expansion of the various forms of day-by-day cooperation with the industrial ministries and with enterprises.

Labor Organization and Personnel Training

As we see, socialist duties touch on practically every aspect of foreign trade activity; they can only be responsibly carried out if an atmosphere of creative ingenuity is created in every foreign trade department, if the methods and forms of labor organization and management are improved, and if the most advanced experience is communicated to others.

A crucial factor in making this a reality is to ensure that every staff member participates actively and creatively in socialist competition. This, of course, depends on many circumstances, but particularly on the level of the organizational and educational work of party, soviet, trade union, and Komsomol organizations and heads of departments. This work should strive to develop a spirit of comradely competition among workers and between groups, to foster communist attitudes toward work, and to raise the level of education and skills among the work force.

A number of studies have shown that competition among workers, departments, and groups helps the effective resolution of these questions. Competition has been organized for the titles: "Best office (section) in the association," "Hero of communist labor," and "Collective of communist labor." Competition to become "Best engineer," "Best foreign language secretary," "Best economist," "Best typist," etc., is widely used.

One interesting aspect of the development of socialist competition in the Ministry of Foreign Trade is the fact that in a number of cases it has extended beyond the walls of the ministry. For example, there may be competition with enterprises and divisions of the industrial ministries (V/O "Mashpriborintorg" competes with "Glavpriborzagranpostavka" of the Ministry of Instrument Construction, Automation, and Automatic Control Systems).

This competition has a considerable role to play in the future in stimulating exports.

In addition the experience collected in organizing socialist group competition between associations, which are under different agencies but linked together by the fact that they deliver components for assembled machinery, should be expanded. An example is the competition between the "Mashinoeksport" and "Tekhmasheksport" associations, on the one hand, and the "Energomasheksport" Association on the other.

Competition between the offices of the V/O "Tekhnopromimport" and V/O "Mashinoimport" is an example of competition between departmental staffs linked together by the fact that they deliver parts for component-assembled equipment.

At the present stage of development of foreign trade, socialist competition is entering into a qualitatively new phase in its organization. Now collective principles are acquiring more and more importance alongside mass competition to win awards as best in profession. For instance, associations are now competing to transform themselves into collectives of communist labor.

The movement for communist labor is a higher form of labor competition among the broad masses of workers toiling to create the material and technical foundations for communism, to inculcate a communist attitude toward work, to establish communist social relations, to improve the moral standards of the Soviet people, and to shape the new man of communist society.

The associations are guided by the "Recommendations for Competition for the Honorary Title of 'Hero, Group, Department Staff, Office, or All-Union Association of Communist Labor,'" worked out by the Industrial Relations Board of the Joint Committee of Ministry of Foreign Trade Trade Unions.

The title "Hero of communist labor" ("Collective of communist labor") is given one year after a worker or collective has joined the movement if he or it has fulfilled certain conditions. The title "Collective of communist labor" is awarded to collectives fulfilling collective responsibilities (offices or departments); 65-70 percent of the workers in such a collective must have already been awarded the title of "Hero of communist labor." The title "Hero (collective) of communist labor" is confirmed by the same bodies that bestowed the award after one year if the recipient has successfully ful-

Labor Organization and Personnel Training

filled individual or collective responsibilities.

The mass movement for a communist attitude to labor began in the all-union associations in about 1967, and since then has grown considerably. The goal is to achieve the titles "Hero of communist labor" or "Collective of communist labor," with offices, departments, and all-union associations as a whole competing. V/O "Prodintorg" and V/O "Tekhmashimport" were among the first to receive the title "Association of communist labor."

At present 12 of the 43 all-union associations in the Ministry of Foreign Trade are competing for the title "Association of communist labor." A total of 5,106 workers and 118 collectives in the Ministry of Foreign Trade have earned the titles of "Hero (collective) of communist labor," while 4,238 workers and 283 offices and departments are currently striving to attain it.

A consciousness of social concern and of the necessity of working for the good of our country takes on many different forms. The third and fourth rallies of heroes of communist labor and pioneers of socialist competition in the ministries (1972 and 1973) were important milestones in raising the level of socialist competition.

As a result of the concentrated efforts of the staffs of all-union associations and other foreign trade organizations, the socialist commitments assumed in 1972, 1973, and 1974 were successfully fulfilled. In addition, the all-union associations were able to improve a number of other efficiency indices. For example, the efficiency of exports and imports was increased; delays were reduced; the quality of delivered equipment was improved; deliveries of turnkey projects rose; the number of contracts signed for the following years was increased, and the amount of earnings in excess of the plan remitted to the state budget was increased; wasteful spending was reduced; the scientific organization of labor and rationalizing work were expanded; labor productivity was increased; the movement for communist attitude toward work was expanded; and the general level of activity in all-union associations was raised.

The USSR's Management of Foreign Trade

Of course, the effectiveness of socialist competition does not just depend on individual willingness; it is also measured by the criteria used to evaluate its results. The Ministry of Foreign Trade has worked out a number of criteria for assessing the results of socialist competition between all-union associations. There are a wide variety of criteria and indices used to assess results, and they do not always reflect the true picture. Difficulties are further compounded by the fact that all-union associations operate under different conditions (different inventories and hence differences in the amount of work performed, etc.).

Within an all-union association the results of socialist competition are assessed on the basis of the findings of a special committee (for the first, second, and third quarters and for the year as a whole). The main criteria for evaluating the performance of the various divisions in an all-union association and for determining incentives for socialist competition, particularly with regard to the fulfillment of socialist obligations, are those spelled out in the Ministry of Foreign Trade order on this subject. Some all-union associations have even expanded this list.

For example, V/O "Tekhnopromimport" adds the following to the list of criteria given in the Ministry of Foreign Trade order:

— placement of orders in percent of the import volume projected in the plan or draft plan (current year — for the first quarter; following year — for the second, third, and fourth quarters) for both capitalist and socialist countries;

— even distribution of order placements in terms of delivery times;

— average volume of deliveries per office worker for one fiscal quarter;

— coordination of imports with exports per year in percent of import plan to capitalist countries for the next year;

— participation of offices in rationalizing programs;

— supply of equipment to turnkey plants.

V/O "Mashimport" adds the following to its "Items for Assessing the Results of Socialist Competition between Offices":

Labor Organization and Personnel Training

— fulfillment of annual plan for delivery of reserve parts;

— fulfillment of deliveries to cover orders resulting from government resolutions made as part of the import plan for the current year;

— the active involvement of offices in the development of the movement for communist labor, participation in the social life of the collective, fulfillment of commissions by social organizations, work to improve the ideological and practical level of awareness of workers;

— also, points are added or subtracted in accordance with the level of results assessed by these criteria.

A number of association boards are rather subjective in the ways and means used in assessing the performance of association departments in accordance with the criteria the particular association has set down. Some have their own guidelines or procedures for assessing the results of socialist competition between offices; others do not. For those which do, the board is easily able to determine objectively how each office is faring as regards socialist competition by means of a point system. As an example of how the results of socialist competition are assessed and how particular offices rank in this respect, let us take V/O "Tekhnopromimport."

In the method used in this association, each office knows where it stands in respect to other offices for each of the competitive indices, and as a result experience can readily be exchanged, with lagging offices being given a boost in accordance with the Leninist principle of emulation.

METHOD
for assessing the results of socialist competition between offices of V/O "Tekhnoimport" for 1974

The results of socialist competition are summed up for each quarter, for each half-year, and for each year. The following indices are compared for each office:

1) fulfillment of the annual import plan from the beginning of the year (first quarter, first through second quarters, first

through third quarters, year) in percent;

2) the same for the socialist countries;

3) the same for the capitalist countries;

4) fulfillment of the annual import plan for a fiscal quarter (for the second and third quarters) in percent;

5) overdue deliveries at end of quarter in percent of planned import;

6) placement of orders in percent of plan or draft plan for imports (current year for first quarter, following year for second, third, and fourth quarters);

7) the same for socialist countries;

8) the same for capitalist countries;

9) uniform distribution of orders with respect to delivery times; ratio of deliveries in first half-year to total yearly deliveries in accordance with the import plan or draft plan (current year — for first quarter; subsequent years — for second, third, and fourth quarters);

10) average volume of deliveries per worker in office for each fiscal quarter (in thousands of rubles for first, second, and third quarters); ratio of total actual shipments to actual number of office workers (for fourth quarter — average volume of deliveries per office worker for year);

11) coordination of imports with exports (commitments of foreign firms in contractual agreements) per year in percent of import plan to capitalist countries for the following year (computed in fourth quarter);

12) office participation in rationalization programs (for second quarter, for first through second quarter, and in fourth quarter for third and fourth quarters);

13) delivery of equipment (separate and assembled) for turnkey projects (computed in fourth quarter for year).

The standing of an office is determined by the sum total of the points received for each of these indices for the particular quarter.

An office with 8 points for each of items 1-9 and 11 is given first place; those with 7 points get second place; and those with one point get eighth place (for items 4, 7, 8, and 11 an 0.5 coefficient is used).

Labor Organization and Personnel Training

Note. For the fourth quarter offices are given 8 points for fulfillment of the annual plan for points 1, 2, and 3 and 0.1 points for each 0.1 percent overfulfillment of the plan, the total not to exceed 12 points, however. Offices that are the first to report (no later than December 30, 197...) fulfillment of the annual plans for imports from both capitalist and socialist countries are given 1.5 extra points for the first, 1 point for the second, and 0.5 points for the third. Offices that have not fulfilled the annual plan are not given any points for items 1, 2, and 3, and their standing cannot be higher than that of offices that have fulfilled the plan.

For item 10 an office receives 1 point for each full 20 percent excess and has 1 point taken away for each full 20 percent deficit, if the average volume of deliveries for the particular quarter in the office is higher or lower, respectively, than the average volume of deliveries for the association as a whole. The volume of deliveries includes both planned and those in excess of the plan.

In item 12 the offices receive 0.2 points for each rationalizing proposal submitted for the current half-year and 1 point for each proposal approved and implemented, but not more than 2 points.

In item 13 an office receives 1 point for fulfillment and has 1 point taken away for nonfulfillment. Offices with no orders for deliveries to turnkey projects receive no points.

In summing up the results for the first half-year, the standing of an office is determined by the total number of points received in the first and second quarters; the standing for the year is determined by the total number of points received in the first, second, third, and fourth quarters.

Offices in first-place standing in the first quarter are given a temporary pennant and an additional money bonus amounting to 150 rubles; those in second and third places are given money bonuses of 100 and 75 rubles, respectively.

Offices that have been in the first three places in the first half-year and for the whole year are awarded the Honorary Achievement emblem.

The bonuses given to offices and departments are provided

by the association board, with the participation of representatives of management, the personnel section, the head accounting office, and party, trade union, and Komsomol organizations.

On the petition of the industrial commission of the local committee or department, the bonus commission has the power to decrease (or withdraw) the bonus funds of a department or deprive a worker of his bonus for nonfulfillment, to the detriment of the department, of the corresponding instructions or principles of foreign trade; for gross infraction of financial discipline, e.g., when association cargoes are left longer than two months in Soviet ports; for refusal to pay bills; for delay of submission of invoices to customers; for wasteful spending, and other valid claims, while an office that has enjoyed an honor standing is not given additional cash bonuses in such cases.

Thus we see from the list of obligations assumed by collectives of foreign trade departments and organizations that socialist competition in the Ministry of Foreign Trade is aimed at mobilizing workers for a massive effort to improve the efficiency of foreign trade activity.

5. Information in Management

The information made available to individuals will differ widely in its aims and objectives in accordance with the nature of their jobs in the administrative apparatus. The principal purposes served by information in management are general clarification, evaluation, persuasion, or the generation of information of another sort, creation of new ideas, problem identification, resolving problems, making decisions, planning, spurring action, supervision, and enquiry.

A considerable amount of the time is spent by administrative managerial personnel on decision-making, but every decision must be based on information. Information is needed:

— to determine markets for the sale and purchase of each type of commodity;
— to plan funds and material and financial resources;

Labor Organization and Personnel Training

— to analyze the orders of foreign firms and to work with domestic industry;

— to draw up contracts, make deliveries, and clear accounts with foreign firms and suppliers;

— to supervise the filling of an order down to the final delivery.

In addition modern management theory views management as a process based on the acquisition, processing, and transmission of information; it analyzes the function of management in this respect as follows:

— accumulation of the current information necessary for carrying out a particular task; such information includes instructions, orders, guidelines, procedures, plans, reports, norms, catalogues, agreements, contracts, etc.;

— transmission (conveying) of information to its point of use; in institutions this is done by means of oral speech, telephones, post, couriers, teletypes, and other means of communication;

— processing of information; this includes the selection, classification, and digestion of incoming information and the working out of a decision for future action or of decisions on operating methods and procedures; this is the most complex function of management and the one bearing the most responsibility, since the more difficult the problem to be resolved, the more complex is the information required to deal with it;

— the transmission of information to executive bodies; this includes commands, directives, procedures, etc.; in institutions it is usually carried out with the same means used to gather information;

— supervision of execution, done with the aid of the processed information; information on the results of an activity enables a manager to determine whether a decision has been implemented correctly, to uncover any problems that may arise, to make necessary corrections in an original decision, that is, to change a plan (program, procedure) of action in accordance with changing experience.

It is easy to envision, therefore, tne management of a foreign trade organization as an information process with feedback.

Practically the entire technological cycle of management of foreign trade involves information, and the success and effectiveness of a manager's performance will to a large extent depend on the quality, completeness, and freshness of the information he receives from both above and below.

The yearly growth in the volume of goods handled in foreign trade, the growth in the number of personnel in the administrative and management apparatus, and the growth in the number of foreign trade transactions are accompanied by disproportional growth in the volume and flow of such information and in the paper flow in general. This process is common to administration and management throughout all the developed countries. A situation has arisen in which the sheer volume of paper and other means of conveying information has reached such proportions that it is becoming more and more difficult to utilize them effectively. Many experts link this phenomenon to today's information crisis.

In 1973 the paper flow handled in the Ministry of Foreign Trade was 22 million documents, which increased to 25 million in 1974. For the ministry as a whole the increase was 10 percent, while in the central apparatus it was 8.5 percent. Handling information occupies 30 to 40 percent of the work time of an all-union association manager and almost 70 percent of the time of a manager in the central apparatus.

At the same time, managers have less and less time for handling paperwork. A time study of the workday of office directors in all-union associations has shown that they have only 2 to 3 hours each day for paperwork; but even this time is not undivided, since they are constantly interrupted by telephone calls, summonses to talks with their supervisors, meetings, etc. As a result there is a chronic shortage of time.

The growth of the paper flow and the shortage of time for work with documents create a conflict between a manager's need for the most complete information possible for making decisions and the quality of the information he receives from the documents. A look at the work of any manager will show that despite the abundance of documents and papers, he frequently does not have a sufficient amount of necessary information at his fingertips when needed, or else information is delayed, which of course results in inefficient, and at times even wrong, decisions. In addition statistics show that 80 percent of the total volume of paper and documents contains superfluous information, and that only about 20 percent actually goes into making decisions.

One way to improve the efficiency of day-to-day activities of managers, and therefore to improve the quality of their decisions, is to improve the system of supplying them with information. A "management information input system" involves a clear classification of the many different types of information in the foreign trade management system; a correct understanding of what the term "information" means as far as day-to-day management is concerned; the establishment of a system to supply decision-making personnel with current information relevant to their managerial functions; and a system of technical facilities for the receipt, processing, storage, and transmission of information.

The importance of information processes for efficient production has been recognized since antiquity, long before information theory or even the word "information" existed. The history of information can be divided into three periods: the first period covers the time before writing was invented, when information was conveyed orally. The human speech apparatus was fully adequate for conveying and processing small quantities of information within the society of that time. The second period begins with the invention of writing, which helped man to remember facts needed in thinking through a problem. The possibility of conveying information by means of texts and figures opened new horizons for mankind. Documentary information appeared on the scene, and paperwork developed. Business relations between people became eclipsed by a thicket of papers and documents. We are now in the third period, the cybernetic period, in which automated means are used to process information. The distinguishing characteristic of this period is the overwhelming growth of information flows, a veritable information explosion.

With regard to the problems of management and the methods used to solve them up to now, we can safely say that given the technical means available, the system of information that had evolved was in general adequate to the needs of management. In any event a state of mutual adaptation was achieved over decades of practical experience: the information system tried to provide management with the data it needed within the limits of its resources, and the management system selected those methods suitable for handling the data received. Today the situation is different, and the factors that have brought about the change are of an enduring nature.

The first of them is the substantial increase in management's need for information. Foreign trade relations and operations have grown in variety and number, administrative apparatuses have become more complicated, the role of science and technology in management is increasing — all these factors contribute to making every wrong decision more costly, so that it has become imperative that every decision rest on as solid a foundation as possible. If, therefore, information is to be the principal instrument in creating these solid foundations, it must be as thorough and accurate as possible. Modern science and technology have created the ways and means for satisfying these high standards, provided that the information also conforms to correspondingly higher standards. Thus the development of special information input systems (managerial information input systems) can be regarded as a second factor responsible for the revolution in information systems.

A management information input system is a team of individuals, a collection of managerial personnel, and equipment for processing data: for gathering, storing, handling, and retrieving data in order to reduce the degree of indeterminacy in decision-making. Such a system should provide management with the information it needs at the moment it is most useful. All incoming information can be classified according to its destination, the time of transformation, the mode in which it circulates in the management system, and its content.

Economic information has a wide variety of functions regarding planning, financing, and accounting, as well as prices, efficiency indicators for different departments, and other parameters characterizing the economic performance of departments.

Economic information differs from all other kinds of information in that it is chronically incomplete; this is due on the one hand to imperfections in existing systems for economic information, inadequate regulation of banks and flows of information, inadequate capacity of channels for conveying information, and the inability to process the entire volume of information needed by management. This problem is gradually being eliminated, or at least alleviated, with the development of scientific bases for an applied information theory, the creation of automatic information control systems, the installation of computers in management, and so on.

On the other hand, the incompleteness of information is due to the very nature of this kind of knowledge: in the first place it is impossible to know everything at once about the objects to be managed or controlled and to exhaustively describe their state at any given moment. This is a much more difficult problem than the first one. In addition economic decisions very often concern the future and must be implemented in the future, and information about the future must perforce possess some degree of indeterminacy, which will be greater the more complicated and the newer the area of human activity it concerns.

Scientific-technical information covers data about the technical characteristics and quality of exported and imported goods.

Administrative information covers the structure of the administrative and managerial apparatus and its functioning, legal information, as well as the following: regulatory information (commands, instructions, memoranda, orders, resolutions), office information (informative letters, telegrams, telexes, office letters), and information on personnel (staff).

This information reflects the organizational methods of management.

Information about personnel is very important. It is not sufficient to know just the level of technical and economic training of office workers, engineering and technical personnel, and managerial personnel at all levels. It is also important to have a factual description of each worker's job performance, so that the most competent can be promoted as quickly as possible. It is easier to detect top-notch workers if an enterprise has access to a management information input system that stores exhaustive information about each employee. No file, no matter how complete, can be compared with information systems using the latest computer technology. Such systems can also be used to obtain information for making decisions to send this or that employee to a retraining or advanced training course.

Day-to-day information is the information needed to carry out the routine functions of managing the administrative apparatus and pertains to all the detailed operations involved in foreign trade. Day-to-day information is unquestionably the most important kind of information as far as running an office is concerned. It cuts across every subsystem and pertains to every department in an organization. However, in spite of its obvious importance, this kind of information is usually not treated as carefully as other types. This is unfortunate because in most organizations it is in this area that the greatest possibilities lie for reducing the cost of and improving management.

Indeed, most of the work done in the recent period to improve the efficiency of management has been related to the emergence of new problems in the area of day-to-day management. In terms of the time required to prepare information, it can be divided into two types: first-hand information, and information that has gone through some process. Information obtained from a worker taking part directly in some process and formulated and written down for the first time is called first-hand information. It is gathered and sent to its point of use for systematization, storage, or developing administrative decisions.

Information is very important for day-to-day management

Labor Organization and Personnel Training

in which the time available for decision-making is limited and mistakes are costly. We shall therefore devote special attention to aspects of dealing with day-to-day information.

The term "information" has received various interpretations, from the purely utilitarian to the purely scientific. It can be safely said that there are as many definitions of the term "information" as there are scholarly books written about information theory, since each author uses the term in his own way. The result has been that we have gotten so used to the term "information" that we have stopped thinking about what the word means practically; it has become simply an affirmative term and covers literally everything we hear or see. In business the term "information" has a quite precise meaning that should be observed in developing an efficient management information input system. Two definitions in particular are of practical interest: the first, a more general definition, reflects the theoretical approach to the concept of information, and the second, a practical definition, is most suited for an analysis of information systems.

The originators of information theory are Claude Shannon in the United States and A. I. Berg and A. N. Kolmogorov in the Soviet Union. The most general theoretical definition of information is Shannon's: Information is a measure of the decrease in indeterminacy. The Committee for Scientific-Technical Terminology of the Academy of Sciences of the USSR proposes the following definition: Information is a set of data that can be stored, transmitted, and transformed. The way information is presented is the message or document. This definition of information has the following correlaries:

1. Information is not the same thing as a document. A document, telex, or other form of message is only paper, i.e., material media for conveying information. In precise terms the administrative managerial apparatus is suffocating not from a superabundance of information (often there is not enough information available when it is needed) but from the colossal flood of documents.

2. A document may contain information for a manager, or

it may not. This will depend on by whom, how, and for whom a document is compiled and what data it contains. It must contain some information, i.e., something new for the recipient of the document. If it does not, a document contains no information. This is why managers sometimes have a pile of papers and documents but are all the same poorly informed. Only if data are examined in detail and organized in such a way that a manager is able to base his actions on them do they become information. Many facts are also retained in a manager's memory. All these data remain merely data until a manager refers to them in performing some act or in making some necessary decision. Data become information when a manager is aware of their significance. From the point of view of decision-making, we can say that information is new data being put to use.

For a document to become a source of information for a manager, he must read it through and understand its content, i.e., the recipient of a document must be versed in those questions with which the document deals; the message contained in a document must contain something new (or something forgotten) for the recipient (manager). If these three conditions are not fulfilled, a document conveys no information for the manager. Understanding the difference between a document and information is necessary to formulate specifications for compiling documents correctly.

3. For a document to contain information, when it is compiled one must know exactly for whom it is intended, i.e., information must have a purpose. Several important points follow from this.

Managerial personnel must be provided only with what is necessary (minimization principle). They can also be given a list of other materials compiled in their administration or association which they can get if they want.

Often managerial workers themselves require "thorough briefings" about everything from their subordinates. This is a natural desire to know everything within as short a time as possible. There is a very good definition of a manager that is one more demonstration of the need to reduce the paper

Labor Organization and Personnel Training

flow for managers, especially at the top level: "A manager is a person who as time goes on knows less and less about more and more, until finally he will know practically nothing about everything." This somewhat allegorical definition unfortunately reflects perfectly the current trend. What questions and problems does a manager not have to deal with during the course of a working day!

The chronic shortage of time and the sheer physical limitations of his capacity to digest volumes of information make a manager practically unable to use such briefings. In fact such a thorough briefing is often a chaos of figures and may even confuse a manager rather than help him.

An American firm carried out an interesting and painstaking study of the system of providing top-level management with information. As a result of its recommendations, the president of the firm began to receive 18 reports instead of 83. He declared: "I think almost 75 percent of all the figures on my desk disappeared as a result of this study; nevertheless, we would be the first to affirm that we have all the really necessary information on all important questions, and we obtain all the data we need to manage our firm and its expansion."

Specialists have come to the conclusion that a person has two kinds of memory: a short-term memory and a subconscious memory. The short-term memory stores for a short period information that is important only at the particular moment, for example, interim judgments or calculations for making decisions. The subconscious memory stores for a long time information pertaining to practice, experience, and facts. A person with a perfect subconscious memory is a walking encyclopedia. Ultimately such persons become efficiency engineers, irreplaceable experts and excellent advisors and assistants, and often even middle-level managers. In addition to having a good memory, a manager must also be able to think and look for and find nontrivial solutions to questions and problems that come up from day to day; the more knowledge and experience he has, the larger the number of alternative solutions he is able to weigh in choosing the best. Hence, in terms of the minimization principle, a manager must have at his disposal a developed, working external memory system. This can be an information retrieval system, a punch-card information storage system, etc.

A manager must be kept informed about what is not working properly; managerial personnel are usually more interested in what is not done or what is done over plan than in what has been done. Of course, in the case of overfulfillment there is usually no shortage of information, so there is no problem. But a manager must demand from his subordinates, first of all, information about hitches that arise in the planned course of operations, i.e., about any deviations from the norm or the plan. Today this is an important principle in the supply of information, especially for day-to-day management. For example, this was the principle followed by the creators of the unified system of accounting and statistics in the GDR, as ratified by the government resolution of May 12, 1966, which reads: "Managers and management bodies of establishments should receive primarily the statistical information they need to make practical decisions. It should be investigated whether it would not be sufficient for supervision of plan fulfillment if they are only informed about problems that arise at key points."

The potential for introducing such an improved system of accounting, statistics, and information for Ministry of Foreign Trade managers into its central administration and into all all-union associations has not yet been fully exhausted. Managerial personnel have sometimes referred to this principle as the "clean desk top" principle. If there is nothing on a manager's desk, this means that everything is proceeding normally.

However, if management is to be informed only about problems that arise, it must be informed promptly. This vital principle is unfortunately not always observed, since our management information system is not yet up to par with our system for handling paperwork.

What do we mean by promptness? Let us start with an example. The fulfillment of the import plan must be completed by December 20. At the beginning of November the inspectorate (commission) checks the maintenance of fixed deliveries of goods to the economy. It is established that of the 29 items, by December 20 only 9 will be delivered. Naturally the inspectorate makes the appropriate report on the results of its check to the main administration, and its head gives an order to promptly assure the fulfillment of the annual plan. But it is already late! The days until the plan period ends are numbered, and the situation remains practically unchanged. Management (and of course the huge administrative apparatus that goes with it) is not needed to determine the situation existing in the system at a given moment but to ensure that targets are met within the time set for them. Subordinates must inform management promptly the minute any hitches arise, i.e., incoming information should emerge in the form of a prognosis. This is what promptness means. It is even better if a manager is himself able to forecast divergences from the plan. That is the art of management.

A management system begins to function smoothly only when it begins to receive prognostic information on a regular basis. The presence of such information on a manager's desk tells us a great deal about the informational competence of his organization and in a certain sense about the quality of department efforts to institute a scientific organization of labor.

Statistical data are an important part of prognostic information. We should distinguish here between "reports" and "information." A statistical report (monthly or for a longer period) must be uniform and compiled only by the appropriate departments (e.g., the automatic data-processing departments) and planning departments, without the assistance of functional or office services. Only data about deviations from the plan should be fed into the management system and passed on directly to managerial personnel.

The distinction between a statistical report and routine information is especially important today, given the work load on the managerial personnel of the Ministry of Foreign Trade; the line must be drawn without delay, since a long, drawn out discussion can only hinder rather than help the development of an efficient management system now that the transition to a two-tiered system is in progress.

The top-level management (heads of main administrations and their deputies, deputy ministers) normally use information for two purposes: to resolve daily problems and to make decisions affecting future situations. Statistics show that the length of time covered by the decisions of managers at different levels is distributed as shown in Table 13.

Table 13

Approximate Time Standards for Executive Decision-Making
(%)

Level of management	Period of activity taken by executives						
	1 day	1 week (ten days)	1 month	3-6 months	1 year	2 years	5 years or more
Minister and his deputies	—	2	8	10	18	27	35
Heads of main administrations	1	4	5	15	25	30	20
Directors of associations	4	6	10	20	30	20	10
Directors of offices	8	10	20	30	20	10	2
Leaders of groups	13	20	30	25	10	2	—
Engineers, statistical engineers, traders	30	40	15	10	5	—	—

At the lower level an influx of information with a regularity corresponding to the flow of real events is necessary. At higher levels it is not so necessary that the influx of information proceed at the same pace as real events, since decisions at these levels are of a long-term nature covering whole years.

One way to ensure a regular flow of information is to draw up schedules for reports for the day-to-day information system. At the level of directors of all-union associations, such reports may be every month. One possibility for such a system could look as follows:

Report (analyzed) Month — April

1. Data enter the automatic accounting section (ACS section) on May 20.

2. Processing and input of the data into the information system should be completed by May 27.
3. Comments on the reports from the auxiliary services (economic plan section, foreign exchange and financing section, etc.) must be received by May 28.
4. Reports of the information system are distributed to the various offices by May 29.
5. Comments are submitted and adjustments worked out by June 4.
6. The problems caused by deviations from the norm or from the plan that require managerial decisions are screened by June 5. At this point information is divided into two classes: statistical report information that is stored, and current information passed on to management for decision-making.
7. Setting of priorities (selection of most important) for the selected problems is done by the association chairman by May 6.
8. Current information is presented to the association management for decision at the directors' board council meeting.

Information can be considered reliable to the extent that it corresponds to reality. Practice has demonstrated that to ensure the reliability of the information recieved by a manager there should be suitable control of its journey through the administrative apparatus, it should be processed and passed on promptly, and the workers who prepare and process first-hand information must have a conscientious attitude toward it. Reliability of information depends in large measure on its source. A serious attitude toward these factors will ensure that the information management receives is reliable and reflects the real state of things.

The most common cause of unreliable information is improper handling of data, especially in calculating average figures. In day-to-day operations the averaging of data results in a loss of information and hence a diminution in reliability. The extreme case of unreliable information is misinformation, i.e., the deliberate distortion of information. Unreliable information can usually be detected by examining the original data, but misinformation is usually concealed by subjective interests; in its case, therefore, a manager must rely on his own intuition, knowledge of his business, and knowledge of his subordinates. Misinformation includes the exaggeration or slighting of data, as when extremes are presented as typical or normal, or when an event is described in exclusively good or exclusively bad terms. Misinformation in management frequently is caused by a biased attitude toward or vested interest in one possible alternative solution to a problem, so that only data that support this alternative are collected.

In the light of the foregoing discussion of the properties of current information and the principles of information supply, the following requirements (instructions) can be set down for gathering current information for management:

1) all informational material should contain facts concerning deviations from the plan or from norms. The factual data included in the compiled information should be set forth in itemized form;

2) in addition to factual data on deviations, information should also contain material on trends, on where these deviations seem to be headed in the immediate and more long-term future;

3) all information should be presented concisely, concretely, and simply. Details should be minimal.

Often a manager gets lost in a mass of details and is unable to glean from a document what is most important in it. One kind of such pernicious fetishism for detail is the presentation of such large figures that a manager finds it difficult to make his way through them or put them to use. In general a human being can comprehend only two-digit numbers, yet current practice in the Ministry of Foreign Trade is to write 22,000 thousand rubles instead of 22 million rubles. Furthermore, the use of a large number of digits in reports, or even just in letters or documents, often creates the deceptive impression of accuracy.

The way information is presented (numerical, tabulated, graphic) should in large measure be determined by the nature

Labor Organization and Personnel Training

of the data and by the desires of the persons who are going to use it. Some like graphs, others do not;

4) information should be presented in such a way that a manager can understand it regardless of how specialized the area or problems with which it deals;

5) information should be reliable and accurate. This is a basic requirement, since information is used as a basis for decisions that are sometimes very important and will have significant economic consequences. For this reason every executive must carefully screen his sources of information, check their fidelity and reliability, and weed out biased information. A specialist in preparing information must compile from his variegated facts and figures information that is as uniform as it can be, eliminating differences in estimates, using the correct exchange rates in calculating costs, etc.;

6) information should reflect both the positive and negative sides of a problem and present an accurate picture.

Thus the answer to the question what information for managerial personnel should be is: information fit to serve as a basis for making decisions.

However, in drawing up instructions it is important to bear in mind that neither a management consultant nor a secretary can prescribe what information a manager should receive. A manager, especially a top-level manager, who has to deal with numerical data must in all cases himself determine what information he will need for fulfilling his responsibilities effectively. Hence the volume of information must be regulated not from below, as is the present practice, but from above; and the higher the level of management, the more should the content of information and the form in which it is presented be adapted to the personal requirements of the manager.

6. <u>Some Methodological and Practical Questions in the Management of Training and Advanced Training of Managerial Personnel</u>

The level of skills and the competence of the staff, particularly the managerial personnel, are important factors in ensuring the successful implementation of measures to improve the organization of labor and management, to introduce computer technology, and to improve the efficiency of foreign trade. L. I. Brezhnev dealt specifically with this question in his speech at a special meeting in the capital of Kazakhstan: "A highly skilled staff is the most important thing; without it there can be no such thing as a really progressive enterprise."[4]

Many factors are involved in this question, one of the more important of which is the correct organization of the management of training and advanced training of foreign trade workers.

The system we have in our country for producing trained personnel for work in foreign economic affairs has basically proven itself. It presently works as follows:

— the Moscow State Institute for International Relations trains middle-level specialists (economists, foreign language correspondents, financial experts, etc.);

— the All-Union Academy of Foreign Trade trains the office staff (managerial assistants in offices, senior engineers, senior economists);

— the College for Advanced Training at the academy provides advanced training for workers at all levels in the foreign trade apparatus. Finally, there is an extensive network of schools for advanced training attached to the all-union associations and other departments of the Ministry of Foreign Trade.

However, training in these areas could still be expanded and improved, and in fact this subject was specifically dealt with at the Sixth Session of the Supreme Soviet (Eighth Meeting) on July 17-19, 1973, in the discussion of the draft entitled "Foundations of Legislation in the USSR and the Union Republics on Public Education." There are a number of reasons dictating this need, among them the contemporary scientific-technical revolution.

As production becomes increasingly complex and as techniques and equipment become obsolete increasingly rapidly, it has become more and more difficult to determine the direction foreign trade should take to achieve maximum effectiveness.

Labor Organization and Personnel Training

The problem is compounded by the instability of the socioeconomic processes taking place in the world at large, so that the traditional forms of foreign trade are no longer adequate.

A worker in foreign trade at any level, and particularly a manager, must not only know how the conduct of foreign trade operations is organized, he must also be able to perceive trends in the development of science and technology and structural changes in different spheres and be able to interpret correctly the influence on the development of foreign trade of progress and of socioeconomic and political processes. This is now all the more important in that the predictions of certain developments in world science and technology indicate the advent of monumental changes that will unquestionably influence the development and hence the content of the training of foreign trade personnel.

For example, predictions about world developments in science and technology published in the United States look as follows: economically feasible desalinization of seawater (1980); computer translations (1978); accurate weather prediction (1980); controllable thermonuclear reactions (2000); laboratory creation of primitive forms of life (1978); mining on the ocean floor (2000); universal immunization against bacterial and viral diseases (2000); chemical control of heredity (2033); control of weather in some areas (2000); industrial production of synthetic protein (2000); communication with extraterrestrial civilizations (not before 2000); prolonged anabiosis for interstellar journeys (not before 2000); universal use of teaching machines (1975); use of logic devices to make difficult and crucial decisions automatically (1979), etc.

These predictions engender a number of questions, of course: What criteria for the progressiveness of foreign trade and economic knowledge are necessary to organize the training of specialists? What is the lifetime of the knowledge they are taught? At what regular intervals should knowledge be renewed? What knowledge can be regarded as established fact? How should future foreign trade specialists be taught? The answers to these questions can be obtained by working out a scientifically sound model for the future foreign trade specialist. To start with, a "goal chart" for the education of a specialist should be worked out; at the top should be a general goal that defines the desired level of training for a specialist. This should then be broken down into a series of subsidiary goals, on whose achievement the reaching of the general goal is contingent. The training of a foreign trade specialist should consist not only of a system of specialized knowledge; it should also organically include the development of physical and intellectual abilities, the inculcation of a coherent philosophical outlook, the acquisition of practical routines for collective creative work in a group, etc. "The problem of training not only a specialist but an educated civilized human being arises in all its acuity because the rough edges of civilization sometimes avenge themselves in unexpected ways and prevent a real specialized knowledge of a field,"[5] says Professor V. A. Venikov.

Thus, according to a "goal chart," the modern foreign trade specialist should have the following attributes:

— a broad professional training in foreign trade that will permit him to deal with a wide range of particular problems in the development of foreign trade and to solve strategic problems concerning the nation's economic development in the context of the major directions of development of scientific-technical progress throughout the world;

— a broad command of advanced methods of analysis and management and the ability to use them creatively;

— continuous improvement of professional competence and general level of culture.

But with the limited time available to train a worker (study time at the All-Union Foreign Trade Academy amounts to 2,460 hours per year) it is difficult to meet these requirements. Many factors are involved, especially a correct balance between the number of study hours for mandatory courses and for independent study, the level of competence of the teaching staff, the content of the curriculum, teaching methods, and so on.

The problem should be approached systematically, i.e., no

Labor Organization and Personnel Training

one particular aspect should be dealt with separately from the others. For example, in fixing the number of hours to be set aside for lectures and independent study respectively, careful consideration should be given to the way instruction is organized, the degree of coordination between the various subjects, etc. It is very important to leave room for options in solving this problem, and the particular aspects should be dealt with according to their importance, interrelatedness, and the way they mutually support one another.

It is also important to have the right approach in determining the blend of all courses with one another, i.e., in determining the role and status of each subject in the overall training of a foreign trade specialist. The end result should not just be the simple accumulation of a store of information by a student but an organically coherent, whole body of knowledge, in which every subject or component has a vital role to play such that its exclusion would mean that the desired level of training for a specialist could not be achieved.

In terms of goals it is clear that a scientifically sound approach is necessary, that is, one which takes into account present practice, future trends, and the nature of foreign trade activity. Initially the procedures used in performing foreign trade transactions and the knowledge required to carry them out should be compared. We have taken the trade transaction as an example, since it is most typical of the kind of activity encountered in foreign trade.

For convenience's sake a foreign trade transaction can be described using grid planning methods; this provides the most graphic illustration of each operation (procedure) and the overall sequence of operations, demonstrates the interrelationships in the technical sequence of foreign trade operations, and shows the plan of detailed time characteristics and other features of each operation and the time required for completing an entire transaction.

Typical export or import transactions should be used, since they involve a whole sequence of operations. A model of a foreign trade transaction is stochastic, i.e., it should show possible alternative ways to perform the same operation.

On the basis of the sum total of knowledge received by a student, we can estimate the role and significance of each course of study as far as current foreign trade activity is concerned. We should bear in mind, however, that a comparison of this sort is based on current practices and does not take into account future trends. For this, predictions of science and technology must be drawn on.

After determining the content of the curriculum and the status and significance of a course, we can construct a model for a foreign trade specialist that should tell us what a specialist should know and what he should be able to do.

An equally important factor in determining the effectiveness of training of foreign trade managerial personnel is the proper choice of the forms of instruction and of teaching methods. This choice should be governed by the specific characteristics of the subjects and by the type of job the trainee is being prepared for (office worker, manager, etc.). But whatever the case, the student should be taught to think creatively and encouraged to keep his knowledge up to date. This means that the methods of instruction used must not only impart information, they must also inculcate the skills for acquiring knowledge independently and for thinking in scientific concepts. In other words, school instruction should be as vigorous as possible.

Programmed learning has an important role to play here. With lecture time limited and given the individual differences in the ability to assimilate knowledge, programmed learning can not only step up the learning process, it can also allow students to proceed at their own pace.

The research being carried out in institutions of higher learning is very important in this connection. The experience of leading Soviet schools shows that an organic link between formal schooling and scientific research is a good foundation for establishing an effective system for training highly skilled specialists.

The training of highly skilled foreign trade specialists is a continuous process of refinement of knowledge already acquired; the life expectancy of specialized knowledge must be carefully considered, so that further training can be effectively organized.

Currently the advanced training of Ministry of Foreign Trade managerial personnel is provided by the Advanced Training College attached to the All-Union Academy of Foreign Trade. A number of unique features must be taken into account in planning advanced training. The same principles as involved in training foreign trade workers apply here as well: What is to be taught? How is it to be taught? Who is to be taught? However, these questions are much more difficult to answer in this case than in training managerial personnel.

The very term "advanced training" when applied to administrators does not always get to the heart of the matter. Only what already exists can be "advanced" further; what is not there cannot. The administrative personnel in foreign trade have considerable managerial experience and a solid store of knowledge, but they are usually unfamiliar with the achievements of modern managerial science. It is therefore important that the curricula for advanced training of managerial personnel reflect accurately all the real problems involved in management. But even though due emphasis is placed on managerial disciplines, the question of what is to be taught is still open. An intelligent balance between theory and practice is extremely important. The cardinal questions here are what is to be done and how.

The pilot studies of the All-Union Center for Scientific Method in Moscow have shown that lectures dealing with theoretical questions should make up no more than 20 to 30 percent of total study time for managerial-level students (in our case this means all-union association deputy directors, heads of sections, and office directors).

Effective instruction is possible only if practical exercises are based on an analysis of concrete situations, backed up by factual reports, surveys, and facts uncovered in special studies. If they are not, they become ordinary, perfunctory exercises. The decisions made by students in dealing with particular industrial problems should be such that they help to develop their capacity to select and use correctly the information at their disposal and give sound reasons for their decisions. Indeed, even the way exercises are done should be changed. Problems should be tackled in teams (5 or 6 students) without the instructor. Then in the classroom lectures, the solutions arrived at by the individual teams should be discussed. The purpose of such a discussion is to bring to light hidden aspects of the problem, to compare different proposed solutions, and to choose the best one.

Practical simulated games with computers should be an important component in the set of methods used for the advanced training of managerial personnel. A game used at the Management Center in Geneva will provide some idea about this method of instruction (the author himself participated in this game).

The participants were divided into six groups that represented six competing firms on six domestic and one foreign market. Before starting the game, each participant was given special materials containing the necessary information about each firm, its principal technical and economic indices, accounting formulas, etc. The participants simulated the functions of management, made decisions, and then passed them on to the lab to be fed into computers, where, in accordance with a predetermined program, the position of the particular firm on the market was determined each time after each decision. The computer's results were handed back to the participants, who then corrected their decisions, returned them to the computer bank, and so on.

The game ended with a broad array of decisions. Each game lasted three days. The use of such practical games to train and improve the training of foreign trade managerial personnel deserves serious attention and should be explored further.

Finally, the question remains: Who is to be taught? There are two aspects involved here. First, a psychological barrier must be overcome, since advanced training in large measure means retraining those who have become accustomed to thinking and working in other ways; second, the students should be grouped according to their level of knowledge.

The training and advanced training of foreign trade managerial personnel is a process that takes place on many levels and requires specialists of various types.

CHAPTER FIVE

Controlling the Quality
of Products Intended for Export

1. General Questions in Controlling Product Quality

Improving the quality of the USSR's industrial products is politically and economically fundamental to the tapping and utilization of the potential reserves for raising labor productivity, economizing on material resources, accelerating the rate of technical progress and economic construction, and consequently to further raising the material and cultural well-being of the population. "A systematic improvement in product quality is a condition sine qua non for the development of the economy," states the Program of the CPSU. "The quality of products in Soviet enterprises must be significantly higher than in the best capitalist firms. For this to come about it is necessary to adopt a broad range of measures, including social control and giving quality indicators a greater role in planning, in evaluating the work of enterprises, and in socialist competition."[1]

The improvement of product quality is especially important with regard to the continuous expansion of the Soviet Union's foreign economic relations, which themselves play a crucial role in improving the domestic economy. "Both political factors, e.g., the need to fortify socialist cooperation and to strengthen the economic basis of peaceful coexistence between governments, and factors that arise from the needs of our national economy make it important for all branches of industry to produce more goods for export. This will facilitate an increase in imports of needed goods. There can be no doubt that the expansion of international trade will have a beneficial effect on the workings of our entire industry," states a report to the Twenty-fourth Party Congress of the Central Committee of the CPSU.[2]

The future development of foreign trade requires the development and manufacture of goods that correspond to the needs of the markets of different countries and increased international specialization of production. This in turn will create favorable conditions for generally improving product quality. If the country is to take an active part in the international division of labor, it must concentrate on producing more effective types of products, increasing serial production of industrial goods, and improving quality. Mutual deliveries of the most major types of products, especially modern technology, and the exchange of scientific ideas and industrial experience are all part of foreign trade, and all promote and speed the pace of technical progress, as well as making the improvement of product quality essential.

There are many factors determining success or failure on the foreign market: prices, the size of contracts, the time required for deliveries and the conditions of payment, the ability to provide maintenance and spare parts for exported machinery and equipment, the conditions of use (or consumption), the peculiarities of the market, and so on. Also, practical experience in foreign trade relations shows that the level of product quality is a factor of growing importance in determining the salability of goods.

The poor competitiveness of domestic export goods forces foreign trade organizations to set low contract prices and, moreover, is one of the major factors retarding the development of exports with a high efficiency index — above all, machinery and equipment. The complaints registered by foreign consumers about defects in delivered goods lead to losses in foreign exchange and undermine the prestige of Soviet products.

The economic problems faced by the USSR in improving the quality of industrial products have been studied quite extensively. Statistical methods for quality control and analysis have been developed. Many of the methods for quality control used in the Soviet Union are widely known outside our country (the Saratov system of delivery on first presentation, the Gor'kov system, and others). A number of studies have dealt with the organization of foreign trade and improving its economic efficiency.

Despite the urgency of the situation, however, almost no study has been made either of the quality of products intended for export and manufactured with the specific demands of different markets in mind, or of the integral role and responsibilities of the state component in the quality control of export products.

The documentary materials setting quality standards for exported products touch only the technical side of the question. The standard instruments of quality control of export goods, i.e., standardization, certification, spot checks, and moral and material incentives have been used, but such economic factors as foreign price levels, receipts and outlays of foreign exchange, etc., which also bear on the question, are virtually unused.

Also lacking are common classifiers for products, such as the number of refusals, defects, and other data that could be encoded and stored in computers.

With neither an established method for assessing this economic aspect of export product quality improvement nor an appropriate system for collecting and analyzing the technical-economic information pertaining to product quality, it is difficult to determine how the state could perform its function, which indeed is an extremely important one, in supervising the quality of export goods.

The current practice of the State Inspectorate for Quality Control of Export Goods, under the Ministry of Foreign Trade, shows that present methods of assessing the quality of goods manufactured for export or already delivered to the foreign consumer cannot provide an adequate idea of how well they are produced.

Thus point-scale rating methods by experts cannot be used

because the specialists themselves tend to be subjectively biased in favor of those they represent (the manufacturer or the foreign trade organization), and because they lack criteria for determining the "relative weights" of a product's various properties. The usual indices of consumer quality, based on durability, reliability, etc., fail to take into account numerous features that are important in the eyes of the foreign consumer: the appearance, finish, and color of an article, esthetic and ergonomic qualities, and so on.

The concept of "export product quality." The term "product quality" refers to the set of properties and characteristics of the products of labor that meet the specific needs of the consumer under fixed conditions of consumption. Under conditions of commodity production the products of labor become commodities "only by virtue of their dual character, only by virtue of the fact that they serve simultaneously as articles of consumption and as bearers of value."[3]

The specific properties that the commodity had by virtue of its being a product of labor intended for exchange are manifested in the process of commodity circulation and consumption.

For the seller, who is the owner of value, i.e., money, the most important thing is use value, that is, the totality of the commodity's properties that most satisfy his needs. Insofar as the commodity holds any interest for the purchaser as a use value, he "evaluates" it, as Marx noted — that is, he studies its quality and evinces a predilection for this or that type of good.[4]

The intensifying struggle to sell commodities and the exacerbation of competition on the world market compel exporters to work out rival tactics and strategies in science and technology, industry, and trade. In recent years the view has become increasingly widespread in business circles in industrially developed capitalist countries that policies relating to product quality must have the same priority as price policy and be based on a thorough study of changes in production technology, market demands, and social relations. It is therefore no accident that this question was widely discussed at the

Tokyo international conference on quality, where it was declared that:

> Although quality is determined by the consumer, the balance between quality and price must be anticipated in advance, so that profit can be guaranteed. Taking variations in quality, quantity, and price as parameters, the production cost of a product that guarantees the necessary profit must be determined beforehand, that is, cost must be planned in the same way as quality.
>
> It is necessary to select the right moment for putting a product with a given quality on the market, and to do so one must use modern planning methods.[5]

A determined effort to make goods more competitive has enabled many foreign firms to achieve a consistently high quality of manufactured goods.

For the countries of the socialist commonwealth to expand their trade, quality must be the watchword, and it can stand considerable improvement. This, along with other factors, is sure to have a positive influence on the efficiency of their domestic economies.

In the Soviet Union, as in other socialist countries, extensive efforts to raise product quality enable more and more goods to be put on the market that meet — or even exceed — present-day demands. On the other hand, despite obvious successes in this field, there are a number of questions whose answers have yet to be worked out: for example, those relating to the demands of different markets for goods of a certain quality, the economic justification for improving the quality of certain products delivered abroad, the application of new ways to attract potential buyers, and several others. N. N. Smeliakov, deputy minister of foreign trade, has written:

> While our industry was just beginning to take heed (and even then not very willingly) of what the workers in our foreign trade organizations were saying about the special re-

quirements that export-oriented machinery had to satisfy, and which industry had only gotten as far as promising to begin to meet, capitalist firms were already building machinery and equipment that took account of special needs for operating in tropical conditions, on stony or sandy ground, using local raw materials, and with different sources of electricity — that is, they were making great strides in the development of their machine exports.

While we were only beginning to understand that before entering the marketplace we had to study it, determining which machinery could or could not be supplied where, as well as how to organize the work involved, capitalist firms had already created a whole science to deal with the question, coordinating production, advertising, and commercial activity into a single discipline.[6]

Let us examine the differences between the requirements of ordinary production and those of production for export in a planned socialist economy.

In socialist countries the quality of products or goods sold domestically is meant to ensure the fullest possible correspondence between the consumer properties of finished goods and the needs of the national economy and, at the same time, to raise the economic effectiveness of their production and consumption.

The quality of export products, on the other hand, must meet the demands of the foreign market and guarantee the highest possible foreign exchange earnings, taking into account cash and capital expenditures on production and transportation.

From what we have said it is evident that the differences between quality requirements for goods manufactured for domestic use and for goods produced for export derive from the objectives for which they are manufactured. While the former must conform primarily to the needs of the national economy where they are for immediate use, products for export bring gain only insofar as they can be sold on the foreign market, which in turn depends on how well they meet the quality requirements of foreign capital.

Each foreign market has its own specific quality requirements, which have evolved along with the historical and industrial development of the particular country and are expressed in national standards and regulations; over and above this, however, production has to correspond to the requirements of the importers, which are dictated by the specific conditions of operation (use) and maintenance: climate and so forth.

Leading European firms, for example, have come to the conclusion that a set of uniform standards had to be worked out for exported automobiles and components, incorporating the American federal safety standards for motor vehicles (EMSS).

Under the American standards each automobile must have an identification plate confirming that its specifications conform to regulations, while the manufacturer is required to keep proper records on the car throughout its life. Failure to comply brings heavy fines or even a ban on selling the car within the United States.

Since the factory does not have the records for each car on hand, it has to recall every automobile that it delivered, even though defects might have shown up in only a few of them.

Thus in 1970 General Motors recalled 37,000 Cadillacs, although only 5,000 were defective. In the same year Ford had to recall 1.2 million automobiles, although defects turned up in only 235.

Western European quality specifications will be based on a plan drafted by the West German quality control organization, according to which all manufacturers that supply assembled goods are obliged to maintain ongoing inspection to see that the safety standards of the importing countries are observed. Both the inspection, which is carried out by an independent organization, and its results must be certified by written documents, which must be kept for a period of ten years.

The vast amount of data involved will be processed by computer. Although records will not have the signature of an inspector, they will still have legal force.

The desire on the part of exporting countries to maintain their prestige on the world market has been a major factor in the development of technical standards for production. For a variety of reasons the quality of products manufactured for domestic use is in a number of cases lower than that of the best models of analogous products put on the foreign market. Production feasibility for certain types of products and their related costs will be determined in particular by how industry has developed in the exporting countries and by natural conditions, sources of raw materials and energy, etc. — all of which make it economically inexpedient to manufacture the same version of the type of good in question for both the domestic and foreign markets.

In consideration of the above and drawing on the terminology of sections 15467-70 of the All-Union State Standards [AUSS], we can define the quality of a product produced for export as the totality of properties that satisfy the demands of the foreign consumer and assure its salability on a given market, to the mutual advantage of both buyer and seller.

Raising the economic effectiveness of exported goods is not the only reason to maintain their quality at a high level. As the socialist countries expand their foreign economic ties and take greater advantage of the international division of labor, the improved quality of their export products will exert an ever greater influence on the development of their domestic economies; and the larger number of sales contracts they are able to conclude because of this improvement will be a good measure of success for those branches of industry and those enterprises that turn out goods for the foreign market.

2. Quality Control of Export Products:
   The Most Important Conditions for
   Raising the Efficiency of Exports

The economic expediency of creating or manufacturing a product for export is determined by comparing the foreign exchange earnings brought in by its sale with the costs of developing, manufacturing, and selling it on the foreign market (design, raw materials, supplies and associated capital investments, outlays for equipment and wages, packaging, transport, maintaining the foreign trade apparatus, advertising, commissions paid to foreign trade organizations, etc.).

The degree to which the tasks confronting export transactions are fulfilled is given by the index of economic effectiveness:

$$X_э = \frac{B_э}{3_э} \text{ foreign exchange rubles/rubles,}$$

where: $X_э$ is the index of relative effectiveness of an export;
$B_э$ is net foreign exchange earnings from the export of a unit product (the price per unit of an exported product in foreign exchange rubles);
$3_э$ is total costs of production and transport (to the border) per unit of exported product.

In many cases other factors besides the above variables are also operative in determining the expediency of effecting export transactions: coordination with the importer, any special conditions involved in marketing a particular product, etc.

The formula is taken from "An Interim Method for Determining the Economic Effectiveness of Foreign Trade," approved by Gosplan USSR in March of 1968; it recommends that calculations be based on a simplified model of cost determination. As the Soviet economist V. V. Savost'ianov notes, "this model for assessing the cost of an article on the basis of its composition differs fundamentally from the model for wholesale prices currently used in the USSR. At the same time, the expansion of profit and loss accounting within the domestic economy requires that the conclusions of the planning agencies coincide with the interests of those carrying out the plans."[7] A new method for determining the economic effectiveness of foreign economic relations — including the effectiveness of exports — is now being developed.

In practice foreign trade organizations use the following formula to calculate the index of export effectiveness:

$$X_{эт} = \frac{\sum q(p^1 - e^1) \cdot 100}{\sum q(p - e)},$$

where: $X_{эт}$ is the index of financial effectiveness of the export of a given article (in %);
q is the quantity of articles;
p^1 is the contracted sale price;
e^1 is the cost per unit of marketing abroad;
p is the wholesale price to industry;
e is the cost per unit of marketing within the USSR.[8]

The current practice has been to leave the influence of product quality out of account when calculating the index of effectiveness.

When we determine that value of the quality index of an export product that maximizes earnings at a given level of cost, the mathematical problem involved belongs to the class of so-called calculus of variations.

In this kind of problem not all the conditions for solving it are known in advance, since besides the quality index, the magnitude of effectiveness also depends on fluctuations in supply and demand, fashion, the conditions under which the product is used, etc.

In its general form the effectiveness of an export is a function of three groups of factors. This can be expressed in the formula:

$$X_э = X_{эт}(C_1, C_2 \ldots; y_1, y_2 \ldots; x_1, x_2 \ldots).$$

We can formulate the problem as follows: Under known conditions C_1, C_2..., which represent the cost of achieving the required quality indices y_1, y_2..., and taking into account unknown conditions of the market that vary independently of our control and are difficult to predict in advance, we must find those values of the quality indices x_1, x_2..., that allow us to maximize the index of effectiveness $X_э$.

In the theory of operations research this problem is called "optimization of a solution under indeterminate conditions."

When the unknown quantities y_1, y_2... are factors whose distribution is at least roughly known, there are two methods that can be applied to determine the optimal solution:

reduction to a determined model;

"optimization of averages."[9]

Reduction to a determined model is carried out by replacing random factors with determinate ones — i.e., with their expected mathematical values.

This method can be used for making rough bilinear approximations when the index of effectiveness depends on random values.

"Optimization of averages" can be applied in cases where the values of the variables y_1, y_2 ... are widely scattered and replacing them with mathematically expected values can produce large errors.

A detailed description of possible solutions to the problem by using operations research can be found in the relevant literature.

Research carried out by the American specialists M. Shekoon and S. Chatterjee is a good example of how operations analysis can be used to build a model for the optimization of quality and price in a competitive market. The distinctive feature of this work is that the authors, applying game theory for the first time, incorporated into their model the psychology of the buyer, who often takes price as an index of quality, reasoning that a higher price indicates better quality.

Their models provide some idea of how far operations analysis can be applied to the modern marketing problems of determining quality, prices, and advertising costs. The practical use of this method requires a detailed study of data on previous sales volumes, the quality of the goods that were sold, their prices, and the forms of advertising used.

If quality control is to be based on a flexible system of standardization that can respond quickly to changes in world market-quality requirements for items of foreign trade, computers will have to be used to determine quality indices.

Quality control in general refers to the achievement and maintenance of the necessary level of quality throughout a product's development, production, and use (or consumption) by systematically supervising and adjusting the determining conditions and factors.

With regard to export products this control refers to the totality of interrelated organizational, technical, and economic measures whose primary aim is to raise export effectiveness. It therefore follows that at all stages in the quality control of export products, it is necessary to measure the costs of attaining a particular quality index against the actual or expected increase in the export prices.

With regard to the organization of quality control, the establishment of the necessary level of quality means ascertaining the quality requirements of foreign markets for the goods supplied to them and analyzing the quality of domestic products to be sent abroad.

Achieving the level of quality entails planning deliveries and producing or developing new products whose quality indices meet the demands of the foreign market.

Throughout the time that the foreign buyer works with (or uses) the product, its quality is kept up by providing technical maintenance, supplies of spare parts, and instructions and manuals for its use and application.

As we have shown, the Soviet Union now controls the quality of industrial products primarily through a set of standards, state certification of product quality on their basis, and state supervision to make sure that standards are being complied with.

Let us look more closely into how standardization and certification act to improve the quality of export products. Even before beginning negotiations over the purchase of goods, the buyer usually forms a clear idea of the range within which quality indices may fluctuate and still meet the needs of the consumer, in the process taking into account a series of factors that, in the majority of cases, are economic.

Product quality requirements can also depend on particular market conditions prevailing at the time a transaction is concluded, e.g., market trends, special quality specification required in the purchaser's country, the conditions of use, consumption and maintenance, tastes, habits, and so on.

Thus on February 1, 1972, a regulation came into force in

England introducing special control over the exportation to that country of oak and chestnut timber, to guard against the possibility of admitting certain types of insects and diseases. Belgium, Denmark, the Federal Republic of Germany, and the Netherlands apply hygienic controls not just to oak and chestnut but to all coniferous species exported to those countries. Oak and chestnut imported from the USSR will be subject to inspection by the English authorities and must bear appropriate certificates.

When a foreign commercial transaction is concluded, the quality of the goods is negotiated between the buyer and seller; it is usually fixed in the sales contract either by reference to a standard to be met or by specifying a number of the most important indicators.

By studying price data for goods with analogous or nearly analogous parameters or technical-economic indicators, the parties can reach agreement on price.

Among the data provided for in the order schedules that foreign trade organizations issue to the enterprises manufacturing export products are the quality requirements specified in the sales contract; if the order schedule does not stipulate any special conditions, product quality must conform to state standards and technical specifications, including those that specifically apply to goods supplied for the export market.

There are two possible types of export transaction. In the first the foreign buyer acquires goods that either already exist or are in serial production and whose quality indices are known in advance. Such goods are manufactured in accordance with the requirements set in existing norms and technical specifications.

In the second the products are either developed from scratch or further processed to meet the demands of the orderer. This is the case (a) when the standards of the selling country are inadequate or do not correspond to the needs of the purchaser, and (b) when the consumer wants the goods to be manufactured either according to the standards of his own country or to others he knows.

As with other industrially developed countries, the Soviet Union has a special system of technical standards and norms that sets quality requirements for export products. In the majority of cases they are either general requirements or supplement those in the basic All-Union State Standards and the technical specifications under which the goods are manufactured.

Thus sections 1015-69 of the AUSS, "Machinery, Equipment, and Instruments Supplied for Export" (replaced at the end of 1973 by resolution of the Scientific-Technical Committee of State Standards Board of the USSR), contain general standards for machinery and technical equipment supplied to foreign consumers. Sections 15140-69 define the design of machinery, instruments, and other technical products for different climate regions of the globe, different grades, and different conditions of use, storage, and transport in connection with environmental influence. These standards apply to both the design and manufacture of the articles in question.

Enterprises and ministries in charge of different branches of the economy work out special or additional technical standards for products designated for export.

In a number of cases the technical standards and norms specify that only one version of certain goods is to be issued for both the foreign and domestic markets.

In 1974 a decision was made to develop or revise more than 300 state standards then in use and about 200 technical norms and standards pertaining to products manufactured domestically, with a view toward creating a single set of standard specifications for particular products produced both for domestic consumption and for export.

The Soviet Union has also done considerable work in compiling a list of the most important types of export articles for which it is necessary to develop state standards of general specifications for products, materials, and assemblies, together with indicators that will ensure their competitiveness and conformity with the contemporary demands of the foreign market.

By standardizing the quality of export products at the government level, it is possible not only to raise the effectiveness of foreign trade as a whole but also to more intelligently select which product groups should be created especially for export.

The problem of earmarking special branches and enterprises to work exclusively (or primarily) for export is tied closely to the need to create special documentation (above all, standards for a branch as a whole) that will define indices for export products and set technical, economic, and legal norms for quality. Such work is being done both in the Soviet Union and in other socialist countries.

In line with the CMEA's Comprehensive Program for the Further Expansion and Improvement of Cooperation and the Development of Socialist Economic Integration between Members of the CMEA, recommendations are being worked out for standardizing the main indicators, so that national standards for products traded within the CMEA can be brought into line with one another. Checks and reviews of the CMEA recommendations for standardization, with a view toward bringing them technically up to world standards, are also provided for.

To standardize the quality indices of export products, industry, scientific research institutes, and foreign trade organizations must, as an integral part of the quality control process, coordinate their work on the basis of information about the quality of both domestic and foreign goods.

It is worth noting that foreign experience in creating special standards for export products testifies to the need to develop a flexible review system responsive to changes in world market requirements for product quality.

In a speech delivered to the Seventeenth Conference of European Quality Control Organizations, held in Belgrade in 1973, Professor K. Isikawa noted, with reference to quality control in Japan, that existing export standards worked out some years ago no longer reflect the requirements of the world market and have ceased to be an effective means for improving quality.

The most important form of government control over product quality is certification, a system used in thirty-two countries. The criterion widely used when evaluating a product for certification is whether it measures up to the standards and present-day requirements of the world market.

Under the Soviet system of certifying industrial products, a procedure has been set up by which newly developed products are placed in a higher category and are awarded the State Certificate of Quality if their technical and economic indices equal or exceed the optimal standards of domestic and foreign science and technology. This system plays a significant role in improving the quality of all domestic products, especially those manufactured for export.

Among the requirements of the state certification system is that it draw up and institutionalize a set of progressive standards. Along with their being responsible for government certification, the ministries of the USSR and the State Committee on Standards of the Council of Ministers of the USSR are in the process of drawing up and putting into operation new standards or altering those already in force. With a progressive system of standards, the quality indices to which certified products must conform are constantly being raised.

Getting products to pass state certification entails a complex network of tasks within which no small measure of importance is accorded to the systematic study of such factors as the demand of both domestic and foreign consumers for product quality; the conditions under which the products will be used; the competitive ability of exported goods; and shortcomings in and complaints about previously supplied products.

Foreign trade organizations play a prominent role in the collection and diffusion of information about all the requirements of the foreign market for product quality. In addition, the Ministry of Foreign Trade has obligatory representation on the commissions that certify products going for export.

Experience has shown that the export of products with a quality seal is economically more advantageous to production, the foreign trade organization, and the consumer, inasmuch as they have greater effectiveness in terms of both production and consumption.

Product certification with a quality seal and the export of

such articles are interrelated and have a substantial positive effect on raising the quality not only of certified goods but of all production. Enterprises that have been producing for export for a long time are usually in a better position to have their goods pass certification.

Nor is it just the system of state certification with a quality seal in itself which positively affects export product quality — the preparations for it within the factory through planning to raise product quality also play a role. In preparing for certification, enterprises incorporate into the shop, section, and department plan such things as measures to raise product quality, prevent defects, and forestall complaints (with an indication of the costs of carrying them out), how long it will take to fulfill them, the percentage of output ready for delivery on demand, values for the various quality indices, etc.

Thus internal certification of group and mass assembly units at the Lenin Komsomol Automobile Factory made it possible to improve the overall quality of the Moskvich so much that the factory was able to produce a single model that incorporated the needs of buyers in different countries.

Despite this, however, the requirements that must be met for certification do not always coincide with those demanded for exports.

There are a number of facts that underscore this problem: products with the quality seal that were not shipped abroad because they did not satisfy the needs of foreign consumers, cases of reported failures once the goods left the country even though they were certified as top quality, and unfavorable reports from representatives of the Ministry of Foreign Trade who have taken part in the work of the certification committees.

Supervision to see that the requirements are fulfilled concerning normative-technical documentation and quality control of export products are part and parcel of the general system of quality control and are carried out at all stages of product development, production, and utilization.

There are further levers for controlling the quality of export products: treating product quality as an element in price formation and providing material incentives to turn out better quality products; planning product quality at the industry or enterprise level; using contemporary methods of active control (the Saratov system of delivering products on demand, etc.) to technically regulate the quality of finished goods; keeping returns on the quality of manufactures.

Settlements for deliveries of export products between all-union associations and manufacturing enterprises are cleared at established domestic wholesale prices; appropriate markups are made depending on the model (whether it is domestic or export grade, for a tropical or northern zone, etc.), assembly, and so on. One form of material incentive is to pay the enterprises a bonus if they maintain their schedules and manufacture export products of particularly high quality.

Through the State Inspectorate for the Quality of Export Products, the Ministry of Foreign Trade is empowered to check that enterprises are properly using the money they are allocated to pay their workers bonuses for overseas deliveries.

Established procedures grant the State Inspectorate the further right to impose fines on those enterprises that sell export products that do not conform to standards and technical norms; the all-union associations are similarly entitled to withhold bonuses.

In a planned socialist economy targets and measures for raising product quality are an integral part of state plans and are formulated in accordance with the basic directions of development of the different branches of the economy, forecasts of technical progress, and the most effective methods for improving quality over the long term.

The basic tasks of planning quality improvement are: ensuring that product quality matches or exceeds that of the best domestic and foreign models; promptly replacing products that are becoming obsolete or withdrawing them from production; seeing to it that standards and other technical requirements are strictly adhered to and that all manufactured goods are of high quality.

The foreign buyer, of course, is not so much interested in

Quality Control

whether products conform to technical standard as in satisfying his needs; and so in planning the quality of products manufactured specially for export, most attention is devoted to improving their consumer properties.

Technical specifications for exported goods are coordinated with the foreign trade agencies.

The main shortcoming of the complex series of measures taken to regulate export quality is the absence of a uniform quality control system based on economic criteria.

To wind up our examination of what we mean by "export product quality," we can say that the most objective indicator of the quality of products delivered abroad is export effectiveness.

The problem of improving the quality of exports must be seen from two aspects: technical and economic.

Product quality is defined by the totality of the physical, chemical, electrical, and other properties that give a product its use value; these are the factors studied by the engineering sciences and product research. By comparing these properties with analogous properties of the same items as they are manufactured in other countries, we can define the level of technical perfection in terms of an international standard.

From an economic point of view it is important to attain the level of quality demanded by the foreign market in order to earn foreign exchange and to modify the costs of development and production. The economic aspect is an integral component of quality control of export products for another reason as well, namely, for setting up economic incentives for the manufacture of export products, since as things stand now, economic levers (prices, profit margins, bonuses, etc.) are the main instruments of quality control.

Both these aspects are closely interrelated and complementary. The totality of an export product's properties determines, along with other factors, export effectiveness; a peak effectiveness index means, in turn, that the product's quality is economically at its optimum.

The interrelatedness of the economic and technical aspects

of export product quality consists of the following list of items: costs of improving the quality of export products; the best quality for products produced for export; the level of quality demanded by the world market; foreign exchange earnings from sales. The second and third terms of the sequence constitute its technical profile; the first and fourth are economic.

The economic input is the cost of improving the quality of export products; the output is the foreign exchange earned from their sale. The inverse relation between them is reflected in the fact that selling better-quality products at higher foreign trade prices should increase the material profits of production.

We can therefore conclude that the main levers used by the state to control the quality of export products (standardization, certification, spot checks, on the one hand, and price formation, material incentives, and planning on the other) must be coordinated with export effectiveness, particularly with the size of foreign exchange receipts, which is a yardstick for measuring the level of quality of domestic products in the light of the latest achievements of world technology and the world economy.

One of the first steps in organizing quality control of exports is to develop evaluative techniques that will provide a working standard for determining the basic lines along which quality is to be improved.

A. Evaluating the quality of export-designated products

Quantitative assessments are necessary at all stages in the development, production, and use of export products, as well as in technical and economic calculations, as far as quality control of export products is concerned.

They involve:

— planning and projecting the quality of an export product, taking into account the requirements of foreign markets;

— determining the optimal level of quality. The optimum quality of an export product is that level which maximizes the difference between the amount of foreign exchange earned from its sale and its cost to the exporter;

— working out standards and technical specifications for the exported product;
— monitoring product quality;
— providing moral and material incentives to workers to turn out export products of high quality;
— studying the dynamics of quality;
— instructions for technical maintenance and use and development of recommended norms for spare parts;
— accounting and information on the quality of export products that have been manufactured and delivered;
— calculating domestic and foreign trade prices;
— calculating the actual effectiveness indices for an export product, including quality.

It follows from the concept of export product quality that the chief purpose of evaluating it is to determine ways to more completely satisfy the demands of foreign markets and, from this, to raise the economic effectiveness of the export and optimize the level of quality of exported goods.

Quality indices can be unitary, compound, or general. Unitary and compound indices respectively characterize either a product's individual properties or a number of them taken together; generalized indices characterize the general level of product quality, i.e., the economic effect and costs involved in improving the quality of finished products.

For each type of product it is necessary to specify which unitary, compound, or general indices (the last two calculated from the first) are to be used to assess quality. The reliability of quality assessments largely depends on a correct selection of the properties to be assessed and the quality indices appropriate to their evaluation.

Here one must keep in mind that the quality of a finished product depends both on the general properties specified in standards and technical norms during its design (i.e., the quality of the model, which determines the technical level of the finished production) and on the actual value of these properties reached in the actual process of production (i.e., on the quality of the product's manufacture). International comparisons are usually made in terms of the technical level of quality.

When evaluating export product quality it is necessary to define indices for:

— the general quality level of the specific type of product being turned out or developed in comparison with analogous products manufactured by competitors;

— the individual physical, chemical, and other properties imparted to the product during the production process in accordance with the specification of standards and technical norms;

— the individual consumer properties of the article (product), taking into account its function, type of model, and conditions of use (consumption);

— the real economic effectiveness of exporting the given product, taking into account its quality.

Quality indices are subdivided into the following basic groups: function, reliability and durability, standardization, esthetic, ergonomic, patent rights, individual safety, and biological and chemical (i.e., social) safety.

Detailed descriptions of the indicators that enter into each of the above-listed groups and their methods of determination can be found in the literature on estimating the quality of industrial products. What is special about the quality indices of export products is that their levels are dictated by the demands of the foreign market and the interests of the exporter.

Be that as it may, the possibility of using these indices to evaluate the quality of an export product will primarily depend on the prompt receipt and collection of information both about its properties during all phases of design, manufacture, storage, and consumption, and their related costs, and about the demands of the foreign market and actual earnings of foreign exchange.

The properties of a product demanded by consumers on a given market are determined by analyzing the competitive data on product quality sent in by the USSR's trade representatives abroad or received from foreign firms and by analyzing information and communications from authorized foreign trade

Quality Control

organizations and industrial specialists, inquiries made by potential buyers, opinions on the quality of delivered goods, and so on.

The main sources of information on prices are contracts, price lists, offers tendered by competitors, economics and statistical periodicals, customs and excise statistics, etc.

Defining the relationship between the quality indices of goods and their export prices means identifying the goods in greatest demand on a given market and then locating those properties that determine the possibility of selling them at their existing prices.

Foreign trade practice shows that for the majority of goods there are basic quality indicators whose change will have a marked effect on the level of export prices.

Thus the following relationship is used to calculate the foreign trade prices of machinery and technical equipment:

$$ Ц_1 : Ц_2 = (N_1 : N_2)^n, $$

where: $Ц_1$ and $Ц_2$ are the prices of assembled units;
l and N_2 are capacity;
is an exponent that expresses the dependence of price on the capacity or productivity of the machine.

The magnitude of the exponent has a wide range of values for different pieces of machinery and technical equipment, from 0.2 to 0.9.

Questions concerning the relationship between prices and product quality indices have been the focus of attention of specialists for some time.

> The creation of high-quality products depends on the ability to correctly estimate their quality at different stages; i.e., during the formulation of technical specifications, the development of a working draft, the manufacture of prototypes, and finally, the finished product.
>
> To establish the correct interrelation between price

and product quality, it is equally necessary to know how to use numerical techniques. Thus the requirements of price formation urgently demand that scientifically sound quantitative methods of estimating quality be developed.[10]

Here we are particularly interested in the use of modern-day computer techniques to collect and analyze information about both a product's quality and the economic indices of its production, sale, and consumption.

The dependence of price on quality is often determined by equations that provide a quantitative assessment of the influence of each product parameter on price.

The general equation for the dependence of price on a product's technical and economic parameters can be written as follows:

$$Y = a_0 \cdot X_1^{a_1} \cdot X_2^{a_2} \ldots X_\kappa^{a_\kappa},$$

where: Y is the product price;
   $X_1, X_2, \ldots X_\kappa$ are the technical and economic parameters of the product;
   $a_1, a_2, \ldots a_\kappa$ are the exponents of the respective technical and economic parameters;
   a_0 is constant.

It is especially convenient if the price-parameter relationship is linear and can be expressed by a linear regression equation:

$$Y = a_0 + a_1 X_1 + a_2 X_2 + \ldots a_\kappa X_\kappa,$$

where: Y is the price of the product;
   $X_1, X_2, \ldots X_\kappa$ are the parameters of the product;
   $a_1, a_2, \ldots a_\kappa$ are the coefficients of the equation;
   a_0 is constant.

The values of the equation coefficients allow us to measure quantitatively the influence of each parameter on the product's price. Thus the dependence of price on the technical and economic parameters of a caterpillar tractor, for example, can be expressed by the following equation:

$$Y = 204.68X_1 + 66.20X_5 + 459.60X_7 + 177.98X_{15} + 390.65,$$

where: Y is the price of the good (in appropriate money units);
   X_1 is the weight of the tractor (in metric tons);
   X_5 is engine capacity (in horsepower);
   X_7 is cylinder volume (in cubic centimeters);
   X_{15} is maximum haulage power (in metric tons).

The constant accounts for the effect on price movement of other factors not specified in the equation.

With this equation it is possible not only to determine the weight of each parameter in forming the price of a tractor but to calculate the prices of tractors manufactured in other countries.

D. S. L'vov cites several equations expressing the relationship between technical parameters of production and prices.[11]

Regression equations yielding a price-quality relationship for machine tools and computers have been worked out at the Institute of World Economics and International Relations of the USSR Academy of Sciences. The equations were derived from data provided by the "Stankoimport" and "Elektronorgtekhnika" all-union associations.

In the United States this method has been used to construct appropriate indices for studying the levels and movements of competitive prices in international trade.

The economists I. Kravis and R. Lipsey[12] provide examples of how regression analysis is applied to the prices and specifications of outboard motors (studying over 100 models from six countries over a period of two years), tractors (using information provided by six American firms on 61 tractors), power transformers, locomotives, Japanese-built ships (using data from 205 ships contracted to Japanese shipyards), and commercial and private motor vehicles.

Also of interest is the use of regression techniques to construct time indices and geographic indices for the sale of passenger cars. The basic data consisted of more than 1,000 price lists on American cars and 700 price lists on cars from five other countries for the six years over which the study was made (1953, 1957, 1961, 1962, 1963, and 1964). The automobiles that were studied represented at least 95 percent of automobile output in each of the countries investigated. The technical characteristics included weight, length, capacity (in horsepower), engine size, number of cylinders, presence of automatic transmission, and the number of doors. The volume of production was also taken into account.

In a number of cases empirically constructed nomograms have proved useful in determining price-quality dependence.[13]

The USSR Ministry of Foreign Trade has developed methods for calculating the dependence of price on technical and economic indices for several types of complex machinery and technical equipment (airplanes, ships, electric power stations, etc.). For less-complicated goods prices are calculated by comparing competitive bids.

The ability to determine product prices on the basis of their technical parameters warrants raising the converse problem — how to determine the level of quality by comparing the prices of analogous goods.

In his book New Forms of Competitive Struggle in Contemporary Capitalism, V. I. Sedov notes that it is possible to use prices calculated from regression equations to obtain quality indices reflecting price relations for a product as expressed in a given currency.[14]

Ph. Cagan, the American specialist, talks in a similar vein about the widely accepted method of measuring quality differences between two versions of the same good by comparing their prices when they are sold concurrently on the open market.[15]

Providing that there is sufficient statistical data, it is therefore possible to derive equations that correlate the market prices of goods with their basic parameters. This in turn makes it possible to estimate the level of quality of a good by comparing the totality of its parameters and its price with those of a comparable item that has been taken as a standard.

Nevertheless, present-day competition between individual monopolies and nonmonopolistic capitals (be they large, medium, or small) has created a situation where estimation of a good's quality on the basis of its price on a particular market is often beset by a number of difficulties.

In many cases prices will depend on other factors besides a good's quality, such as the relation between supply and demand, the level of technical maintenance and supplies of spare parts, the tax system, customs imposts, fashion and consumer tastes, the insurance system, and so on.

There are any number of reasons that can cause two qualitatively identical versions of the same good to be sold simultaneously at different — and sometimes widely divergent — prices.

Many foreign firms intentionally list prices that are deliberately wrong, without any indication of how a shipment was made up. At other times prices are set simply in error, without adequate economic justification.

Iu. Ia. Iakovets and E. I. Punin note in their book <u>Price and Quality</u> that foreign firms maintain a flexible system of pricing, mainly through the use of discounts. It is the opinion of these specialists that there are dozens of different ways in which discounts are offered in capitalist countries. Aside from reductions for buying in quantity or serial discounts for large sales, the most commonly used are discounts to dealers, bonuses, discounts on exports, special discounts, and discounts for paying in cash.

A more objective indicator of how the market actually evaluates product quality can be found in the prices of items of mass consumption. These prices do not depend on the will of the manufacturer but are set by the consumer, who is more interested in economic results than in fashion.

In the United States prices on this category of goods are widely used to determine the level of quality (both present and as it is projected to change over time) of such items as automobiles, machines for mass production, airplanes, and widely owned consumer durables.

It is interesting that in many cases regression analysis shows no significant difference between price-quality correlations of new and second-hand goods, so that this difference can thus be ignored. Z. Griliches notes that the relative weights of technical parameters given by equations based on current automobile prices are in the majority of cases practically identical with those obtained from similar equations for automobiles produced one year before.[16]

Generally speaking, estimation of the quality of a given export product involves:

— defining those properties of the product that have been determined by the demands of the foreign market;

— establishing the relationship between the quality indices of goods sold on a particular market and their export prices;

— selecting a list of quality indices needed to estimate the product's quality and choosing the methods for their measurement;

— determining the base values of the quality indices;

— determining the real quality index values for the product being assessed;

— comparing the quality indices of the product with the corresponding base values;

— providing economic grounds for industrial recommendations;

— determining the extent to which the properties of the good under analysis correspond to the demands of the market.

The choice of a list of indicators for making an assessment depends on the nature of the problem that the investigator is dealing with.

Thus in order to forecast the quality of an export product, one must know which are its most likely markets and how demand and consumption will develop over time; from there the quality indices can be selected that will prove most decisive in getting the product sold.

In order to determine the optimal level of quality, primary attention is given to those indices that have the greatest weight in setting domestic and foreign prices.

Quality Control

When it comes to choosing the base indicators that are to serve as the point of comparison, some problems can turn up.

It is usual when estimating the level of quality of export products to take standard indices as the base indicators.

There are a number of possible standards of export product quality that can be applied here: an actually existing product whose sale on a given market is most economically advantageous to the exporter; a hypothetical product whose quality would maximize the satisfaction of both exporters' and importers' needs; or a standard selected from the buyer's own country.

When determining the general quality of a given type of product (whether it is being put on the market or developed) by comparing it with analogous products manufactured by competitors, the evaluation should be made by measuring the totality of the basic technical and economic quality indices against the same indicators for the product that has been chosen as a standard. Where there is sufficient statistical information available to derive regression equations for the relationship between the contract prices of homogeneous goods and their basic parameters, the evaluation can be made by comparing prices rather than the totality of technical indices (this cannot be done when dealing with a new product just coming onto the market, since there the exporter sets prices mainly on the basis of market conditions and other considerations). In this type of assessment prices must be suitably corrected for the influence that other factors exert on price formation (the commercial and political climate, market trends, the tax system, foreign exchange rates, etc.), so as to reduce them to comparable magnitudes.

One of the methods State Standards Board of the USSR recommends for making compound evaluations of the level of product quality is to use an integral index, which can be represented as a ratio of the total useful effect obtained from the utilization of the product to the total costs incurred in creating and consuming it:

$$K_и = \frac{П}{З_с + З_{п.п.}},$$

where: $П$ is total useful effect;

$З_c$ is costs of creating the product;

$З_{п.п.}$ is costs of consuming the product.

Only the foreign consumer can calculate the total useful effect of a product put on the foreign market. The useful effect for the exporter is what is left after taking the foreign exchange earned from selling the product (equal to the contract price) and deducting any outlays that might be made on marketing it outside his own country and any losses suffered because the level of quality was inadequate or the goods were defective. In this case the formula assumes the form:

$$K_э = \frac{B_э}{З_э},$$

where: $K_э$ is the integral quality index of the export product;

$B_э$ is net foreign exchange earnings from the export of a unit good;

$З_э$ is total costs of producing a unit product and transporting it to the border.

This formula for the integral quality index of an export product is none other than the formula for the relative index of effectiveness of exporting a unit product. It is necessary to use comparative values when calculating the relative integral index.

The integral quality index of an export product can for practical purposes be written as:

$$K_э = \frac{B - B_д - B_y - B_o - B_p}{C + З_6},$$

where: B is contract price in foreign exchange;

$B_д$, B_y, B_o, B_p are expenditures (or price reduction) in foreign exchange associated respectively with: poor-quality manufacture and the elimination of factory defects; raising the quality of the product to the level demanded by the given market;

pre- and postsale maintenance; selling the product (advertising, agents' commissions, delivery expenses, etc.);

C is industrial wholesale price or cost price in rubles;

3 is additional expenditures on eliminating defects, including those discovered during state quality inspection.

All the indices that enter into this formula are average values, calculated per unit product. Some of them can be used. as direct indices of the product's technical level and of the quality of its manufacture.

Depending on the aim of the investigation, it is also possible to assess export product quality by applying unitary indices or index numbers for defects; in this case the "weight" of the defect must be determined on the basis of economic indicators.

B. <u>Quality control of export products. The work of the State Inspectorate for the Quality of Export Products of the Ministry of Foreign Trade</u>

Quality control is usually taken to mean the verification of how well the product's quality indices correspond to established requirements throughout its design, manufacture, and utilization.

As in other technologically developed countries, quality inspection in the Soviet Union is an integral part of quality control and is performed by intra- and suprafactory agencies in charge of the inspection, supervision, and receipt of products to see that they conform to specifications.

Intrafactory agencies inspecting product quality include technical supervisory services, technical inspectorates of enterprises, factory laboratories, and weights and measures offices.

Intrafactory technical control offices are mainly responsible for seeing that the factory's products conform to the requirements of state standards, the norms for that branch of industry, technical conditions, and design and measurement specifications. Enterprise technical control offices also check that technology is kept up to par throughout all stages of production, check on the quality of raw materials, supplies, and assemblies, and take part in receiving and checking prototypes of basic products.

As an organizational subdivision of the enterprise, the technical control office must ensure that all of the Soviet Union's quality requirements are enforced within the factory, including those that apply specially to products turned out for export.

Both suprafactory departmental supervision and state supervision of quality are done by agencies of the State Committee for Standards of the USSR Council of Ministers and by state and branch inspectorates belonging to the various ministries and administrative departments. The work of these organizations, as well as the activity of popular supervisory agencies, constitute the basic methods of control within the state system of quality control. It is worth mentioning that even though social control takes on ever greater importance as socialist society develops, this in no way means that state supervision in the USSR plays a weaker role in seeing to the observance of product-quality requirements.

Quality inspection is carried out at the state level by a number of independent institutes for checking and supervision.

The legal position of these institutes (inspectorates) is defined in each separate case by decision either of the government or of a plenipotentiary government agency for the establishment of state inspectorates, and by the regulations concerning the organization in question promulgated within the given decision.

In carrying out their functions, the state inspectorates act in the name of the state; their authority to carry out checks and supervision extends to all enterprises, organizations, and institutions whose activity is concerned with meeting the requirements of juridical and technical norms under the given inspectorate's supervision.

Despite their separate legal status, state inspectorates can, depending on the nature of their work, either be subordinated to particular ministries or be completely independent, acting as a department with special rights within governmental institutions.

The state supervisory bodies with the greatest authority to introduce and enforce standards and technical conditions are the agencies of the State Committee for Standards of the Council of Ministers of the USSR. They are empowered to make spot checks on the quality of all types of products, as well as on the techniques of measurement and checking used in their production; their checks extend to enterprises, organizations, depots, and warehouses. Similarly, they have authority to prohibit the delivery of products that do not conform to established requirements and to apply economic sanctions if they discover that products have been sold which were manufactured in violation of technical standards and norms.

Besides the specialists from the ministries and from manufacturer and consumer departments, the State Committee for Standards has the right to enlist representatives from enterprises and quality inspectorates into its supervisory activities.

The USSR has a number of special organizations whose job is to supervise and control compliance with the established state norms and regulations that define the requisite quality of different products, including those designated for export.

They include the State Inspectorate of Mine Engineering of the USSR, the USSR Union Registry, the Soviet Naval Ministry, the State Grain Inspectorate of the Ministry for Procurements of the USSR, and a number of others.

The state inspectorates have full powers to organize and carry out the supervision and control of product quality within enterprises and to apply coercive measures when the latter violate the established norms and regulations.

Inspectorate representatives have the right of unlimited access to the units under their supervision for the purposes of performing inspections and obtaining necessary records and information.

On the basis of the data obtained by these checks and inspections, inspectors draw up a balance sheet of the violations they uncover and the reasons for them and request the management of the unit in question to rectify them.

The requests are usually presented as acts, rulings, or directives. These documents have the force of administrative rulings, and the enterprises being checked are obliged to carry them out.

Responsibility for checking the quality of export products falls to a special agency, the State Inspectorate for the Quality of Export Products of the Ministry of Foreign Trade (with the exception of certain types of products, such as cereals, furs, live animals, etc., which have their own specific features and are specially checked). Equivalent agencies exist abroad.

The state has two main tasks in controlling the quality of export products:
— to prevent defective goods from being shipped abroad;
— to secure improvements in export product quality.

Looking at the history of state control, we see that the agencies involved have always linked their work directly to industry's efforts to improve product quality, as well as to the development of our country's foreign economic relations.

Currently the most salient aspect to the improvement of the state system of control is the gradual transition from the simple inspection of export products to participation in actual quality control.

What role the state inspectorate plays in controlling the quality of exports is determined by what stage of the work is involved:
— it helps prepare for the production of products for export by assisting in the testing of prototypes, in the work of interdepartmental committees, and in the state certification of products;
— it ensures that manufacture is up to required quality by checking the quality of materials, parts, assemblies, and export products at all stages in their production; by checking on the status of the planned measures for improving product quality and their fulfillment by enterprises; by participating in test series, etc. On the basis of their findings the state control agencies draw up reports and proposals for presentation to

Quality Control

the agencies for industrial management or to higher levels;

— it guarantees that product quality will be maintained during transport, storage, and processing prior to shipment to the foreign consumer through its inspection of ports and rail distribution depots.

As the tasks of the state checking system indicate, the effectiveness of the inspectorate's work can be measured in terms of the level of product quality that is attained as a result of its actions.

One possible index of the effectiveness of checking is the ratio of the additional foreign exchange earned as a result of the activity of the checking agency to the costs of the checking system, of eliminating defects, and of raising product quality.

Other indices that provide a relative measure of the level of a good's quality, and hence of the effectiveness of checking, are:

— the number of complaints that the foreign consumer makes about the quality of a product and the total monetary losses involved in satisfying them;

— the number and character of defects discovered at different stages of state checks that require the product either to be returned for further work or to be withdrawn from export; the percentage of output not permitted to be shipped;

— the stability of manufacturing quality attained as a result of the checks.

In the course of their work, the various subdivisions of the State Inspectorate make use of the most advanced methods of quality control, including statistical verification and different forms of assessing and analyzing information gathered during the processes of checking and inspection. Nevertheless, the fact that our foreign trade activity lacks a unified system for ensuring the receipt, collection, collating, and processing of all existing data on the quality of exported goods means that the state checking system does not permit control of the quality of our export products at the level of contemporary requirements.

For this reason it was proposed that an information and inquiry system be developed and installed for the State Inspectorate for Quality Control (IIS-SIQ).

The aim of creating the IIS-SIQ is to ensure collection and analysis of all information on quality possessed by the suprafactory agencies that supervise quality control and all of the data received during the process of a good's use (consumption) abroad.

As a complex of administrative and mathematical economic techniques, computer technology, and communications facilities, the IIS-SIQ allows the central apparatus of the State Inspectorate to more rationally manage the work of its local agencies and to more intelligently select the basic directions in which the state quality control system can be improved.

It is envisaged that the information provided by this system will enable the workers in the State Inspectorate to make appropriate decisions, prepare proposals, and bring them to the attention of the enterprises and organizations. In the long run the IIS-SIQ should serve as a basis for incipient efforts to develop an automatic control system by the state quality control system (ACS-SIQ).

The creation of the IIS-SIQ was prompted by the fact that the rapid growth in the Soviet Union's exports, the changes that have taken place in their structure, and the development of trade with such countries as the United States, the Federal Republic of Germany, France, and Japan all demand that quality be checked more effectively. To raise the effectiveness of state quality control it will first be necessary to determine how far this system goes toward fulfilling the tasks confronting the Soviet Union's foreign trade and then proceed to plan both what is to be inspected and the forms and methods by which checking is to be done. With the situation that exists at the moment, the amount of technical information that the State Inspectorate receives is insignificant, and the amount of economic data it receives is for all practical purposes nonexistent. In order to acquire the information that is needed — both from state inspectors and from abroad — the necessary conditions must be created: forms must be drawn up, proper instructions given as to how to fill them in, etc. To increase the quantity of information coming into the State Inspectorate and to improve the prospects of obtaining it in significantly large volume, data will have to be processed by computer. Computer processing will substantially reduce the time lag between when a product is put on the market and when information on the results of its use (consumption) is received.

The installation of such a system will make it possible to obtain sufficient data to meet the needs not only of the government control agency but also those of enterprises, ministries, agencies, and foreign trade organizations for the quality control of export products. The use of computers to collect and process information on the quality of goods will make it possible to incorporate, where necessary, a "quality" subsystem into the ACS currently being developed by the Ministry of Foreign Trade.

The first stage in the creation of the IIS-SIQ must be to develop a system capable of collecting information on the results of state checks on a particular product, the elimination of its defects, and the refinishing that has to be done on the product abroad. In addition, the system must be able to present appropriate quarterly reports.

During the second stage it is proposed to expand the system and to both collect and analyze information on basic methods used at the supraplant level for quality control of various types of products (including clients' agents) and to issue questionnaires for the different branches of the economy, for different countries of destination, and for all-union associations.

The third step in developing and setting up the IIS-SIQ will be to organize the collection, collation, and analysis of data on the quality of Soviet goods delivered abroad. This work should be based on a precise calculation of economic indices (foreign expenditures on quality per unit of output, foreign exchange losses incurred through removing defects in production, the integral quality index, etc.).

The IIS-SIQ consists of a functional and a service part. The functional part includes subsystems for technical and economic information on the quality of exported goods and for records and accounts on current operations. The other part of the IIS-SIQ provides informational, mathematical, and technical services.

The general principle used in designing the IIS-SIQ was that used in setting up the technical facilities for an ACS in the Ministry of Foreign Trade, i.e., a unified informational base for the system and centralized data processing, using the technology available at the Ministry of Foreign Trade computer center ("System 4-50").

There are also local units belonging to the State Inspectorate responsible for the following functions:

— to take the masses of information that have been examined and sorted out and collect and prepare them for the computer;

— to transfer this information to the computer center for further processing;

— to autonomously decide on day-to-day tasks and to duplicate the information processed by the computer center.

The preparatory work that went into setting up the IIS-SIQ has made it possible not only to specify and plan how long it would take to carry out the basic steps involved in its development but also to identify a number of new directions in which the government quality control of export products could be improved. One such improvement was to draw up a standard format for the quarterly reports submitted by local departments; this will facilitate the compilation of records and make it possible for the central apparatus of the State Inspectorate to maintain up-to-date information on the results of its work until such time as the IIS-SIQ is in a position to handle these data. Similarly, State Inspectorate document forms were standardized, a method for coding all incoming information was developed, and the basic stores of data on enterprises, products of various countries, subbranches of industry, reasons for defects, State Inspectorate personnel, and so on, were created.

In line with this plan and in light of the quantity of incoming information, it was decided to test the system by collecting information on the quality of automobiles produced at the Volga Car Factory. This decision was made official in the appropri-

Quality Control

ate protocols between the Volga Car Factory, V/O "Avtoeksport," and the State Inspectorate.

A number of conclusions follow from the above discussion.

Since quality is often the most important determinant of whether a product will be successfully sold, and thus of whether foreign trade fulfills the tasks required of it, there is currently an urgent need to create a unified system for controlling the quality of export products.

Both in developing a system of state standards for export products (currently done by the State Board for Standards together with the Ministry of Foreign Trade) and in certification of export products, account should be taken of a product's technical properties and the economic results obtained by selling it on the foreign market.

The calculation of the costs of eliminating specific faults and raising a product's quality to the level demanded by a given market, and of the outlays that would be required to improve it on the basis of information regularly received from abroad, makes it possible to make running technical-economic estimates of the actual quality of individual goods and to determine the optimum level of quality for particular products manufactured for export.

State quality control of export products plays an indispensable role in foreign trade activity. By ensuring that the economic effectiveness of exports continues to rise and that the Soviet Union's prestige on the world market is not damaged by the delivery of poor-quality products, and moreover, by its adoption of positive measures to raise product quality, it occupies a central position in the system of measures applied for the quality control of export goods.

As far as export goods are concerned, the following basic measures can be taken to improve the effectiveness of state quality control of exports:

— applying up-to-date forms and methods of product quality control and analyzing their results;

— making objective technical-economic evaluations both of how well the inspected products have been manufactured and of the consumer quality of goods sent to the foreign consumer; comparing the results of these evaluations and using them to determine the effectiveness of state controls;

— selecting the main points around which work is to be oriented, using as its starting point the level of quality of export goods actually achieved by industry (selecting which items are to be inspected, taking part in drawing up and implementing measures to raise the quality of finished products, supplies, and assemblies, drawing up proposals for submission to agencies in charge of industrial management, etc.);

— upgrading the setup and supervision of staffs, the training of specialists employed as state inspectors, taking into account that the nature of the activities performed by state agencies responsible for overseeing the quality of export products is changing and broadening in scope.

Government control of export quality is part of the overall mechanism of export product quality control. If it is to have proper economic criteria for performing its assigned tasks, modern methods must be used to collect and analyze technical and economic data on product quality and to use this information to make decisions on how to utilize the material and labor reserves of the local supervisory agencies. Setting into motion a system for gathering information being developed by the State Inspectorate for the Quality of Export Products under the Ministry of Foreign Trade would make it possible to do away with having to rely on fragmentary information on product quality and to replace it with the systematic, computerized collection and analysis of all available data. To set up the IIS-SIQ it will be essential to work out (or use already developed) classifiers for enterprises, products, defects, countries, etc., so that the data can be coded for storage and processing by computer.

CONCLUSION

The preceding investigation points up the timeliness and importance of the question of the development of foreign trade. By posing it we have been able to shed some light on the tasks and functions of foreign trade management and to define the driving forces behind its development. Obviously much remains unresolved. Still, we can say that we have taken one major step: we have described the administration of foreign trade and have delimited the problems with which it must cope. The problem now is to unveil how, and along what basic lines, that administration can be improved — that is, the forms and methods of organizing labor. This is a unique "social imperative" determined by peculiarities and practical requirements of developing foreign trade.

The fact is that the present and future development of foreign trade are an integral part of historically larger tasks being addressed by the Soviet people — tasks whose solution lies in organically joining the achievements of the scientific-technical revolution to the advantages of a socialist economic system. So far as foreign trade is concerned, this means finding the most effective means and methods of harnessing the potential advantages of the international division of labor, particularly that within the socialist world.

As has been spelled out in the recommendations of scientific-technical conferences on the scientific organization of labor and management in foreign trade, to do this requires the further extension of planning in foreign trade; improvements in the organizational structure of its administration (i.e., the system must be made more amenable to managerial control, the operational efficiency of its most important structural elements must be raised, and the multiplicity of steps involved in preparing and making decisions has to be reduced); the consistent application of profit-and-loss accounting; the intensification of moral and material incentives to prompt foreign trade agencies and workers to improve the economic indices of their performance and to work out and apply more ambitious planning targets.

One important step in this direction will be the more efficient management of relations between industrial and foreign trade organizations; this will come when they both see that the production of export products with high profitability is in their mutual interest. At present dealings between the two are seen to by the several main product aministrations and all-union associations; this is as it should be, since it merely expresses what is obviously the objective situation at the moment.

The negative side of this type of organization is that questions of improving relations with industry are not decided in any comprehensive fashion, but episodically, as they arise. The reason is that there is no agency within the Ministry of Foreign Trade capable of generalizing the experience of these dealings and of transcending the piecemeal preoccupation with narrow departmental problems in order to approach the job of improving them from the point of view of the interests of the system as a whole.

We are not just talking about inducing industrial enterprises to produce goods for export. What is needed is a wide range of measures, including the working out of a uniform technical and commercial policy for the export of Soviet products.

Here we stand in complete accord with the view of Deputy Minister of Foreign Trade N. N. Smeliakov that

> industrial might is no longer enough to stimulate exports. The scientific-technical revolution demands research, design and engineering, and care in the production and sale

Conclusion

of a product, as well as in its technical maintenance and servicing. There is also a time factor involved. Whoever swiftly adapts production to the demands of the buyer, whoever offers the widest range of appropriate technical services, whoever thinks ahead to the needs of tomorrow will win on the world market. Long-term success requires serious forecasting and anticipation of long-term tendencies and of the necessary preparation for production and commercial services. In short, a whole series of measures is called for.[1]

Without this the efforts that the foreign trade divisions have made to develop exports — especially those of machinery and equipment — will not produce the desired results. From this it follows that with foreign trade expanding in quantity and scale and with the increasing diversity of both products and the ways and means of exporting and importing them, to manage foreign trade means to forecast. And the more long-term and precise the forecasts, the easier it will be to manage.

Yet we often find a situation in which the heads of foreign trade divisions are so mired in day-to-day work that they have no time to look into the future. In other cases we have numbers of division heads who believe that forecasting is something to be left to higher levels of administration. Obviously there is no need to prove that either of these tendencies is less than healthy: the division head who indulges in forecasting (regardless of whether he has time for it) will invariably come up against "unforeseen circumstance," emergency situations, etc.

All of this means that any improvement must be premised on due account being taken of present and future changes in the development of foreign trade. In other words, the system of management must maintain maximum possible correlation between the organizational structure of the system and the nature of foreign trade processes. It is for this reason that it is so important to develop an overall design for managing foreign trade. Such a design must build on the new technical facilities that the scientific-technical revolution has made available to management, on new methods of management, and of course, on suitably trained managerial personnel.

Technical office equipment, the material underpinnings of management, ranges from computer and reproduction techniques to means of communication. Heading the list are computers, which greatly expand the technical capacities of management. Together with various mathematical tools and organizational measures, computers constitute the foreign trade automatic control system. However, the introduction of an automatic control system in the Ministry of Foreign Trade will have an effect only if it goes beyond traditional management procedures and concentrates on those managerial problems which, by virtue of their scope, have not been solved and have, as a result, led to the irrational use of financial and labor resources.

And so while in the first case the use of an automatic control system to deal with traditional tasks may speed up paperwork and reduce the number of managerial personnel, in the second case the main effect will come not from economizing on the labor expended on managerial work but from a fundamental improvement in the process of management itself. It is therefore extraordinarily important that the development and installation of an automatic control system be directed by top-level leadership.

In the Ministry of Foreign Trade such ideological and organizational leadership for this work comes from the level of the deputy minister of foreign trade of the USSR. This is as it should be, since the question of radically improving the methods of management of foreign trade could not even be formulated, let alone solved. Foreign experience also testifies to the importance and necessity for the installation of an automated control system to be directed by top-level personnel. In his article "The Advantages of Systems," Academician D. M. Glushkov points to the experience of Japan. Wherever company leadership was directly involved in drawing up and instituting an automated control system, the economic effect was considerable (profits rose by 10 to 40 percent). Where responsibility was entrusted to second-rank personnel, the result was insignificant (a few percent) or altogether lacking.

The use of computers and other technical equipment must necessarily lead to essential changes in the forms, methods, and style of work in the administrative apparatus. The methods of mathematical economics, particularly grid models, deserve a prominent place in this work.

Finally, the third element that must be considered when developing a general design for management, and which for all practical purposes will determine the effectiveness of the entire administrative system, is the training of managerial personnel, particularly divisional heads. Hence it is customary to treat any social expenditures on the training of highly skilled managerial personnel as always justified and as yielding the highest returns. This is why it is so important to incorporate into the general design the skill requirements for leading personnel, a specific description of the work they will do, the scope and nature of the knowledge they need, and consequently, the nature of the specialized and advanced training they should undergo.

All of these elements must be provided in the general design systematically. They cannot be treated in isolation, either from one another or from the overall organization of foreign trade.

NOTES

In Lieu of a Preface

1. L. I. Brezhnev, Leninskim kursom. Rechi i stat'i, vol. 1, Moscow, 1970, p. 211.
2. V. I. Lenin, Polnoe sobranie sochinenii, vol. 15, p. 368.
3. L. I. Brezhnev, Leninskim kursom. Rechi i stat'i, vol. 2, Moscow, 1970, p. 522.

Chapter 1

1. V. I. Lenin, Polnoe sobranie sochinenii, vol. 3, p. 56.
2. See Tibor Kiss, Problemy sotsialisticheskoi integratsii stran SEV, Moscow, 1971, p. 22.
3. See Moskovskaia pravda, November 11, 1973.
4. See Izvestia, April 14, 1973.
5. See Naukovedenie i informatika, ninth issue, Kiev, 1973, p. 80.
6. Ibid., p. 81.
7. See Pravda, March 3, 1972.
8. Vizit L. I. Brezhneva v Soedinennye Shtaty, Moscow, 1973, p. 79.
9. See Veneshniaia torgovlia SSSR za 1973 god. Statisticheskii obzor, Moscow, 1974.
10. L. I. Brezhnev, O vneshnei politike KPSS i Sovetskogo

gosudarstva. Rechi i stat'i, Moscow, 1973, p. 507.

11. SU 1918 g., no. 33, article 432; Vneshniaia torgovlia, 1968, no. 4, pp. 2-3.

12. See L. A. Feonova, M. L. Postolenko, and S. P. Nikitin, Organizatsiia i tekhnika vneshnei torgovli SSSR, Moscow, 1974, pp. 8-9.

13. See K. G. Voronov, K. A. Pavlov, and V. A. Pripol'tsev, Uchebnye materialy po kursu "Organizatsiia i tekhnika vneshnei torgovli," Moscow, 1970.

Chapter 2

1. V. I. Lenin, Polnoe sobranie sochinenii, vol. 42, p. 290.
2. Materialy XXIV s"ezda KPSS, Moscow, 1971, pp. 68-69.
3. S. Kovalevskii, Rukovoditel' i podchinennyi, Moscow, 1973, p. 17.
4. Materialy XXIV s"ezda KPSS, p. 69.
5. Ibid., p. 68.

Chapter 3

1. O. V. Kozlova and I. N. Kuznetsov, Nauchnye osnovy upravleniia proizvodstvom, Moscow, 1970, p. 70.
2. B. Gurnei, Vvedenie v nauku upravleniia, Moscow, 1969, p. 161.
3. See V. G. Vishniakov, Struktura i shtaty organov sovetskogo gosudarstvennogo upravleniia, Moscow, 1972; Funktsii i struktura organov upravleniia, ikh sovershenstvovanie, edited by G. Kh. Popov, Moscow, 1973.
4. See Vnutrifirmennoe planirovanie v SShA, Moscow, 1972, pp. 41-43.
5. S. M. Kirov, Izbrannye stat'i i rechi, Moscow, 1957, pp. 411-12.
6. Materialy XXIV s"ezda KPSS, p. 101.
7. Dun's, August 1970, p. 32 [retranslated from the Russian].

8. Materialy XXIV s"ezda KPSS, p. 172.

Chapter 4

1. See V. D. Voronkov, Organizatsiia truda v promyshlennosti GDR, Moscow, 1971.
2. V. V. Vorovskii, Stat'i i materialy po voprosam vneshnei politiki, Moscow, 1959, p. 136.
3. K. Marx and F. Engels, Soch., vol. 23, p. 392.
4. Pravda, March 16, 1974.
5. V. A. Venikov, Rol' nauchnogo issledovaniia v vysshem obrazovanii, Moscow, 1962, p. 21.

Chapter 5

1. Programma Kommunisticheskoi partii Sovetskogo Soiuza, Moscow, 1972, p. 86.
2. Materialy XXIV s"ezda KPSS, p. 61.
3. K. Marx and F. Engels, Soch., vol. 23, p. 56.
4. See K. Marx and F. Engels, Soch., vol. 19, p. 387.
5. Y. Akao, "Quality in Indirect Departments," Proceedings of the International Conference on Quality Control, Tokyo, 1969, p. 470.
6. Novy mir, 1973, no. 12, pp. 216-17.
7. Vneshniaia torgovlia, 1974, no. 6, p. 44.
8. See V. K. Shishov, Analiz khoziaistvennoi deiatel'nosti vneshnetorgovykh ob"edinenii, Moscow, 1969, pp. 74-75.
9. See Sovetskoe radio, 1972, no. 6, p. 20.
10. Standarty i kachestvo, 1970, no. 11, p. 30.
11. See D. S. L'vov, Ekonomika kachestva produktsii, Moscow, 1972, pp. 230-31.
12. See Irving B. Kravis and Robert E. Lipsey, Price Competitiveness in World Trade, New York, 1971.
13. See I. I. Punin and Iu. S. Iampol'skii, Parametricheskie metody opredeleniia tsen na morskie transportnye suda, Mos-

cow, 1970; I. I. Punin, <u>Zavisimost' tsen mashin ot ikh tekhniko-ekonomicheskikh parametrov i kachestva</u>, Moscow, 1973.

14. See V. I. Sedov, <u>Novye formy konkurentnoi bor'by v usloviiakh sovremennogo kapitalizma</u>, Moscow, 1971, pp. 122, 125.

15. See Phillip Cagan, "Quality Changes and the Purchasing Power of Money," <u>Price Indexes and Quality Changes</u>, Cambridge (Mass.), 1971, p. 217.

16. See Zvi Grilliches, "Hedonic Price Indexes for Automobiles," <u>Price Indexes and Quality Change</u>.

Conclusion

1. <u>Novy mir</u>, 1973, no. 12, p. 237.

GLOSSARY

Glossary

This glossary lists all the acronyms or abbreviations that occur in the text. Most are transliterations of Russian terms — e.g., Gosplan — that mean nothing to those not familiar with Soviet economic and trade jargon or institutions. A few, however, of the less well-known terms have been given English initials to remind readers of their translated sense — e.g., IIS-SIQ. The Russian initials and the words they stand for are also given in each of these cases.

Finally, it should be noted that the list of foreign trade organizations is not up to date but reflects the structure of the Ministry of Foreign Trade when this book was published (1975).

ACS	Automatic control system (ASU: avtomaticheskaia sistema upravleniia)
ACS-SIQ	Automatic control system of the State Inspectorate for Quality Control (ASU-GIK: avtomaticheskaia sistema upravleniia-gosudarstvennaia inspektsiia po kachestvu)
AAUS	All-Union State Standards (GOST: gosudarstvennyi obshchesoiuznyi standart)

Glossary

Gosplan	State Planning Committee (Gosudarstvennyi planovoi komitet
Gossnab	State Committee for the Material Supply of the National Economy (Gosudarstvennyi komitet po material'no-tekhnikheskomu snabzheniiu narodnogo khoziaistva)
IIS-SIQ	Information and Inquiry System-State Inspectorate for Quality Control (ISS-GIK: informatsionno-spravochnaia sistema-gosudarstvennaia inspektsiia po kachestvu)
NIKI	Scientific Research Institute on Business Cycles (Nauchno-issledovatel'skii kon'iunkturnyi institut)
SOL	Scientific Organization of Labor (NOT: nauchnaia organizatsiia truda)
VAVT	All-Union Academy of Foreign Trade (Vsesoiuznaia akademiia vneshnei torgovli)
VK	All-union bureau (Vsesoiuznyi kontor)
V/K "Dal'intorg"	Far Eastern Trade Bureau
V/K "Lenfintorg"	Leningrad-Finland Trade Bureau
V/K "Novoeksport"	Innovation Export Association
Vneshtorgbank SSSR	USSR Foreign Trade Bank
V/O	All-Union association (Vsesoiuznoe ob"edinenie)
V/O "Almaziuvelirtorg"	Diamond and Jewelry Association
V/O "Aviaeksport"	Aviation Export Association
V/O "Avtoeksport"	Motor Export Association
V/O "Avtopromimport"	Automobile Industry Import Association

The USSR's Management of Foreign Trade

V/O "Eksportkhleb"	Grain Export Association
V/O "Eksportlen"	Flax Export Association
V/O "Eksportles"	Forest Export Association
V/O "Elektronorgtekhnika"	Electrotechnical Association
V/O "Energomasheksport"	Energy Machinery Export Association
V/O "Litsenzintorg"	Licensing Association
V/O "Mashinoeksport"	Machine Export Association
V/O "Mashinoimport"	Machine Import Association
V/O "Mashpriborintorg"	Machine Tool Association
V/O "Medeksport"	Medical Export Association
V/O "Metallurgimport"	Metallurgical Import Association
V/O "Mezhdunarodnaia kniga"	International Book Association
V/O "Prodintorg"	Supply Association
V/O "Prommashimport"	Industrial Machinery Import Association
V/O "Promsyr'eimport"	Industrial Raw Material Import Association
V/O "Raznoeksport"	Miscellaneous Exports Association
V/O "Raznoimport"	Miscellaneous Imports Association
V/O "Soiuzgazeksport"	National Gas Export Association
V/O "Soiuzkhimeksport"	National Chemical Export Association
V/O "Soiuznefteeksport"	National Oil Export Association
V/O "Soiuzplodimport"	National Produce Import Association
V/O "Soiuzpromeksport"	National Industrial Export Association
V/O "Soiuzpushnina"	National Fur Association
V/O "Soiuzvneshtrans"	National Foreign Transportation Association
V/O "Sovfrakht"	Soviet Freight Association
V/O "Stankoimport"	Machine Tool Import Association
V/O "Sudoimport"	Ship Import Association

Glossary

V/O "Tekhmasheksport"	Technical Machinery Export Association
V/O "Tekhmashimport"	Technical Machinery Import Association
V/O "Tekhnopromimport"	Industrial Technology Import Association
V/O "Tekhsnabeksport"	Technical Supply Export Association
V/O "Traktoroexport"	Tractor Export Association
V/O "Vneshposyltorg"	Foreign Consignment Association
V/O "Vneshtorgizdat"	Foreign Trade Publishing House Association
V/O "Vneshtorgreklama"	Foreign Trade Advertising Association
V/O "Vostokintorg"	Eastern Trade Association
V/O "Zapchast'eksport"	Spare Parts Export Association

ABOUT THE AUTHOR AND EDITOR

V. P. Gruzinov, a specialist on Soviet foreign trade management, was at the time this book was published a member of the Faculty of the All-Union Academy of Foreign Trade in the USSR Ministry of Foreign Trade.

Edward A. Hewett has published a book and numerous articles concerning various aspects of Soviet and East European foreign trade, with a particular focus on trade within the Council for Mutual Economic Assistance. He is Associate Professor of Economics at the University of Texas at Austin.

GPSR Compliance
The European Union's (EU) General Product Safety Regulation (GPSR) is a set of rules that requires consumer products to be safe and our obligations to ensure this.

If you have any concerns about our products, you can contact us on

ProductSafety@springernature.com

In case Publisher is established outside the EU, the EU authorized representative is:

Springer Nature Customer Service Center GmbH
Europaplatz 3
69115 Heidelberg, Germany

www.ingramcontent.com/pod-product-compliance
Ingram Content Group UK Ltd.
Pitfield, Milton Keynes, MK11 3LW, UK
UKHW041430180426
11947UKWH00007B/377